TASTING

WHISKEY

*The mission of Storey Publishing is to serve our customers by
publishing practical information that encourages
personal independence in harmony with the environment.*

Edited by Margaret Sutherland and Nancy Ringer
Art direction by Alethea Morrison
Book design by Kimberly Glyder
Indexed by Christine R. Lindemer, Boston Road Communications

Illustrations by © Andrew Heath
Maps by Bart Wright/Lohnes+Wright, except for page 85 by Dan O. Williams
Cover photography by © Keller + Keller Photography, front; © Attitude/Shutterstock, front and spine
(fabric texture); © Blaine Harrington III/Alamy, back (right); © Madredus/Shutterstock, back (wood
planks); © Mary Evans Picture Library 2008, back (bottom left); © Mountain Laurel Spirits, Todd
Trice, back (top left); © Stephen Lyford, back (author)
Interior photography credits appear on page 255

Storey Publishing
210 MASS MoCA Way
North Adams, MA 01247
www.storey.com

Printed in China by Printplus
10 9 8 7 6 5 4 3 2 1

LIBRARY OF CONGRESS CATALOGING-IN-PUBLICATION DATA

Bryson, Lew, author.
  Tasting whiskey / by Lew Bryson.
    pages cm
  Includes index.
  ISBN 978-1-61212-301-1 (pbk. : alk. paper)
  ISBN 978-1-61212-302-8 (ebook) 1. Whiskey. I. Title.
TP605.B79 2014
663'.52—dc23
                              2014023260

*T*o my late grandfather, Newton Jay Shissler,
who always kept a bottle of 'shine stashed in
the kitchen cupboard.

*T*o Jimmy Russell, Parker Beam, and the
late Elmer T. Lee and Ronnie Eddins,
giants of bourbon from whom
I learned an immense amount.

*A*nd to the memory of Truman Cox, a good
man who was taken from us way too young,
before he could achieve the greatness
as a master distiller that I solidly
believe was his destiny.

TASTING WHISKEY

WHISKEY

AN INSIDER'S GUIDE TO THE UNIQUE PLEASURES OF THE WORLD'S FINEST SPIRITS

LEW BRYSON

Storey Publishing

Contents

FOREWORD

There are very few people on this rocky sphere of pain and tribulation I'd rather have a drink with than Lew Bryson, and most of them are dead. I've known Lew as an occasional drinking buddy, a friend, and an editor for going on 15 years, and even despite that editor business I still look forward to our next tipple, much like the giant panda looks forward to nibbling the first succulent bamboo shoots of spring. Lew is just that pleasant to spend time with.

In fact, he's so agreeable that you tend to forget just how damn smart he is and how much he knows: about whiskey (he's written and edited for America's leading whiskey magazine for years), about beer (four books on the topic), and, well, about everything, or so it seems talking to him. At the same time, he's not one to talk a bunch of junk just to make you think he's a bigshot. But ask a question, and you'll get a good answer (it helps that he used to be a librarian, I suppose). When it comes to the matter at hand — whiskey — he's one of the most knowledgeable people I've ever met, without descending into trivia, one-upping, or blather. Which is good, because the literature on the topic is prone to be precisely that sort of bothersome stuff. Not this book.

Tasting Whiskey is a book that I would have loved to have had close at hand when I first started getting into whiskey, back when Ronald Reagan was president (I needed the stuff then, but I feel the same under every administration). Like its author, the book is clear, patient, thorough, and even-handed, all without taking itself too seriously. It cuts through the old myths and marketing hooey that form such a large part of whiskey lore, without introducing new hooey of its own. I learned something on every page. I'd say more, but I've got a column to write and Lew is, as usual, waiting for it.

Sláinte,
David Wondrich

Founding member of
The Museum of the American Cocktail

Author of two books on cocktail history,
Punch *and* Imbibe

INTRODUCTION

There's a feeling I get whenever I land at the airport in Louisville and walk into the terminal, under the big "Welcome to Louisville" sign, past the Woodford Reserve tavern, and down the escalators. It's a weight off my shoulders, a weight I'd forgotten I'd been carrying: the weight of being a bourbon lover among people who often giggle at the mention of the word. I walk down that terminal . . . and I'm with my people. This is the place where I once slipped up and packed a bottle of Booker's in my carry-on bag going home, and the TSA guy honestly said, "Look, we'll just forget it this one time. That's really good bourbon; take better care of it." Yes, sir!

There's another feeling I get when I'm in the presence of an ancient and rare Scotch whisky. It's awe, and something close to reverence. As long ago as 200 years, an acorn took root, grew into an oak, and was cut, seasoned, sawn into billets and staves, and shaped into a barrel. Bourbon or sherry was aged in the barrel, for however long, after which the barrel was shipped to Scotland, reassembled, and filled with new whisky. After at least 10 years, the barrel was emptied again, and more new whisky was put into it, somewhere around the year I was born. Then here I am, say 40-odd years old, and I'm handed a glass of it, drawn from the cask. My grandfather hadn't yet been born when the whole process started. And it tastes marvelous.

Then there's the feeling I get when I have a glass of a new whiskey in my hand: anticipation. I have a good idea of what it's going to taste like from my previous experiences, but I don't know exactly what *this* is going to taste like. That's exciting, and it whets my appetite and fires my curiosity.

More and more people feel that way about whiskey these days, but it's been a long time since whiskey was held in such general high regard. Whiskey has seen boom times, such as the huge surge in interest in Scotch whisky during the Victorian era, but the twentieth century was for the most part a lean time, from the rough restart of American distillers after Prohibition through the rise of vodka and light rum in the 1960s and '70s. However, whether you're talking about Scotch, bourbon, or Irish, whiskey has made an amazing comeback in the past 20 years, and it's continuing to rise. Scotch whisky (the two different spellings of *whisky* and *whiskey* are quirkily applied; see page 14 for an explanation), for example, has seen the emergence of single malts as a high-priced, high-growth market niche. Sales continue to climb despite steep price increases, and rare bottles are seen as investment-grade purchases at auction houses in New York and Hong Kong.

But while Scotch is still what you hear the most about, the world of whiskey is broader, as is its rise. Bourbon has left its decades-long glide path into regional obscurity on the strong lift of the cocktail culture revolution and a new appreciation for authenticity; Jack Daniel's is booming internationally; and rye whiskey is resurgent after a near-death experience in the 1990s. Japanese whisky has come solidly into its own, with global critical acclaim that is translating into export sales. Irish whiskey is simply amazing, having posted double-digit sales increases for the past 20 years,

eclipsing the much-talked-about growth of craft beers and blossoming with new brands and new styles. There is even growth in the long-declining Canadian whisky segment, as distillers rediscover the strengths of blended whisky.

People don't just want to drink more good whiskey; they want to know more about it. They want to know about Scotch, bourbon, Irish, Canadian, Japanese, and all the new craft whiskeys. They want to know what's good and what's not, they want to know how it's made, they want to *see* it being made, and they want to know more about the people who make it. They go to the Kentucky Bourbon Festival, they go to the Fèis Ìle (the Islay Festival on Scotland's "peatiest island"), and they make pilgrimages to their favorite distilleries on the Kentucky Bourbon Trail, the Malt Whisky Trail, and the new Ireland Whiskey Trail.

The purpose of *Tasting Whiskey* is to get you ready for those next steps. I'm going to share with you what I've learned in years of studying whiskey, sampling whiskey, visiting whiskey distilleries and talking to the people who make it, and writing about it for a living. It's a shame how much misinformation about whiskey is out there. I know that when I started I had some laughably wrong ideas about how it is made, how it is aged, and why it tastes the way it does. Those are common misconceptions, and I want to get you up to speed all at once, so you can move forward to enjoy your whiskey.

I'm going to tell you about how whiskey's made, the unique challenges of tasting it (and what it is you're tasting), and what I've found to be the best ways to taste it. Then we'll talk about the different regions of whiskey, how they differ, and why their whiskeys are made the way they are, where they are. Then I'll tell you how to drink your whiskey, what goes well to eat with it, and how you can build a collection of whiskey.

I hope you enjoy the process, and I hope you learn how to enjoy whiskey more by learning more about it. It's a great clan, a broad family you'll be joining, with branches all over the world. Happy to have you on board!

THE STORY OF WHISKEY

Whiskey is a unique spirit, with a unique taste. Other spirits do have some traits in common with whiskey. Vodka, for the most part, is also made from grain. Brandy is also barrel-aged. Rum has a similar range of unaged and aged expressions, as does tequila. Those last three often benefit from aging in used whiskey barrels. Gin may not seem to be related, but it's a grain spirit, and its ancestral cousin, genever, is barrel-aged in the Netherlands to make a surprisingly whiskey-like spirit.

But no other spirit inspires as much passion as whiskey! There are many more vodkas than there are whiskeys, but are there books that examine the differences among them? Do people collect them? Tequila inspires brand loyalty, but can you name the master distiller of your favorite brand? Do rare bottles sell for over $50,000 at auction? Cognac reaches those heights, but does cognac command the huge sales that whiskey does? Whiskey got the jump on brandy over 100 years ago and has never looked back.

Like my boss at *Whisky Advocate* says, a lot of people drink vodka. But have you ever seen a vodka magazine?

Let's make the difference clear: whiskey is a spirit that is distilled from the product of fermented grains and aged in wooden barrels (which are almost always oak). It is not made from potatoes, fruit, or molasses; any spirit made from such things and calling itself "whiskey" is an imitation.

Why do I say that so emphatically? Whiskey has centuries of tradition behind it that make it so, and government regulations behind it that insist upon it. Whiskey came from Ireland and Scotland; it emigrated from there to Canada and Japan; and although the early distillers in colonial America were mostly central European (the British settlers primarily made rum), they had a similar grain-based distilling tradition and picked up on barrel aging as early as the Scots and Irish.

Those centuries of tradition stand on the shoulders of thousands more years of brewing tradition, which in turn stand on the foundation of civilization. Here's how whiskey fits into the history of humankind.

IN THE NAME OF THE SPIRIT

IF WE START FROM THE very beginning, whiskey is about civilization. One theory of how civilization started is that it came about when humans settled down to grow grain, in order to have a steadier supply of grain than they got from gathering wild grains. They ate the grain, of course, but the theory rests not on eating, but on drinking. Some anthropologists believe that humans learned to grow grain in order to have a steady supply of beer, an important part of ceremony and celebration.

Beer, wine, and mead were potent enough for humans for millennia; they're still potent enough for us today on many occasions. But about 2,000 years ago, alchemists discovered (among other things) purification through distillation. At first they distilled only water, but soon they learned to distill essences, oils, and eventually crude, fiery beverages.

Distillation is dependent on the different boiling points of liquids. To separate pure liquids from a mixed liquid, we gently raise the temperature and capture and condense the vapors as the different liquids boil. This works only if the liquids have sufficiently different boiling points. Happily, water and ethanol are such a pair.

Although we tend to think about distillation in these simple terms — a matter of the boiling points of water and ethanol — there is a large number of liquids being distilled, including other alcohols, oils, and aromatic compounds. The process is not perfect; not all the alcohol is captured, nor all the water and heavier liquids left behind. But as we have more perfectly understood how distillation works, we have been able to get better at it, and get out what we want, while leaving

WHISKEY? OR WHISKY?

*L*et's get this out of the way right now. Many words have been written about why some countries — and by extension, their distillers — spell the word "whisky," and others spell it "whiskey." (The Welsh, just to be different, spell it "wisgi.") Generally speaking, in Great Britain, Canada, and Japan, it's "whisky." In the United States and Ireland, it's "whiskey," though there are a few American brands that prefer the other spelling — Maker's Mark and George Dickel, for instance. Just to add to that little bit of confusion, where the U.S. Code of Federal Regulations defines what the spirit is under American law, it consistently spells it "whisky."

That should make it plain, but I'll spell it out for you: it doesn't make any difference which way you spell it, except for national pride. "Whisky" and "whiskey" are two virtually identical words for the same thing. I don't even know why we have discussions about it. No one has ever proposed that a Canadian's "neighbour" is any different from an American's "neighbor." An ingot of "aluminium" is the same stuff as "aluminum," right down to the subatomic level.

That's not to say there is no difference between the spirits from the different countries, because there are differences, very significant ones, and we'll get to that later. But the differences have nothing to do with spelling!

To appease the purists (though some sticklers will certainly still find fault), I will use "whisky" when talking about Scotch, Canadian, and Japanese whiskies. When I'm talking about American and Irish whiskeys, or about whiskey in general, I'll use "whiskey," because I'm an American, writing in America; it's how we do it here. But it's only spelling.

Whisky or whiskey: it's only a letter.

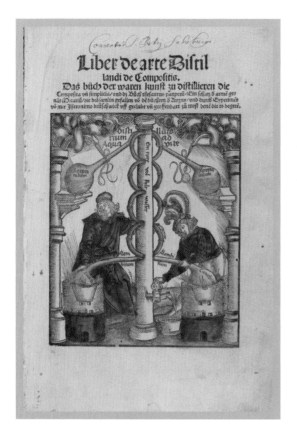

It's more important to realize that by modern definitions, we aren't talking about whiskey here at all. We definitely have a spirit distilled from the product of fermented grain — in this case, almost certainly malted barley — but then we run into the issue of aging. While the monks, and soon farmers and millers, were making the rough spirit, and smoothing it with spices, honey, herbs, and God knows what else, one thing they weren't doing was aging it in barrels. They had barrels, and they had spirits, but the two didn't come together for quite a while.

INTO THE WOOD

BEFORE WHISKEY GOT AGED, it largely got smuggled. Taxation has been the lot of booze for centuries, because kings and politicians know a good thing when they see it, and usually put a tax on it. That's when the long, intricate dance of the distiller and the exciseman, the moonshiner and the revenuer, began. Clandestine Scottish and Irish distillers had natural advantages in their home turf: plenty of streams and lakes for mashing and for cooling the vapors, and hills and deep valleys for hiding from the tax collectors.

This may be why barrel aging first started. Small wooden barrels were lighter and less prone to break than ceramic jugs, and a smuggler could move quickly with small kegs. Given today's craft distillers' experience with small barrels and quick aging, it's completely believable that a month in a 5-gallon barrel could have a significant and desirable effect on raw spirit, especially if it were sloshed about.

Oddly enough, over in the American colonies, distillers were generally considered pillars of the community; sometimes they were sponsored by the community so the town could have a distillery. As I said, the British

Hieronymus Brunschwig's *Liber de Arte Distillandi de Compositis* (Strasbourg, 1512) describes the manufacture of aqua vitae, one of the world's first distilled spirits.

behind that which is foul-tasting, impure, and watery.

We have only a foggy idea of when these distilled spirits were first made. To begin, there are records of *aqua vitae* ("water of life/vitality," the alchemical Latin name for alcohol) being consumed in Ireland in the very early 1400s, and malt sent to a friar to make *aqua vitae* in 1494. *Aqua vitae* would be translated as *uisce beatha* in Gaelic, which — probably with the application of years of drinking — would eventually become linguistically massaged to "whiskey."

A re-creation of George Washington's eighteenth-century gristmill and distillery at Mount Vernon, one of the largest of its time

settlers, especially those in New England, mostly made rum, but my Pennsylvania Dutch ancestors made whiskey, usually from rye, the grain they were most familiar with.

Come the Revolutionary War, this rye whiskey would become the patriot's drink: rum came from molasses imported from the British West Indies, subject to taxes before the Revolution, hard to get after it began. Rye whiskey was indigenous, and the lore is that Pennsylvania rye helped keep the Colonial soldiers warm and well tempered during their time in winter quarters at Valley Forge. General Washington must have liked it; he built a distillery at his estate at Mount Vernon, and after retiring from the presidency, he would become for a short time the nation's largest distiller of rye whiskey. Now that's a pillar of the community.

NEW WHISKEYS, AGED

THE WORLD WAS CHANGING, and whiskey would change with it. Americans had tasted liberty and wanted more: when the war was won and the United States tried to grapple with the debt it had run up fighting it with an excise tax on distilling, farmer-distillers in western Pennsylvania refused to pay it, a defiance that became the Whiskey Rebellion.

In Scotland, about 30 years later, distilling would be revolutionized by government rule when legal distillation was made easier (and enforcement against illegal distillation was made stronger).

Meanwhile, a new kind of whiskey made largely from corn was being made down the Ohio River in Kentucky: bourbon. Another new whisky-making tradition was growing up in Canada: blended whiskies, which quickly became the norm. And in America, France, and Canada (and later Scotland), a hybridization with French brandy technology — storage in barrels that were toasted or charred on the inside — would change whiskey from the fiery, off-clear spirit it had been since its birth to the amber beauty we know today.

Bourbon and rye benefited suddenly from this new aging technique, getting the nicknames "red liquor" and "Monongahela red" from the deep color the charred wood imparted. The oak made a perfect container for the whiskey, and the longer a distiller (or retailer — whiskey was sold in full barrels at the time, and a store or tavern would pour from the barrel) kept it, the better it got.

Scotch whisky started to benefit from barrel aging at around the same time. The ports of England and Scotland received barrels of wine from continental Europe; in the thriving economy of the post-Napoleonic era, Britain grew rich and drank up the best of France and Spain and Portugal, particularly sherry. Distillers stored their whisky in these second-hand barrels and made the same

discovery about their properties that American bourbon distillers had. It was a new world.

Two things then cemented whiskey's place in the world: steam power and the phylloxera aphid. Steam power and the industrial revolution came to distilling and made possible great breweries and distilleries. The invention of the steam-heated column still allowed the production of great quantities of mild-flavored grain whisky, which blenders used to tame the full flavors of pot-distilled malt whisky. This blended Scotch whisky was more popular than its predecessors — it fit the tastes of more people.

But what really made Scotch whisky the power it still is today was the destruction of Europe's vineyards by the phylloxera aphid. The French were making and selling vast amounts of cognac to the British; sales in the UK tripled in 15 years in the mid-1800s, to about 65 million bottles annually. Then the aphid struck, feeding on and destroying the roots of French grapevines. By the time

Moonshine whiskey, on its way to market in the southern Appalachians, 1860s

the cognac producers had grafted their vines to phylloxera-resistant American rootstocks, they found that thirsty Britons had switched to the newly drinkable blended Scotch, and now it was selling around the world as the empire expanded.

Though the market for Scotch whisky expanded tremendously toward the end of the nineteenth century, it crashed as the century turned and the speculative bubble burst. The Irish at first picked up the slack, only to crash along with the Americans when Prohibition burst onto the scene after World War I. Prohibition, far from being the free-for-all for whiskey smuggling portrayed by popular fiction, was a disaster for whiskey companies around the world. Imagine, after all, America as a thriving market for whiskey, from both its own distillers and distillers around the world, importing shiploads of whiskey from overseas and carloads from Canada, shipping Kentucky and Pennsylvania whiskey across the country on its modern rail system. Then suddenly the only way to move whiskey into the country was on tiny motorboats landing on beaches, and the only way to move it around the country was on rickety trucks on back roads. Production and sales plummeted. Things didn't get a lot better after Repeal; there wasn't any aged whiskey left in America, and Scotch and Irish whiskey hadn't recovered.

Then whiskey went to war. World War II demanded full mobilization of national industry, and whiskey distillation was deemed nonessential. (Churchill must not have been consulted.) Instead, whiskey makers converted to making industrial alcohol for chemical feedstock. When the war was finally over, whiskey had been banged around for decades, but distillers believed that the good times were coming back at last. As we all know from watching *Mad Men*, for at least a while they were right.

FALL AND RISE

THE GOOD TIMES didn't last. Beginning in the 1960s, consumers around the world began to turn away from whiskey and increasingly embraced vodka and light rum. The change hit hard in the early 1980s, when a glut of Scotch whisky — the "Whisky Loch" — led again to a crash in the industry. Bourbon and Canadian whisky began a long, gradual decline.

Vodka would continue to rise in popularity until the 2008 recession, taking over a third of U.S. spirits sales. But the seeds of whiskey's return had been planted in the scorched fields of whiskey's fall. The 1980s saw an increase in single malt Scotch releases, a new thing for Scotch whisky. Independent bottlers such as Elgin grocers Gordon & MacPhail had for years been buying casks from local distillers, aging them in their own warehouse, and bottling them for sale as singles, but now single malts were being released on a much larger scale, led by Glenfiddich.

Bourbon began its turnaround with the growth of Maker's Mark, a smoother wheated bourbon, and the creation of Blanton's single-barrel bottling and Booker's unfiltered cask-strength bourbon. The small but growing acceptance of these bottlings would set an example for the industry and get bourbon some of the attention it deserved.

Irish whiskey began the process of survival and revival by consolidating: by 1966 all the distillers left in the Republic of Ireland had united in one company, Irish Distillers. Ten years later they built a modern distillery in Midleton and bought Bushmills, the remaining distillery in the north. They decided to reformulate Irish whiskey as a lighter, blended whiskey, and that laid the groundwork for the

In "Woman's Holy War" (1874), armored women with lethal-looking battleaxes shatter casks of liquor. The crusade for temperance led to Prohibition in 1920, with devastating and long-lasting effects on the burgeoning whiskey industry.

tremendous growth that category has seen over the past 20 years.

That's about where I entered the fray, in the supporting role of whiskey media. The increasingly sure and respected voices of people like Michael Jackson (he's best known in America as a beer writer, but in the UK his reputation is for whisky writing), Jim Murray, David Broom, John Hansell, Gary Regan, Charlie MacLean, and Chuck Cowdery brought respect and interest to the category, and the launch of two magazines for the whiskey consumer, *Whisky Advocate*, where I've worked for 17 years, and *Whisky Magazine*, made the reach even greater. Social media, blogging, and the instant "tell me more" magic of Google added powerful immediacy to it all.

But whiskey truly works best at a personal level: face to face, glass in hand. When whiskey festivals, such as WhiskyFest and Whisky Live, were launched and began to thrive, they changed the public's perception of whiskey. When the real aficionados thought of their brands, they didn't think of Wild Turkey and Glenmorangie; they thought of master distiller Jimmy Russell and whisky creator Dr. Bill Lumsden. These were the people who'd been quietly working for years in relative solitude, known mostly only to the distillery workers they saw every day. These events brought them into the public eye; they made them rock stars.

That changed things even more. It gave whiskey authenticity. It had always had it, of course, but now the public actually saw it. Real people made the whiskey, and the public could meet them, talk to them, ask them questions, and thank them. It was an explosively powerful shift, realized in such events as the Kentucky Bourbon Festival, the Islay Whisky Festival, and the Spirit of Speyside Whisky Festival — celebrations of whiskey right in the heart of where it's made, and where tens of thousands of people now visit every year. They

come to see where *their* whiskey is made, and has been made, for over 200 years.

It's been a wild ride for whiskey, this past 20 years. It was a complete turnaround, from declining sales to the most powerful force in the world of alcohol beverages, as beer falters (except for the flavorful, authentic craft category; see a connection?) and wine climbs out of a glut. We drank our way through the wonderful aged whiskeys left over from the glut of the 1980s, and now prices are rising. Production's catching up, and there are more whiskeys to try than ever.

We see more differences in whiskey as well, and this will be a waking time for new tastes and flavors in whiskey. I remember something Anchor Distilling founder Fritz Maytag, one of the early pioneers of craft distilling, said a few years back at a rye whiskey roundtable interview we did for *Whisky Advocate*. We had 10 rye whiskey distillers, bottlers, and retailers sitting around talking about the renaissance of rye whiskey, and about the amazing super-aged stuff that was coming out of warehouses at the time.

We knew the supply of older whiskeys wouldn't last, but Maytag said that not only was it not a bad thing, but that it would lead to something else. "Broadly speaking, the whiskey world thinks that older whiskey's better," he said. "And older whiskey is different. Wonderfully different. But I submit to you that, especially because we have a big shortage of rye whiskey, you are all going to discover the beauty of young rye whiskey." As I taste some very young, very interesting ryes from craft distillers these days, I know how right he was, and how true that thought holds for a lot of new whiskeys.

That's what whiskey's been through, and where it is now. In the next chapter we'll talk about how it goes from grain to the state of the original whiskey: raw, clear spirit. Let's get to work.

MAKING SPIRIT:

FERMENTATION AND DISTILLATION

If you want to learn about tasting whiskey, you need to find out what it is, how it's made, and what goes into it. You could simply walk up to a glass, have a sniff and a sip, and taste it completely blind, ignorant of everything but the moment in front of you . . . but why on earth would you want to?

That's the kind of thing distillers and writers and other whiskey experts are asked to do in competitions, in formal judging situations. We're not tasting for pleasure, for enjoyment, or for celebration; we're working. That's not to say there aren't great moments! But it's better when you're placed in the full knowledge of where the whiskey came from, how it was aged, who picked the barrels. You can put the whiskey in context, and then you'll not only know what it tastes like, you'll understand something of why, and you'll know more about what to expect from your next whiskey from that distiller, or that blender, or that region or type.

The most elemental things to know about a whiskey have to do with how it is made. There are similarities in how the world's whiskeys are made, but the differences, the delicious variations, are in the details. Almost everything can be played with, tweaked, or changed wholesale, and has been, by some distiller, somewhere, at some time. The good results are still around.

There's a simple start to it. The first thing you have to learn is that all whiskey starts as grain — no exceptions, no "potato whiskey" or "apple whiskey." If it ain't grain, it ain't whiskey.

Barley, corn, rye, and wheat are the most common, but there are whiskeys out there made with oats, quinoa, hybrid grains like triticale, and buckwheat (which is not *technically* a grain, but it malts like one and can be ground to flour like one). Sometimes it's a matter of necessity — you make it with

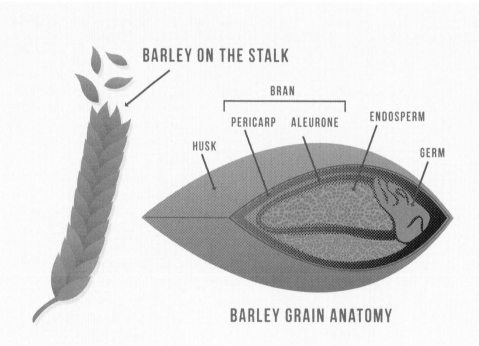

BARLEY ON THE STALK

BRAN

PERICARP   ALEURONE

ENDOSPERM

HUSK

GERM

BARLEY GRAIN ANATOMY

The barley grain's endosperm holds the starches that are converted into sugar through the whiskey-making process.

what you've got — but most often there was a choice, and usually either the most tasty or the most economical grain wins out. It's not far off the process you go through when you look at the selection at the liquor store; that one tastes exceptional, but I can buy three bottles of this pretty good one for the same price.

Grain may seem like an unnatural source of liquid upon first look: dry, dusty, and usually turned into bread or cattle feed. It's what's chemically bound in the grain that makes it an exceptional way to make whiskey (and beer). Take a kernel of barley, or corn, and slice it open. Inside you'll find tiny, tiny clumps of hard, insoluble starches, held in a matrix of proteins. Whiskey needs neither. But the starches can be chemically converted to sugars, and that's just the ticket for whiskey.

Grain gets made into whiskey through a series of chemical changes, actually. We'll get into each of the changes in general throughout this chapter, but here's a general overview: after the plant does its chemical job of turning water and dirt and sunlight into stalk and grain, it is harvested and cleaned. If it's barley, headed for Scotch whisky, it's *malted*, a natural process that gets the grain to sprout. Sprouting releases enzymes that convert the hard starches to softer starches. The *malt*, as it's now called, and any other grains, are then ground and cooked. Cooking activates plant enzymes that chemically convert the starches to sugars. (Distillers of other whiskeys, such as American bourbons, add malt to their recipes, not for the flavor but for these enzymes; Canadian distillers culture the enzymes and add them directly.)

That's the cue for the next player: yeast. This little fungus eats sugar, reproduces like mad, and gives off carbon dioxide and alcohol. Up to this point, the process is practically identical to that of brewing beer. But now the alcohol needs to be extracted and concentrated

(that is, *distilled*). The mixture is heated in a still, where, with its lower boiling point, the alcohol evaporates faster than the water. The alcohol vapor is collected and condensed. It is usually distilled again at least once to clean it up a bit, and then it is reduced to a standard barreling *proof* (the percentage of alcohol in the whiskey) and put in oak barrels.

That's where the next chapter begins, though, so it's time to dig into the details on grain, fermentation, and distillation.

THE MOTHER GRAIN

WHISKEY IS GRAIN, as much as bread is, but in liquid, concentrated form. Think of how different breads are: a dark round of pumpernickel, a sweet golden wedge of cornbread, a dense and chewy loaf of whole wheat. Similarly, whiskey's character derives largely from the predominant grain — the mother grain.

BARLEY AND MALT

EACH WHISKEY AROUND THE world has its mother grain. For Scotch it's clearly barley, or malt, as it's called when it's been through the malting process. Although just about any grain can be malted, the overwhelmingly most commonly malted grain is barley (mostly because of the popularity of beer), and so it is usually generically referred to as "malt," as in malt whisky or single malt whisky.

Barley is a preferred grain for whiskey for the same reason that almost all the world's beer is based on malt: it is relatively easy to malt, a controlled process of partial sprouting. The grains are stuffed with starches, which serve as concentrated food sources for sprouting and are easily converted to sugars. The sugars are the part of grain that eventually becomes whiskey. That's another reason malt

How to Make Whiskey

GROW GRAIN → HARVEST/CLEAN → MALT (SOMETIMES)

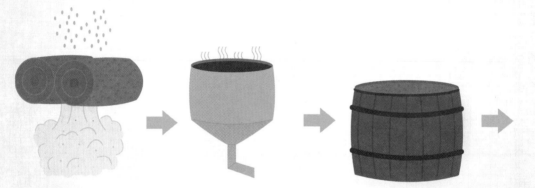

GRIND/MILL → MASH/COOK → FERMENT

DISTILL → AGE → BLEND → BOTTLE

is used for making beer and whiskey: it tastes good.

That's why it's been around for so long. Malting is an ancient discovery, dating back to the beginnings of civilization, in Mesopotamia. We know malting took place that far back because there is physical evidence and written records of brewing from the period of the Sumerians, around 4000 BCE.

It's a simple enough concept, though a bit more complicated in execution. Grains sprout in the spring, when they warm up from winter and are wet by spring rains. This sprouting, or germination, serves the true purpose of the grain: reproduction. When the conditions for sprouting occur, enzymes are released in the grain and break down the protein matrix that holds the hard starches in place. The shoot begins to grow, consuming the starches as they are converted to sugar.

That's not good for whiskey, though; distillers want to get as much sugar out of each kernel as they can. That's called the yield, and it's the kind of cost-crunching number that a volume business lives and dies on. So malting is a tightly controlled process, with temperature, humidity, and timing all carefully monitored.

The barley is steeped in water for perhaps 2 days. Then it is drained and allowed to germinate. During that time, the barley has to be turned, either by hand or with machines, to

Once soaked, barley kernels are spread across a distillery's maltings floor to germinate, modifying the starches that will eventually be converted to sugars and then whiskey. They're turned regularly to keep them from clumping.

WHAT IS PEAT?

*P*eat isn't hard to describe, but it's somewhat hard to understand. It is partially decayed vegetation, mostly sphagnum moss, that builds up over centuries, or even millennia, in bogs, swamps, and moors. Why doesn't the stuff just rot away? It's covered in water.

If you've ever gardened, you may have used peat moss to give sandy soil better water retention or simply to hold water around plants. That's how peat accumulates. As the moss dies the new moss holds water in place, slowing the rate of oxygen transfer to the dead moss, so it doesn't rot. A peat bog holds just enough water to keep that process slowed.

As the decayed matter accumulates, it weighs more and more and exerts enough downward force (from gravity) that the bottom layers are compressed into a denser layer, something like particleboard. The peat is cut from the bog in long pieces, called turfs or turves, and laid out in rows or stacks to dry. You can see those drying turves along the road on Islay, cut by townspeople as free fuel for their fireplaces.

A distillery that wants that smoky peat essence in its whisky will burn the peat in its kiln during the malt drying process. It's a controlled slow burn; you don't want very much open flame, because that's burning too clean. What you want is voluminous, pungent smoke to rise through the green malt and bind itself to the husks.

The interesting thing about peat for the whisky maker is that every place's peat is different. Peat is found all over the world, from the tropics of Indonesia to the cold, high latitudes of such places as Tierra del Fuego, the Falkland Islands, Canada, northern North America, Finland, Russia, and Scotland. It's estimated that 2 percent of the world's land surface is peat bogs, so we won't run out too soon. (There are already plans in place to conserve Scottish peat. Distillers are doing their part by investigating new techniques to get the most out of every curl of smoke.)

The plants that grow in these bogs give each particular peat its character. Irish peat is different from Islay peat; Islay peat is different from Highland peat; Highland peat is different from Orkney peat. To a chemist it's a simple matter of analysis. To a whisky drinker, it's a matter of nosing; you can often smell the difference.

Peat is a strong aroma/flavor, but if you've been to a peat bog that's being cut for burning, or you've smelled unburned peat, you'll know that's *not* the smell in whisky. You might be told that some whiskies have a light peat character from using water that passes through peat on its way to the distillery; don't believe it. Eddie McAffer, manager at the Bowmore distillery: "Just a romantic notion." The only way to get that distinctive smell from peat is to burn it.

For Scotch whisky that uses peated malt, the peat itself is an ingredient as surely as the malt or water. It's part of the location, the *terroir* that makes whiskies different. I've been at the cutting face of Hobbister Moor, Highland Park's peat source on Orkney. Standing on the clay sublayer that's at the bottom of the moor, there was about 6 vertical feet of peat, representing about 5,000 years of accumulation. The top layer was loose, light brown, and full of heather stems and leaves and blades of rank grass. Farther down, the peat was more compacted, though still friable, and you could still see stems and leaves.

All the way down, dating 5,000 years back, it was quite black and much harder . . . and I still saw some stems of plants that grew in that bog 3,000 years before the birth of Christ, 3,800 years before the Vikings arrived on Orkney. By now that peat, those stems, has probably been burned to flavor the malt of a batch of spirit for Highland Park, and in 15 or 18 years . . . *Sláinte!*

Peat is cut in turves, or strips, that are stacked and left to dry for a couple of weeks, then collected and burned in a distillery's kiln to produce peated malt.

starches will make a mark, while a kernel that hasn't changed enough — "undermodified" — won't. He knows what he's talking about; he started with Bowmore in 1966, turning malt by hand on that same maltings floor.

When it's fully modified, the green and still damp malt is put in a kiln, where hot air blows through it, drying it and killing the sprout. The idea is to get it hot enough to stop growth, but not so hot as to roast the malt or denature the enzymes.

This is where peat smoke will be introduced, if desired. Malt kilns today use hot air that is free of any smoke or combustion smells, but 200 years ago that wasn't so easy, and malt often had a smoky aroma from the drying process. There are two uses of malt where that smell is still wanted and steps are taken to preserve it: brewing in the style of the German *rauchbier* ("smoke beer") and a significant number of Scotch (and Japanese) whiskies.

If peating is on the program, it's the first thing that happens in the kiln, because it works only on wet malt. The kiln will be stoked with smoldering peat, and the smoke will pass through the kiln for up to 18 hours. The smoke is not particularly hot; you can comfortably stand in the kiln during this stage. It's humid, but it's not even that smoky, because the malt's absorbing it.

The amount of smoke the malt absorbs is measured in parts per million (ppm) of phenols, the aromatic compounds that give the smoky aroma. They can range up to 60 or 70 ppm in the heavily peated malts. You may hear people talking about phenol numbers in the whiskeys themselves, but those numbers are not exact. The phenols in malt versus the phenols in the actual spirit run on about a 3:1 ratio, as a lot of the smokiness is left behind in the mashing process, locked in the husks of the malt. There are other variables in how

keep the sprouts from intertwining and forming unmanageable clumps. The enzymes are at work during the sprouting, breaking down the protein matrix to expose the starches.

When the conversion is at its peak, and before the shoot begins to consume significant amounts of food, the germination process is cut off by heating the malt in a kiln. Eddie McAffer, manager at the Bowmore distillery on the island of Islay, showed me an old maltster's trick called "chalking the malt" to see if the malt's getting ready for the kiln. He picked up a kernel of malt from the maltings floor at the distillery and scraped it down the grayish plastered wall. It left a white streak. "Close to done," he said, explaining that the softened

Whiskey Grains

MALT WHISKY
(SCOTCH, JAPANESE, SOME IRISH)
100% barley malt

GRAIN WHISKY
(SCOTCH, JAPANESE, SOME IRISH)
Varying grains; often wheat

SINGLE POT STILL IRISH WHISKEY
A mix of malt and raw barley

RYE WHISKEY
51+% rye, plus malt and corn

CANADIAN WHISKY
Corn, rye, and malt; actual ratios vary widely

BOURBON
51+% corn, plus malt and either rye or wheat

smoky a whiskey is, with one of the biggest being how it is distilled. The best measure of smokiness is still the human nose!

After peating is done, the heat is turned up; of course, that's an immediate step if the malt is not to be peated. After about two days, the malt is dried. The whole malting process takes about a week, one maltster told me: grain goes in, malt comes out, and there's not a lot you can really do to speed it up.

That's malt, the basis for single malt Scotch whisky and Japanese malt whisky. Irish whiskey is made with malt; the whiskeys from the Irish Distillers company (e.g., Jameson, Powers, Redbreast, Midleton) also contain a varying amount of unmalted barley. Although American whiskeys like bourbon and rye use a portion of malt for their enzymes, their main grains are different. Bourbon revolves around corn, and rye is centered on its namesake, but both use some of the other. Let's have a look.

RYE

RYE IS NOT A PARTICULARLY well-behaved grain, which is not so surprising: it's young, one of the most recently domesticated grains. Archaeological evidence for rye only goes back to about 500 BCE, making it a relative adolescent among grains — and it acts like it.

Rye grows exceptionally tall for a grass, 6 feet or more, and it often grows where it is not wanted. Its so-called volunteer stalks will pop up postharvest, and the grain is exceptionally quick starting. When it crops up in a wheat field, it damages the value of the harvest. It is also noted for its bitter, earthy taste, which was despised by the Romans, or at least by Pliny the Elder.

Pliny found almost nothing good to say about the poor grass. In his *Natural History* he describes it as "a very inferior grain . . . only employed to avert positive famine." He didn't like how it tasted either: "Spelt is mixed with this grain to modify its bitterness and even then it is very disagreeable to the stomach."

But even Pliny had to admit rye's good side: "It will grow upon any soil, and yields a hundred-fold; it is employed also as a manure for enriching the land." Farmers say rye will grow on rock, and indeed, on a rye farm I visited in Alberta, there were shoots of rye springing up anywhere there was the barest amount of soil or dead grass: on rock, on buildings, on farm machinery.

Rye is so tenacious, quick growing, and heavily rooted that it needs no weeding; it simply chokes out anything that tries to compete with it. It holds the soil against erosion, and as Pliny notes, it can be grown on a 2-year cycle, plowed back into the soil for fertilizer the first year. Those are the qualities that made rye popular in eastern Europe and Scandinavia, where pumpernickel and *rugbrød* are staple breads.

Of course, if it makes bread, it will make whiskey, and rye can be readily malted. The Germans knew that as well as anyone. When they emigrated to North America in the 1700s, they brought rye and a knowledge of distillation with them. Pennsylvania was soon dotted with farm distilleries, and the flavorsome rye whiskey they made became an American classic. Canadians learned about rye the same way, and the tall, unruly grass took well to the uneven soils of the East and the broad sweep of the prairie.

CORN

THE OTHER BIG AMERICAN distilling grain is corn. It may seem hard to believe that corn is a grass, particularly when you're looking at a span of trimmed lawn next to a cornfield, but both plants are true grasses, members of the family Poaceae. Wheat, rye, and barley are clearly grasses — just bigger — but corn has a much thicker stalk, and the kernels, the grains themselves, grow on a fairly large cob, wrapped in a protective husk. It's a strange-looking grass.

Grass it is, though, and that's why it works so well for distilling. Corn is king in North America, and it's been bred to be so. Maize, as it's called in much of the rest of the world, descends from a grass called teosinte, a wavy frond-like plant. Native Americans successfully crossbred teosinte until it was a single stalk, bearing increasingly large and grain-covered cobs. The increase in yield is nothing short of astounding, and corn has become a crop so important to American food technology that it shapes it in ways most of us can't conceive.

But for our purposes it's easy to see why American distillers chose to use it: its incredible fecundity. Given good soil and the right climate — and corn has been bred to expand that range quite a bit — corn will put forth a huge amount of grain. It is difficult to malt, but there's more than one way to husk an ear; once corn has been milled and cooked to split open the starchy matrix, a relatively small addition of malt provides the enzymes to convert corn's plentiful starches to sugars in the mash.

Corn's only problem is that it's a bit of a one-note song; the flavor is sweet and strong. So farm distillers learned to create a recipe, what we now call a mashbill, with a lot of corn for the sweet flavor and fermentation-fueling sugar, a portion of malt for the enzyme power to convert the starches to sugars, and a couple of sacks of rye (or sometimes wheat) to spice things up and put some flavor into the liquor. They had the grains milled (probably leaving either a portion of the meal as payment — millers were often distillers as well — or a promise of the whiskey to come), and then it was time to mash.

COOKING THE MASH

WHATEVER KIND OF GRAINS you're using, whether malted or smoked, or not, they'll undergo mostly the same process now. The grains are milled to the consistency of flour to make a grist, which is then mixed with water. The water matters — quite a bit — and distillers are usually located near good sources of water. To begin, distilling requires plentiful water for cooling; the alcohol vapors need to be cooled and condensed as they come off the still, and fermentation needs to be cooled in the summer so the yeast doesn't run riot and ruin the mash. But cooling water can be from almost any clean source. The actual distilling water is more important. Calcium in the water supplies needed nutrients to the yeast; iron in the water will ruin whiskey, making it turn black and foul. The limestone layers under much of central Kentucky provide iron-free, calcium-rich water that is so good for whiskey making that I've heard distillers say that historic distilleries failed because they were "off the slab."

You need good water, then, and the proper consistency of grist going into the mash tun, the vessel where the starches in the grist, now called the mash, are converted to sugars. Depending on the distillery, the mash is either set at the appropriate temperature for this conversion or the mash is gently heated in rising "steps" to get different sets of enzymes to work at their most efficient levels.

Pine "washbacks," or fermenting vessels, at the Ardbeg Distillery on the Isle of Islay in Scotland

SOUR MASH

Ask whiskey drinkers what "sour mash" means, and they might tell you, "It's Jack Daniel's, that's the real sour mash whiskey; it's got that sour mash tang." Really? The sour is just in the mash. By the time it gets through the still, the sour's gone, and as anyone can tell you, Tennessee whiskey (and bourbon, its kissing cousin) is sweet.

You may also hear that sour mash is like a sourdough starter, with the distiller holding over a small part of the already fermented mash, now sour, to the next fermentation, to ensure continuity between batches. Except that the sour mash — also called stillage or setback or, confusingly, backset — is what comes out of the column still, after a trip through live steam. There's nothing alive in there. It's a thin, sour liquid full of dead yeast — just what your mash needs.

That "sour mash" is added to the fermenter with a new mash; as much as a third of the volume in the fermenter will be sour mash. The sour mash does two things: it feeds the yeast; the dead yeast is perfect food for the next generations of yeast, and there are leftover enzymes in there to boost the ones in the fresh mash. It also drops the pH of the mash, making it slightly acidic — just the way the yeast likes it — and headed for the sour state that will make the next batch of sour mash.

Why does the yeast like acidic mash? According to Jeff Arnett, master distiller at the Jack Daniel Distillery, which rather famously uses sour mash, it doesn't . . . not exactly. He compares yeast to a racehorse with a reputation as a "mudder," a horse that performs well on a wet track. "A wet track does not make a mudder run faster," Arnett noted, "but it can run faster on a wet track than the other horses."

Similarly, an acidic mash slows the yeast, but it slows the bacteria in the mash even more. Bacteria are a problem for distillers. They eat sugars, but they don't make alcohol, and they usually produce off-flavors. Slowing them down allows the yeast to overpower and outreproduce them.

So sour mash is about continuity and consistency, but not in the sense of a sourdough starter. It's about making sure the distiller's yeast strain is the dominant activity in the fermentation, and that every fermentation is a healthy and vigorous one, just like all the others.

Sour mash is part of almost every bourbon made; there are a very few one-off bottlings that are made without it just as experiments. Almost everyone thinks he knows what it means . . . and now *you* really do.

The temperature is crucial: too low, and conversion doesn't happen; too high, and the enzymes will break down and nothing will happen. When the conversion does happen, it's almost mystic. The starchy mash is thick and heavy, like oatmeal. Then the enzymes work their magic, and suddenly the mash is slippery and slick with sugars, a stunningly evident physical transformation.

At this point there is a divergence in practice. In most distilleries the sugary liquid (called "worts") is strained out of the mash, and the sugars left behind will then be washed out of the mash with successive applications of hot water, called "sparges" or simply "waters." That hot water also brings a final conversion with some more complex sugars. The complete run of worts and sparge

Whisky stills at Glenfiddich's distillery at Dufftown in Scotland; note the three different geometries.

waters (except the last sparge, which usually becomes the grist water for the next batch) is then cooled in a heat exchanger and sent to fermentation. Traditional American distillers don't strain the mash; the whole thing goes to the fermenters, floury grain bits and all.

FERMENTATION

THE MASH WILL FILL about two-thirds of the fermenter. The remaining volume in the fermenter will be filled with sour mash, what's left after previous fermentations have run through the still. The distiller's particular strain of yeast is added and fermentation begins, converting the sugars in the mash to alcohol and carbon dioxide.

Fermentation speed and temperature can have an effect on the aromas created by the yeast. Fermentation is a heat-producing (or exothermic) chemical reaction, so the wort will get warmer as it ferments (unless it is cooled by the distillery). Heat will make it run faster and create more aromatic compounds. Some of this can be desirable; too much is not. Which strain of yeast is used can also have an effect (see the section on Four Roses's five yeasts on page 148), which is why distillers are so careful to keep their yeasts clean and healthy. They'll subject samples to microscopic analysis to make sure the strain isn't mutating.

The product of fermentation, at between 8 and 18 percent alcohol by volume (ABV), depending on the distillery and the yeast, is now called "beer" by American distillers and "wash" by the Scottish and Irish. It's ready for distillation.

HOW A POT STILL WORKS

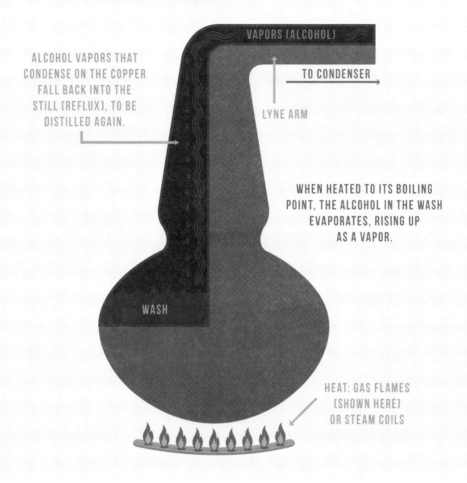

ALCOHOL VAPORS THAT CONDENSE ON THE COPPER FALL BACK INTO THE STILL (REFLUX), TO BE DISTILLED AGAIN.

VAPORS (ALCOHOL)

TO CONDENSER

LYNE ARM

WHEN HEATED TO ITS BOILING POINT, THE ALCOHOL IN THE WASH EVAPORATES, RISING UP AS A VAPOR.

WASH

HEAT: GAS FLAMES (SHOWN HERE) OR STEAM COILS

DISTILLATION

THE MECHANICS OF distillation at the different distilleries can be a confusing subject, and it's no wonder. There are pot stills, column or continuous stills, hybrid stills, and extractive distillation stills. They all work differently, but they also all work the same, by concentrating alcohol through separating it from the wash or beer, the initial product of fermentation. Most whiskey distillation relies on a series of two or more distillations, each one either bumping up the alcohol content or cleaning the spirit of unwanted impurities.

BATCHES OF POTS

DISTILLATION ON A POT still is a batch process; you put a "charge" of wash into the still, you heat it till it's done, then you clean the still and start over.

Pot stills are easy to understand; everyone's seen a pot. To see how a pot still works, take a cooking pot, put water in it, and put it on the stove. Put the lid on it, and turn on the heat. As the water boils, the steam hits the lid,

COPPER: THE GUARDIAN

opper pot stills gleam in a distillery. Copper-walled column stills hiss and bubble away, sometimes with an extra load of copper scrap in the top. Copper abounds in a stillhouse. But it wears out and gets dented; it tarnishes and can look ratty. Why are distillers in love with copper?

"Originally copper was used because it was available," Dr. Bill Lumsden explains. "It was malleable, you could shape it fairly easily into the shape of a still, and it had good heat transfer capability. That's not so crucial nowadays, because most of the heating is done by steam coils inside the still, but in olden days it would be heated over a coal fire or something like that, so we needed to conduct the heat to whatever was inside. It was by chance that it was discovered that the copper chemically reacts with the condensing vapors."

The copper combines with sulfur in the vapor — the sulfur comes from the grains; it's a component of some proteins — to create copper sulfate. The sulfate, a black noxious-smelling compound, stays behind, leaving the spirit to flow clean.

At Woodford Reserve the runoff from the first still is caked with copper sulfate; here the copper reaction also is pulling out the oils from the corn in the mashbill. "The grunge," says master distiller Chris Morris. "We call it the grunge. Don't touch it, you'll be washing the smell off your hands for three days."

Take the copper out of distillation, and that's what your whiskey would smell like. "It would be very pungently sulfury, meaty, almost a cabbagey smell," says Lumsden. "Not really what you would want. Not only would there be too much of the sulfur itself, it would mask a lot of the fruitiness and subtlety of the whisky."

Interestingly, the binding of copper to the sulfur takes away copper as well as sulfur. The stills, the condensers, the lyne arm: everything copper in the distilling path has to be replaced at some point as it gives itself up to make the whiskey tasty and aromatic. If the best examples of humanity have hearts of gold, surely the best whiskey has a gleaming heart of copper.

---

which is cooler than that hot metal below. The steam condenses; you can see it on the inside of the lid when you lift it off.

That's exactly how a pot still works, with two important differences. The first is the whole key to distillation: alcohol boils at a lower temperature than water. So heating the still and its contents to a point between the boiling point of alcohol (ethanol) — 173°F (78°C) — and the boiling point of water — 212°F (100°C) — will give you a long yield of vaporized alcohol that can be condensed and captured.

That's assuming you've provided for the second important difference between a pot and a pot still: an outlet. Stills need an exit for the alcohol vapors. When those vapors come out of a pot still, they go through a neck at the top, then into a sideways tube called the lyne arm. Lyne arms may bend down sharply, or gently, or more horizontally; some angle up. It's all about reflux: redistillation within the distillation.

Reflux is something that doesn't get talked about much by whiskey drinkers, but it can have a huge effect on the taste of the

HOW A DOUBLE COLUMN STILL WORKS

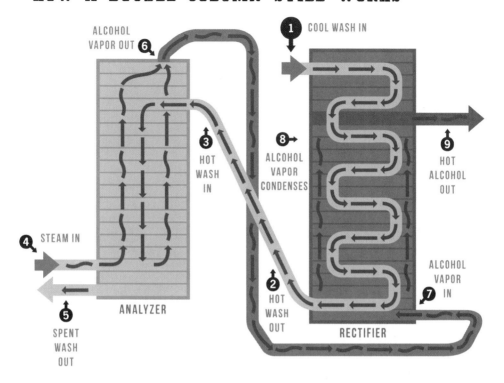

1. Cool wash enters the rectifier column and flows through a system of piping, heating as it goes.

2. Hot wash flows out of the rectifier and is run to near the top of the analyzer column.

3. The hot wash flows into the analyzer column and down through a series of perforated plates. (Note: This is where cool fermented mash would enter the column for bourbon, rye, and Tennessee operations as a first step.)

4. As the wash trickles down, live steam moves up through the plates. The hot steam evaporates the alcohol, turning it into a vapor, and carries it along to the top of the column.

5. The leftovers — spent wash and mash solids — flow out of the bottom of the column. In the bourbon-making sour mash process, the watery mash solids — called "slops" or "stillage" — will be added to unfermented mash as "setback."

6. Hot, impure alcohol vapor flows from the top of the analyzer column. Alcohol levels vary at this point, but they are well over 50%. For grain whisky, the vapor goes to the bottom of the rectifier column, as shown here; for bourbon, the vapor goes to a pot still–like doubler for further purifying.

7. Hot alcohol vapor enters the bottom of the rectifier column and rises through another series of perforated plates. As it rises, it comes into contact with the gradually cooler piping that holds the wash. Some impurities — and water — condense and are left behind (in most cases they drain to the bottom of the column and are pumped to the analyzer for further distillation).

8. Alcohol vapors hit the "spirit plate" and condense at this particular height and temperature. Higher alcohols and other more volatile impurities continue to rise (in most cases they are condensed and returned to the incoming wash feed for redistillation).

9. Hot alcohol flows to the condenser and spirit receiver at approximately 90 to 95% ABV.

whiskey. Aficionados will tell you all about the water source, and the barrels, and the warehouses, and the peat, but it's not often you'll hear someone mention the amount of reflux.

It's not that hard to understand. Reflux refers to the amount of vapor that condenses and falls back into the still before "escaping" to the condensers. The more that happens — that is, the more "reflux" there is — the more the spirit gets cleaned up before it is passed on to the next stage. Short, squat stills have less reflux than tall stills and will produce a heavier spirit; similarly, an upward-aimed lyne arm will drain condensing vapor back into the still, passing only the hottest, purest vapor and producing a lighter spirit.

Some of cleaning is through the evaporative process, a purification through boiling, but a lot of it is in the contact with the copper skin of the still, another thing that doesn't get talked about much. Copper isn't just pretty; it's crucial to the distillation process.

That's why, according to Dr. Bill Lumsden, head of distilling and whisky creation for Glenmorangie and Ardbeg, the two different types of condensers used at Scotch whisky distilleries make such a difference in the spirit. Shell and tube condensers enclose up to 250 copper tubes in a copper shell that the vapor passes through from the lyne arm; cold water runs through the tubes and encourages condensation, and thus reflux. The other type of condenser is a simple worm tub, where the lyne arm feeds a copper worm, the familiar spiraled tube that runs down through a tub of cold water.

Lumsden used to work at a distillery where both types of condensers were used. "I could pick out the difference, nosing and tasting blind," he recalls. "There was such a distinct difference. The whisky made in a distillery with worm tubs is typically much more meaty and sulfury in character."

After the first distillation in the "wash still" has fully begun and the condensed, cleaned-up spirit starts to flow, there's a decision to be made. Is this spirit good enough to become whiskey? This is where the makers earn their keep: the cut. When spirit first flows from the wash still, it's not what they want. It is at a much lower proof, contains undesirable components, and has a character to it that will never become good whisky. This first part of the runoff from the still is called the "foreshots." It will be diverted to a tank and added to the next run to be redistilled.

When the runoff reaches the proper high percentage of alcohol (there are many "alcohols"; the one whiskey makers are looking for is ethanol), the flow is directed to a holding tank; this is the "heart cut." The heat is carefully adjusted to maintain the flow of heart cut for as long as possible, but eventually the time comes to divert the runoff again; this is the final part of the runoff, called the "feints." The feints are also redistilled with the next wash run.

The heart cut — now called "low wines," at around 20 percent ABV — will be distilled in a smaller spirit still, and again, the cuts will be made. This time the cuts have a much greater effect on the character of the spirit; the foreshots and feints remain behind (to be added to the next run). A tighter heart cut will give a cleaner, lighter spirit; a broader cut will yield a spirit with more of the various esters, aldehydes, and higher alcohols, known as congeners (see page 81), giving it a deeper, somewhat oily character. The overall proof of this runoff will be much higher, closer to 70 percent. It is now ready to be put in barrels to age.

COLUMNS:
UGLY AND EFFICIENT

COLUMN STILLS ARE EVERYTHING pot stills are not. They're ugly, just tall columns of bolted-together sections with screwed-down access plates, often tarnished or even rusty, and usually not included on tours. They're quite similar to each other, varying mostly in scale rather than geometry. They're loud, hissing and roaring with the rush of live steam. They run 24/7, not in batches — they're also known as "continuous stills" — and there's no heart cut to be made, just a steady stream of high-proof alcohol.

Not very exciting, right? It's actually fascinating once you learn what's going on in there, and how nineteenth-century distillers cracked the problem of efficient distillation. Pot stills produce good-quality spirit, but there is a necessary downtime between each distillation when the still is being emptied of waste, cleaned, refilled, and then heated for the next distillation. Distillers wanted a way to produce a lot more spirit, quickly, efficiently, and consistently.

The key to the column still is the idea of wash, or beer, moving in one direction — falling downward in the column — as live steam moves up through it in the opposite direction. The wash meets the steam, and as it moves downward the alcohol evaporates and moves upward with the steam; the steam (water) cools and falls downward, and the alcohol vapor becomes more concentrated as it reaches the cooler top of the column. As long as wash and steam are being fed into the column, distillation continues, and high-proof alcohol comes off the top in a steady stream. All a distiller has to do is keep up with fermentation and keep an eye on outputs.

It's a bit more complicated than that. The wash doesn't just fall through rising steam in an open column; it would fall too fast to be heated above alcohol's boiling point. Instead, there are perforated plates in the column that hold the wash, spaced about 15 inches apart. Steam rises through the holes, stripping away the alcohol as it evaporates (some distillers call the column still a "stripper still"). As the weight of the wash overcomes the pressure of the steam, it moves downward to the next plate, where the process happens again and again, the wash dropping down and the alcohol vapor rising, until all the alcohol is stripped out and the liquid waste drains out the bottom (that liquid waste is then cooled and used as sour mash in bourbon fermentation).

Bourbon distillation uses a single-column still and, you'll recall, unfiltered beer, with the grain passing down through the still. The vapor is condensed, and the spirit, now at about 140 proof (though every distiller is different) and at this point called "low wines," is sent to the doubler, essentially a classic copper pot still. Here the whiskey may be slightly raised in proof, cut to leave undesirable flavors behind, or simply run through to react with the copper; again, every distiller has different techniques. Regulations require that the distillate be no more than 160 proof after this final distillation step to make whiskey.

Grain whisky in Scotland is made with a slightly different setup. Scottish distillers use the classic two-column still as perfected by Aeneas Coffey — ironically, an Irish exciseman, or whiskey tax collector — in 1830. The Coffey still (as some distillers call it) has two columns, the analyzer and the rectifier. The wash is preheated and introduced into the top of the analyzer. This is like the single column of the bourbon still, and after the alcohol is stripped out through the plates, it passes to the bottom of the rectifier.

The rectifier is designed to pull off alcohol while allowing more volatile and undesirable congeners to rise to the top of the column. The alcohol stream vaporizes and moves upward through another series of plates, again concentrating as it moves up. Unlike a bourbon distillation, the idea here is to get a much cleaner, purer stream of alcohol, and for grain whiskey that usually means the spirit comes off the rectifier at above 90 percent alcohol, a whopping 180 proof. The flow from the bottom of the rectifier is recirculated into the wash to be sure all the alcohol is recovered; the higher volatiles from the top of the rectifier are either released to the atmosphere or used for chemical feedstock.

Confused? Don't feel bad; it takes a while to figure out everything that's going on in there. If it helps, think of the column still as a series of pot stills perched on top of each other, each one working a batch and sending the vapors up to the next one.

There's a third type of still that involves *adding* water to pull off more congeners, but I'm going to address that in the chapter on Canadian whisky (see page 164), since that's where I saw this still in operation, and because Canadian distillers seem to be the ones most interested in the clean spirit that this extractive distillation can give them.

At the end of the distillation process, the results are roughly the same: a clear, high-proof spirit that's ready to be entered into barrels for aging (or to be bottled as "white whiskey"). The spirits that are lower in proof have more flavor and aroma, but not all of it is desirable. The spirits that are higher in proof are cleaner and without undesirable character, but they have much less aroma and flavor. The barrel will help filter the former, add flavor to the latter, and give both color.

We started in a field of grain, then malted it, milled it, mashed it, fermented it, and distilled it. Malting took a week; mashing and fermenting took another 5 or 6 days, and distillation another day. Two weeks of constant activity will now lead to the filling room, where the spirit will go into a barrel, then into a warehouse . . . and then will sit there for years. We'll talk about wood in the next chapter.

HYBRID STILLS: WHEN YOU JUST CAN'T CHOOSE

The pot still makes for great single-batch control and allows a careful distiller to cut the spirit right where he wants it. The column still allows greater reflux, a clean spirit, and much greater efficiencies. Many craft distillers, faced with the choice, have opted to do both.

Modern still makers offer a hybrid still, with a column sitting atop a pot. The appeal is that the column is adjustable. If distillers want to run it as a pot still, they can open up the plates, and it's . . . kind of like a pot still. If they want to run a bourbon-type spirit, they can close off some of the plates. If they want a cleaner spirit for vodka or for "white whiskey" (the unaged whiskey often sold by craft distillers) they can close up the plates and recirculate within the column, or even send it out to another column, using the pot mainly to heat the spirit. They can even put a bulbous "gin head" with no exit pipe on the still and recirculate spirit through botanicals, allowing it to fall back into the pot.

If you see one of these hybrids in a craft distillery, don't be fooled if your tour guide tells you it's a pot still. It's not really a column still, and it's not really a pot still either. It's something else, quite flexible, and able to be changed up as the distiller wants.

AGING

Take the clear spirit we saw at the end of the previous chapter. That's what our ancestors of 200 years ago would probably have recognized as whiskey. They may have mixed it with hot water and sugar and flavorings, or infused it over a period of days or weeks with herbs, bark, fruit, flowers, or other natural flavors, or they may have bolted it straight.

But 200 years ago whiskey was, for the most part, raw, or unaged. If it was aged, it was by accident, not intent. That was about to change, and whiskey would be transformed from a rough mental anesthetic to a world favorite with a distinct air of sophistication. The transformation would arise from a piece of ancient technology: the barrel.

Scotch whisky maturing in oak casks in a classic earthen-floored "dunnage" warehouse

BARREL AGING

Barrels had been a major advance for the ancient world long before whiskey came along. The practice of steaming wood in order to bend it is believed to have been first developed for boat building. Some bright person, most likely a Celt, borrowed the technique to bend and piece together wooden staves into a cylindrical shape that curved inward at top and bottom and was capped at each end with a lid, or head, fitted into a groove in the staves. The earliest barrels were held together with rope; eventually the rope was replaced by metal hoops that were riveted together and hammered onto the bulge of the barrel.

The barrel was actually quite ingenious and much more than a simple container. It was a way that one person could control a heavy load, well past his or her ability to lift or hold. Every year at the Kentucky Bourbon Festival, you can watch the Bourbon Barrel Relay,

where bourbon warehouse workers roll barrels (filled with water, not whiskey, for the event) down a set of tracks and into a simulated warehouse rick, the set of wooden rails that hold the barrels. They roll the barrels as fast as they can, make right-angle turns, and can rock the barrels up on end to make them turn or bring them to a stop. The barrel's round shape and curved sides allow one person to quickly and precisely control a little over 500 pounds of bourbon, while the uniform size makes it possible, with experience, to roll a barrel down the rails of the rick in such a way that the bung stave — the one with the hole in it, where the barrel is filled and then plugged with a poplar plug, called the bung — ends up topmost, where it can't leak.

Early whiskey makers turned to barrels because they were better containers than earthenware jugs or leather skins for holding the liquid. Like the copper still, though, the barrel was capable of making the whiskey better in ways that hadn't even been thought of.

PARTS OF A BARREL

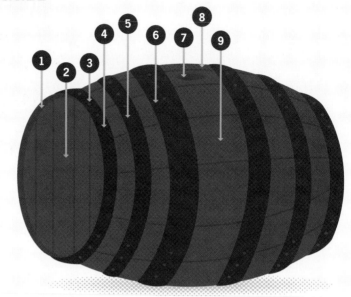

1. CHIME
2. HEAD
3. RIVET
4. HEAD HOOP
5. QUARTER HOOP
6. BILGE HOOP
7. BUNG HOLE
8. BILGE
9. STAVE

CHARRING

ONE OF THE KEYS TO maturing whiskey is charring the inside of the barrel by placing the open-ended barrel over a burner and blowing a hot flame into it. This controlled burn creates physical changes that transform the oak barrel from a mere container to a chemical reaction chamber, a filter, and an infusion vessel.

American bourbon makers were among the first to use charred barrels for storing and aging their whiskey. No one's quite sure exactly when they started charring the barrels; we'll get more into that in chapter 6. But the difference it made was immense, and it would have an effect on whiskey making around the world.

Charring does several things to the wood. First, it creates a layer of charcoal on the inside of the staves. Charcoal has well-known properties as a filtering agent; when wood is converted to charcoal, it gains a huge amount of effective surface area to adhere to

and to contain chemical compounds. A mere gram of charcoal has about 200 square meters of effective surface area, an astounding figure. The char on the inside of a whiskey barrel grabs and sequesters unwanted aromatics, like sulfur.

The heat of charring also changes the oak beneath the char. The sugars in the wood are caramelized in what's called the "red layer," a thin but noticeably colored layer in the wood that can be seen in a disassembled barrel's staves. The alcohol in the whiskey, a natural solvent, permeates the red layer as summer's heat expands it and pushes it into the wood. The caramelized sugars dissolve and become part of the whiskey, adding to both the flavor and the color.

Charring also begins the breakdown of the oak's lignin. Lignin is a natural polymer in the wood, a big and complex molecule that adds strength to the wood. As alcohol continues the breakdown of lignin that the charring began, it creates flavor compounds that will give the whiskey familiar characteristics, such as vanillin, the source of bourbon's creamy vanilla notes, and wood aldehyde compounds, which become aromatic esters. Three of the major esters formed are ethyl syringate (which gives an aroma of tobacco and fig), ethyl ferulate (a spicy cinnamon aroma), and ethyl vanillate (a smoky, burnt aroma), all producing aromas familiar to the bourbon drinker. Another group of compounds, lactones, can give a coconut note. As the alcohol continues to break down other parts of the wood, it releases melanoidins, which deepen the flavors and add more color.

In general, charring is so beneficial and crucial to whiskey maturation that used casks are sometimes recharred for further use. We'll talk more about reuse later.

Live flames and bent oak: charring a barrel

LEAKS AND LEAK HUNTERS

*M*uch of the smell of a whiskey warehouse comes from the slow "breathing" of the barrels. But some of it comes more directly, from leaking barrels. The coopers make them as tight as they can, and each barrel goes through a pressure test before leaving the cooperage: it is filled with water and compressed air and tightly stopped to see if any water forces its way out. Any leaks are repaired; substantial ones involve taking down the barrel and replacing or reshaping individual staves, while smaller ones can be plugged with "spiles" (small wooden spikes) or bits of dried rushes for linear leaks.

Still, leaks may develop. As summer heats the warehouse and the whiskey expands, it will force its way through any small crevice and ooze down the barrel. As it dries, the sugars from the oak are left behind as a sticky brown stain, the source of much of that rich, sweet warehouse reek.

Distillers have generally come to accept this amount of loss as part of the price of aging whiskey. A few distillers, though, still keep leak hunters on staff. They will prowl the warehouses, crawling over the ricks with flashlights, checking for barrels with significant amounts of whiskey drooling down the sides. When they find one, they'll repair it in place if they can, or roll it out if they have to do a bigger job, hoping that it's not too far back in the line of barrels that have to be removed to get at it.

BREATHING

THE UNCHARRED PART OF the oak has an equally significant effect on the whiskey's maturation, and it's because oak does a great job holding liquids, but it isn't perfect. Whiskey barrels are built to close enough tolerances that they can hold liquid for months or years without leaking — much — but the cellular structure of oak is such that a slow exchange of liquid and oxygen takes place over the long weeks, months, and years in the warehouse. You can smell it happening. Whiskey warehouses have a rich, almost overpowering smell that hits you as soon as you walk through the door, like richly sweet, musty caramel; over-ripe fruit; and damp wood, with, of course, a boozy hint of alcohol (only a hint in *some* warehouses, that is — I've been in some where I would have been scared to light a match).

Distillers and warehouse workers grow so used to the smell that they don't really notice it. "The only time I smell it is when there's something wrong and it smells different," Wild Turkey's long-time master distiller Jimmy Russell told me, which is astounding; the smell of Wild Turkey's warehouses in high summer isn't so much an aroma as it is like walking into a huge, soft caramel and vanilla pudding.

Some of that smell comes from the small leaks that develop in the barrels over the years, from the drips and drops that are spilled over years of sampling — official and unofficial — and from the wood of the barrels and the wooden frameworks that hold them in place. But largely that smell comes from the "breathing" of the barrels, the slow exchange of air and liquid that steals away whiskey at a rate of up to 5 percent a year (even more in craft distilleries that are using small barrels or aging in a particularly hot or dry climate), what distillers call the "angel's share."

On the whole, Scotch whisky loses more alcohol than water in this breathing process, and older barrels have to be watched carefully, lest they fall below 80 proof and become no longer legally whisky. On the higher, hotter floors of American warehouses, more water is lost to evaporation than is alcohol, and the proof will rise, meaning whiskey could go in at 120 proof and come out, say, 7 years later at around 135 proof, stronger but reduced in volume.

Loss to evaporation is one of the unavoidable costs of making whiskey, as certain and unyielding as taxes. It will be less in cooler climates or wet conditions, but it happens every year, without fail. Along with the growth of undesirably harsh and drying wood character as a whiskey ages past its prime, evaporation is the true endpoint of aging a whiskey. Eventually the angels can claim so much of the whiskey that the barrel dries out and leaks copiously, or even collapses when touched.

At the same time, barrel breathing is one of the basic elements of whiskey maturation. Without this exchange, the whiskey simply will not mature properly. Why? Let's go back to the cellular structure of oak. In the living tree there are slow-moving exchanges in the wood, through a maze of fibers and channels, for the transport of water, air, sugar, and minerals. As the oak develops more woody outer layers, the living wood — that part that is wet with sap when you saw through a tree — will develop *tyloses*, blockages that close off the channels. The tyloses serve to cut losses of living tissue during drought or infection. For the cooper, tyloses are what make oak a favored wood for waterproof (and whiskeyproof) barrels. They block the channels and will not pass liquid. They will, however, pass air as the liquid ever so slowly seeps out through interstitial spaces.

SIZE MATTERS

*C*raft distillers have stirred up controversy by using barrels that are smaller than the industry standard. (In America that's a 53-gallon barrel.) They wanted to age their whiskey in wood, but they needed it faster, because they had bills to pay. They looked at the effects of relative proportions of surface area of wood exposed to whiskey and decided that smaller barrels would age the whiskey more quickly. Quite a few small distillers made the decision to age their whiskey in 30-gallon, 15-gallon, 5-gallon, and even 2-gallon barrels.

Does it work? The whiskey picks up color very quickly from the proportionately large surface area, but the flavor is different compared to "large barrel" whiskey aged to a similar color. Evaporation losses are steep, and the barrels cost more per gallon of whiskey aged, but it is a trade-off with speed of return on investment. The question is whether the whiskey is actually aging faster or aging differently.

Scott Spolverino, a whiskey chemist who's looked specifically at the aging process in these smaller barrels, describes the difference as aged versus matured. "Aging is what you put on the bottle: how old is it?" he says. "It has more to do with wood compounds, wood-based flavors, more extraction, and literally the time it's in there. Maturation is the culmination of chemical reactions and evaporation."

Evaporation is important, but Spolverino also describes a process that takes place over time, unaffected by the barrel size. This is "ethanol clustering," a structural coming together of ethanol and water in a way that makes the ethanol sensation on the palate smoother. "A small barrel can't force the hand here," he says.

How do small-barrel whiskeys taste? I was wary of the idea at first. Even with only 20 years of drinking whiskey behind me, I've already encountered folks who thought they could speed this up and have been disappointed. But I've had some young whiskey aged in small barrels that I liked — the Ranger Creek .36 Texas bourbon, for one — and I've decided that maybe small barrels aren't necessarily the horror that I'd originally thought they were.

I've noticed that some small distillers are moving to large barrels as their sales and production increase, though. Larger barrels mean less evaporation — even balanced against a longer time to maturity — which means more whiskey to sell, and that's a powerful argument. But some distillers will, I think, continue to use small barrels for at least part of their stock. The flavors are robust, and with regular sampling to stop aging when it's peaked, that can make an appealing whiskey.

Over successive summers, whiskey moves out of the barrel and air moves in. The whiskey moving out has an effect we already know about: we lose whiskey, and all we get for it is a pleasant smell in the warehouse! But as the air moves in, it contributes to all of the chemical reactions that are going on in the barrel, from the charcoal filtering arising from the char to the breakdown of lignin and subsequent development of various flavor compounds. As compounds in the whiskey mix with the incoming oxygen and are oxidized, fruity esters arise, giving whiskey those signature aromatics that simply can't be explained by mere grain and wood. All these amazing aromas and flavors are coming from the wooden barrel . . . and all the whiskey makers were looking for was something to hold whiskey on the way to market.

TIME IS MONEY

AT THE SAME TIME THERE'S a lot more to barrel aging than simply airing up the spirit. The late Lincoln Henderson, a long-time Brown-Forman distiller who oversaw the production of such iconic whiskeys as Jack Daniel's, Old Forester, and Woodford Reserve, told me about some experiments his team ran at Brown-Forman over 30 years ago.

They assigned chemical engineers to study the aging process, to better understand it and to see if there was a way to shorten or improve it. Shortening the aging process is a constant attraction for whiskey makers (and their accountants); time truly is money in this business, stemming from the evaporation losses, increased taxes, and the physical needs of warehousing.

"We made bourbon in 5 days," he said, with a grin that was still a bit sour with the memory. "You need that air to get in the barrel, so we were feeding oxygen into the whiskey, running it over wood. It looked beautiful! But it tasted like crap."

What is the aging magic? Is it the speed of the exchange? Is it the atmospheric pressure, the pressure in the barrel? Is it something going on inside the wood that changes things? All good questions, and all part of the reason that we don't make whiskey in 5 days.

NEW WHISKEY IN OLD BARRELS

SCOTTISH, CANADIAN, AND IRISH whiskey makers use very few new barrels, and those few they do use are a relatively recent innovation. They've aged their whiskey in used casks for a long time, and they've become very good at using them to get a variety of different flavors. Bourbon casks are the most common type they use, if only because there are so many.

There's an element of necessity to it. American whiskey makers buy the barrels newly made and charred, and, for the most part, they use them once. American regulations require that bourbon, rye, wheat, malt (American-made; there are separate regulations for Scotch whisky), and rye malt whiskeys must be aged in *new* charred oak barrels. Whiskey that is aged wholly or partly in used barrels — done to get less of the strong flavors the new barrels impart — must be labeled as "whiskey distilled from bourbon (rye, wheat, malt, or rye malt) mash," but currently the only major brand so aged is Early Times, though there are some craft whiskeys that are aged in used barrels.

Since American straight whiskey makers can use a barrel only once, they've become a source of barrels for most of the rest of the world's whiskey makers. "We've got the flavor out of them, now you can have them" is the joke from the Americans. "We'll use them now that you've soaked the harshness out" is the response.

It's all in good fun, but there's truth to it. Scotch whisky makers don't want the strong vanilla notes that a new barrel brings, and that first use extracts most of it, which is what the bourbon makers want.

That's also part of the reason you'll see much older age statements on Scotch whiskies than on bourbons. I've had Scotch whiskies that were older than I am, but the oldest American whiskey I've seen was the 27-year-old Parker's Heritage Collection bourbon from Heaven Hill that came out in 2008. It was a beauty, a majestic whiskey that tasted much younger than it was, but that's extremely rare. I've had 18-year-old bourbons that were overoaked, tannic, and astringent. There's much more flavor potential in a new barrel, and once it's been knocked down even by a 4-year exposure to high-proof spirit, it has a slower cumulative effect on new spirit.

Sherry casks are the other major source of used wood for aging whisky. Usually the sherry barrels are made with European oak, which has more tannin and a different structure from that of American oak. The sherry barrels will retain some of the character of the fortified wine that was in them, and that varies with the type of sherry: dry fino, nutty/vanilla oloroso, rich, sweet Pedro Ximénez. Bourbon wood can give the vanilla and coconut aromas bourbon drinkers are familiar with. Combine the flavors of these "first fill" barrels in their

first reuse with the distillery character, and you can develop delicious whiskey.

But it's not just bourbon casks and sherry casks, or even the occasional port, Madeira, or new oak cask, being reused. Some distillers are using second- and third-fill casks to get less wood character and more of the individual taste of the spirit and the evaporative effects. The results of these different casks can then be blended together in new ways to give interestingly varied single malt bottlings from the same distillery. In other words, don't assume that a GlenWhatsit 18-year-old single malt is the same whisky as the GlenWhatsit 12-year-old, just six years older. It may be another prospect altogether.

WAREHOUSING

SCOTCH AND OTHER distillers can play mix and match with reused casks to create different flavors in their whiskies. Bourbon distillers may take a different tack; Four Roses,

Oak barrels in Woodford Reserve's stone-walled warehouse in Versailles, Kentucky

CASK VS. BARREL

*Y*ou'll mostly see me using the word *barrel*, but sometimes I'll say *cask*. What's the difference? Well, *barrel* is mostly an American usage, while it's usually the Scots who say *cask*. (The Irish mostly say *barrel* as well, but then, they spell *whiskey* the right way, too.) Nevertheless, there's a significant difference between a bourbon barrel that's in an American warehouse and a bourbon cask that's in a Scottish warehouse . . . sometimes the Scottish one's bigger.

Bourbon barrels are sold to Scottish distillers, but they're not shipped to Scotland as barrels. They're knocked down into parcels of staves and hoops to save space on shipping. When they get to Scotland and go to a cooperage (often the Speyside Cooperage in Craigellachie) for reassembling, they may be put back together at the American standard of 200 liters (almost exactly 53 gallons), but they may instead be put together with more staves as a traditional hogshead size, at 225 liters (63 gallons).

That's one reason I call them *casks* — they're not the same barrels as they started out — but the other reason is cordiality: that's what the Scots call them.

---

for example, makes and blends 10 different bourbons (more on that on page 148), and Beam has two different mashbills, one with a higher proportion of rye. But the usual way of getting varied flavor profiles within a distillery's portfolio is warehouse selection.

There are a variety of types of warehouses; that's true in America, Scotland, Ireland, Canada, and Japan. The bizarre half-tube concrete warehouse at Kilbeggan in Ireland comes to mind; it looks like the inside of a whale in there. The craft distillers rarely have anything normal in the way of warehouses at this point in their development; Ranger Creek ages its small-barrel whiskeys in metal shipping containers that bake in the hot Texas sun. Warehouses can be on hills, by rivers or the ocean, in wooded glades, in wide-open fields, or on city streets; they can be made of wood, brick, or stone; they can be short or toweringly tall; and it can all affect the aging whiskey inside.

This is where the American distiller gets the most chance for variety in its bottlings. Think about it: the barrels are *all* new, charred oak, usually from the same supplier. The char can be varied slightly, and there is a trend toward toasting the heads rather than charring them, but barrels are usually done the same for all of a distillery's whiskeys. The mashbill varies among distilleries, but again, within a distiller's confines, there are usually no more than two at most for making bourbon. Yeast, with the glaring exception of Four Roses, is usually one strain per distiller, and the column stills are virtually identical in their output.

The warehouse, then, provides a chance for real variety. Go to the top levels of seven-story "ironclads" (wooden-frame warehouses with corrugated metal skins) for barrels that have been subjected to greater heat, and you'll find their whiskeys have strong oak character. Lower, cooler levels are where you'll find the best candidates for super-aged whiskey. The deep center of middle floors, insulated

HOW STORAGE LOCATION AFFECTS THE FLAVOR OF BOURBON

*R*ule of thumb: bourbon gets at least 50 percent of its flavor from the barrel. The longer the bourbon spends in the barrel, the more oak flavor it has. Equally important is how and where the bourbon is stored.

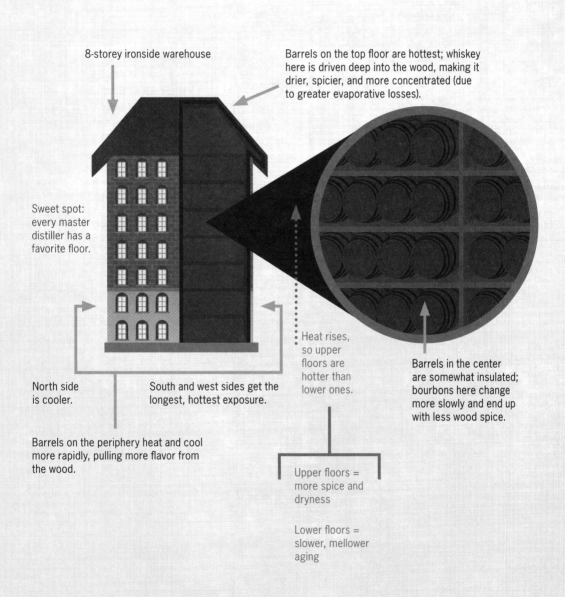

8-storey ironside warehouse

Barrels on the top floor are hottest; whiskey here is driven deep into the wood, making it drier, spicier, and more concentrated (due to greater evaporative losses).

Sweet spot: every master distiller has a favorite floor.

North side is cooler.

South and west sides get the longest, hottest exposure.

Heat rises, so upper floors are hotter than lower ones.

Barrels in the center are somewhat insulated; bourbons here change more slowly and end up with less wood spice.

Barrels on the periphery heat and cool more rapidly, pulling more flavor from the wood.

Upper floors = more spice and dryness

Lower floors = slower, mellower aging

Whiskey barrels and bar codes: a mix of old and new technology that has revolutionized whiskey making

by a surrounding thermal damper of thousands of barrels of whiskey, will be where the temperature swings are the most moderate and the character of the aging whiskey will be the most predictable, the heart of standard bottlings.

All experienced master distillers have their favorite floors (and the warehouse workers know where their favorites are, too), and some that they know just never make good whiskey. There are floors that are not used (sometimes they're left empty, sometimes they're used to age other spirits); there are even some warehouses that are no longer used, awaiting demolition. (Bad decisions can take years to come to light in this industry.)

But when warehouse variety is being used to create consistent bottlings of familiar brands, it's a matter of taking a parcel of mature barrels from one warehouse floor, another from a different warehouse, and so on, and then mingling them. That's why as a month's distillation is barreled and put away

to age, it's not all stuffed into one warehouse, on one floor. It's spread around, to be sure that whiskey is always coming to maturity in different conditions. It's also protection against losing an entire "vintage" of whiskey in case of fire.

Because of the much greater volume of whisky Scottish distillers produce, and the other differences they have to work with, their warehouses tend to be more uniform. But they still have warehouses that have a definite cachet, a mystique to them. Some of the best known are on Islay — warehouses that face the ocean and are occasionally slammed by waves during storms. Bowmore's No. 1 Vaults are perhaps the best known of all, the oldest whisky warehouse in Scotland and actually just below sea level. The ceiling is low, the light is scattered, and the smell is tremendous: sherry, wood, sea freshness, and the strong, sweet smell of malt whisky. This is where the cultiest of cult whiskies came from: Black Bowmore was tucked away here in oloroso

HOW OLD? AND HOW MUCH?

A couple of things about age statements. First, not all whiskeys have them. They're generally not required; age statements are usually just selling points. A whiskey that doesn't have one is often younger, but not always. Distillers are doing more "no age statement" labeling these days; they say it's because it gives them more freedom to bottle a whiskey when it's mature, and not be bound by a preprinted age statement. That's true, but it is also a reflection that whiskey stocks are on average younger than they were 10 years ago, which in turn is a reflection on whiskey's greater sales in recent years. It's our fault: we drank up all that older stuff!

Second, an age statement means that the youngest whiskey in the bottled blend spent that many years in wood in the warehouse. Once a whiskey leaves the barrel for the final time, aging is officially over. Time spent in the bottle doesn't count, and a whiskey won't change in glass unless the closure — cork, screw cap, or whatever — starts to pass significant amounts of air. So just because your great-uncle bought a bottle of J&B in the 1970s doesn't make it a 45-year-old whisky.

Finally, you'll have noticed by now that older whiskeys cost more. I hope that after reading this chapter you'll have a pretty good idea of why, but let's be sure. First, not many barrels will make it to the extremes of age, simply because most barrels are not the right barrel or in the right place to be able to take a whiskey that far without ruining it. The whiskey may evaporate too fast, or the cask might develop a sudden leak as it gets old, or the wood may not be right and the whiskey gets puckeringly astringent, or it may just not be in the right part of the warehouse. Not every barrel can do it, and the cost of the ones that failed has to be factored into the price of the one that makes it.

Then the evaporation, the angel's share, is chewing away at the whiskey in a barrel steadily over the years. Often when a bourbon gets to 20 years in the barrel, or a Scotch whisky gets to 40 years in the barrel, there's just not much left, even if it's wonderful. The yield can be less than a hundred bottles, from a barrel that was filled with enough spirit to fill three hundred.

Then there are the hard facts of rarity: unusually rare bottlings command higher prices from auctions and collectors, and that's how the bottles are going to be priced. If there are buyers out there who will pay $4,000 for a 40-year-old whisky at auction — and there are, in increasing numbers — then distilleries are leaving money on the table if they price their 40-year-old whisky at $2,000. They may bottle it in an artful crystal decanter and put it in a beautiful presentation case to soften the blow, but there's the price.

Of course, there's Glenfarclas . . . which recently released its 40-year-old whisky, without a lot of fanfare, in the same bottle it uses for all its whisky, with a label only slightly changed from its 12-year-old bottling. It was a delicious whisky, everything you'd ask for from a 40-year-old Speyside sherry-cask whisky: fruit, nuts, lush complexity with a drying bit of leather, and that heavier short-still body. Price? $460. Apparently a bottling for the drinkers rather than the collectors.

sherry casks in 1964. If you can find a bottle of the first bottling, you'll have to pay over $10,000 for it.

SELECTION AND BOTTLING

THAT BRINGS US TO the final stages in the process. This is where the parcels of barrels are selected, dumped, mingled, and bottled. It's nowhere near as simple as it sounds.

The whiskey has been followed, sampled, and monitored from the moment the grain came through the gates. Samples are kept and records made of every step: milling, mashing, fermentation, distillation, and representative samples along the way. Arguments continue in the industry over the benefits of automation in the distillery — does it create better consistency, or does it take the individual genius out of the equation? — but very few argue about the benefits of computers and barcodes in tracking individual barrels through the maturation process.

POSSIBLE COMPONENTS OF A 15-YEAR-OLD WHISKEY

5%

10%

50%

35%

15-YEAR-OLD WHISKEYS

16- AND 17-YEAR OLD WHISKEYS

18- AND 20-YEAR-OLD WHISKEYS

21-YEAR-OLD WHISKEYS

As groups of barrels reach maturity for their particular purpose — blended whisky, flagship bottling, single malt, extra-aged single barrels — sampling may increase to determine whether the whiskeys are properly matured, as opposed to being a certain number of years old. The older the whiskey, or the more divergent from the distiller's usual bottling, the more care is taken.

A new bottling, or "expression," is always exciting. Sometimes a new expression is the result of production staff — distiller, warehouse manager, master blender, distillery manager — letting management and marketing know about something special that's cropped up; sometimes it's the result of marketing coming up with an idea or requirement and asking the production folks to make it happen if possible.

That's how it works in a perfect world, but sometimes it's the result of running out of stock for another expression that has sold better than expected. This is the source of the old industry joke about marketing calling up production: "That 16-year-old is great, it's great! Great job! We're sold out; can you make more of it for next week?" "How about in 16 years?" production responds.

The back end of selection is planning, deciding how much whiskey to make (and what types), what barrels to put it in, and where to age it. The planners are working with a lead time of 4 to 9 years or more for bourbon, 3 to 6 years to start for Canadian, and more like 8 to 12 and up for Scotch, Irish, and Japanese . . . and a market that took two major directional changes in the past 30 years. Ask an honest distillery manager about long-range planning, and the first response you're likely to get is a grin.

Once the parcels are selected, it's time for my favorite part of the whole process: dumping. The barrels are lined up, the bungs are drilled and extracted, and the whiskey gushes forth, free flowing, into a trough (some distillers actually use pumps to suck the whiskey out of the barrels, which is okay, but not as visual). It's fun to watch, it smells great, and you can sometimes get a sample right out of the barrel, the way the distillers and blenders drink it. (That's strictly illegal, of course. But it happens.)

The contents of the barrels are mixed; then they are often placed in a tank or a large wooden vat for a length of time (it varies from distillery to distillery). This is called "marrying," and it ensures an even blend of the flavors of the different barrels.

The whiskey is usually chill filtered. If whiskey gets very cold, down around the freezing point of water, there are some proteins that will precipitate, turning the whiskey slightly hazy. This is considered visually unappealing, so the whiskey is chilled and the haze is filtered out. This may also filter out some flavor compounds (ethyl esters and attached fatty acids). Some of us believe that makes the whiskey taste different, less flavorful, so there is a growing movement among distillers to forgo chill filtering, and the bottle may say so.

Some whiskeys may also get a small amount of caramel coloring at this point, if it's legal in their country of origin. The caramel is made from the same malt sugars the whiskey is, and it's in the name of having all the whisky in a brand expression uniformly colored, but again, some connoisseurs object, and there are uncolored expressions that make that distinction.

Then it's off to the bottling line, the loading dock, and the shelves of your favorite store or bar. That's not including all the marketing that gets attached (kidding!) or all the taxes that are levied (sadly, not kidding), but it's best if you not think about those. Focus on tasting the whiskey in light of everything you've learned. You'll be better off that way!

THE WALL AND THE WORK:

THE CHALLENGE OF TASTING WHISKEY

The long wait is over. The acorn was planted, it grew, and it was felled, seasoned, and made into a barrel, which may have then taken years to season wine or other whiskeys before aging the whiskey now before you. The grains were sown, and they grew and were harvested. The barley, corn, rye, and wheat were mashed, the yeast did their happy work, and the beer's been through the stills. The whiskey has been cradled and crafted by the barrel and the climate for years. It was dumped, bottled, shipped, and sold. Finally, after years of preparation that may well have reached back to before your mother's mother was born . . . the whiskey is ready.

Are you?

Because I wasn't. I had been drinking for about 15 years when I first faced a whiskey I actually wanted to *taste*. I drank beer and was tasting it for reviews; I was lucky enough to be learning about tasting from some of the earliest, best craft brewers.

But when I drank whiskey it was either a frat-boy dare and a fiery shot, or a mix with a soft drink — ginger ale, cola, lemon-lime — to make what I found to be a palatable drink. I didn't sip, and therefore I was barely getting more than the most obvious flavors whiskey had. Whiskey tasted like smoke (the Johnnie Walker I drank to appear sophisticated), or burning vanilla (Wild Turkey shots fired back in manhood-chasing moments), or a really bad idea (Canadian Club dumped randomly in fruit punch to see if it worked like rum; it didn't).

So mostly I drank beer and wrote about it. One magazine I wrote for regularly (and still do) was *Malt Advocate* (now *Whisky Advocate*), and it was a beer magazine, founded by passionate enthusiast John Hansell and run out of his basement at the time. We were having a great time keeping up with the rapid advance of microbreweries in the mid-1990s, and I'd just been named managing editor. Then there was an adjustment in the industry as the number of breweries outpaced the demand (and the number of trained brewers). Underfunded breweries started to close, or downsize, or simply cut back on expenses . . . like advertising in beer magazines.

Luckily, John was also a whiskey drinker, a bit obsessed about it really, and we'd been running the occasional whiskey article. When this great readjustment in the microbrewery niche occurred in 1996, John quickly decided that there was room in the market for a whiskey magazine, and we shifted focus without much hesitation.

Well, *John* didn't hesitate much. I did. I knew next to nothing about whiskey! We had a meeting I still remember, just the two of us, in his backyard, over cigars, dark Baltic porters, and, eventually, glasses of whiskey. Here's the deal, he told me. If you want to keep writing for the magazine, if you want to stay on as managing editor . . . you have to learn to drink whiskey.

That might sound like an easy requirement to meet, but there was a problem. I didn't know the first thing about it, except that the ways I *had* been drinking whiskey weren't going to cut it if I were going to write about whiskey in the same way I wrote about beer. I had to understand whiskey, learn how it was made, see it made, understand all the building blocks that went into the liquid. . . and then learn how to discern aromas and flavors, pick out distillery character, develop my own preferences, and finally hone my senses to really taste whiskey, to determine which ones I liked, which ones I didn't care for, and which ones I loved.

That didn't seem likely, because when I drank whiskey, all I could taste was *Hot! Burning! In my Mouth!* When I put whiskey in my mouth, it was like drinking fire. That's why I slammed shots or mixed it with soft drinks — to get it over with as quickly as possible or to take that fiery edge off. I would read detailed tasting notes on whiskeys, about maple, citrus, mint, fudge, warm honey, tarry rope, tangerines, lavender . . . and all I got was the roar of heat from what felt like raw alcohol on my tongue. Was it me? Was I genetically challenged? Or was it them, making this stuff up?

I went back to John and asked him, what the heck do I do? How are you getting all this out of whiskey? That's when he told me about The Wall, and how to get past it. That's what I'm

EXPLAINING THE WALL

What is The Wall, and how does drinking every day eventually get you past it? In *Buzz*, his 1996 book on the science of alcohol and caffeine, science writer Stephen Braun explained why alcohol feels like fire. After showing how the compounds in a sip of whiskey (he playfully specifies an 18-year-old Macallan) are chemically sensed by the ion channels of the taste buds, he notes that none of the taste impressions you're getting are from ethanol. Pure ethanol is, as the government's definition of vodka requires, odorless and tasteless; it makes no impact on the taste buds.

Alcohol does, however, affect a set of nerve receptors called polymodal pain receptors. Braun notes that they respond to three kinds of stimuli: physical pressure, temperature, and specific chemicals. When these receptors are overstimulated, we feel pain. Ethanol in higher concentrations — whiskey, for example, but not beer or wine — will stimulate the pain fibers in these receptors, to the point where we perceive the sensation as burning.

Capsaicin, the active element in hot peppers, has a similar effect. You may see where I'm going here . . . that's right: as with hot peppers, you can build up a tolerance to the physical heat and pain of the ethanol in whiskey. If you eat a jalapeño every day, you will find that the burning sensation you initially feel will be lessened over time, and soon you'll be happily crunching away and tasting the deliciously herbal flavors you couldn't even notice before, when you were too busy crying. You've broken through The Wall, and the pain no longer obscures the flavors that were there all along.

---

going to tell you, and it's the most important thing about tasting whiskey and enjoying it.

First, you have to want to enjoy the whiskey. Unless you're coming to this having already been drinking neat liquor, you'll need to break through The Wall before you can really get it. I'm assuming you know that learning to drink whiskey is worth it. Maybe it's because someone told you; maybe it's because of something you read; maybe it's because you want more of those flavors you get in cocktails or highballs. If it's none of those, and someone just gave you this book as a well-meaning gift, well, just take my word for it. It's going to take some work, but it's worth it . . . once you get through The Wall.

Actually getting *through* The Wall is a matter of practice. "You have to drink whiskey every day," John told me, and he wasn't kidding. I didn't have to drink a lot, but I would drink at least an ounce of whiskey every day. I tried bourbons, I tried blended Scotch, I tried single malts. It got to be a bit like getting kicked in the face by a mule every evening after a while. I didn't look forward to it, but I kept doing it. I was smelling good stuff, so I knew it was there, but the mouth still rebelled.

Then one day, after about 3 weeks on the Whisky-a-Day Program, I put a glass of Dalmore single malt (I'd tell you which bottling, but I simply don't recall) to my lips and sniffed — I smelled some fruit and a hint of cocoa — and then sipped . . . and

I tasted fudge. I remember the moment: my eyes widened, I opened my mouth again and breathed in, and I tasted the sweet creaminess of fudge, with just a twist of dry baker's chocolate. I was finally tasting whiskey.

It's also worth remembering that most of what you're doing when you "taste" whiskey is actually *smelling* whiskey. Our actual sense of taste is a fairly limited instrument compared to our sense of smell. You don't need to read physiological reports to understand this. Just think of how things taste when your nose is completely stuffed up and you can breathe only through your mouth; they taste dull, blunted.

Have a good fresh French fry with your nose wide open, and you get the earthiness of the potato, the slight caramel notes from the browned crispiness around the edges, the notes of the fry oil (let's hope it's clean and fresh; if not, you may smell fish or burnt corn), and the hot salt. Now clamp your nose tightly with your fingers and eat a fry from the same batch, still fresh and hot, and you'll still taste the salt, still taste the fullness of the oil, still sense the texture, but all those top notes are gone, and you're left with a much less appetizing mouthful.

When you eat or drink, you're tasting with the tongue, but you're also smelling, as the aromatics ride the airflow through your mouth and up into your nose. It's best to think of it the way the eighteenth-century French gastronome Jean Anthelme Brillat-Savarin so perspicaciously put it: "The taste and the sense of smell *form but one sense*, of which the mouth is the laboratory and the nose the chimney."

What makes whiskey and other spirits so much more exciting in this realm is the physical presence of alcohol. Alcohol, beyond its well-known effects on the mind and body, is also a powerful and volatile solvent. As we saw

earlier, it dissolves and then absorbs aromatic compounds in the beer and in the barrel, carrying those to the finished whiskey. When it encounters the heat of your mouth — and the heat of your hand on the glass before even entering your mouth — it begins to evaporate and thus carries a stronger dose of those aromatics to the "chimney" of your nose.

Whiskey is, in this sense, similar to perfume — also alcohol based — and carries its bouquet on a floating, volatile bed of alcohol. It's a synergistic whole. The creation of alcohol in fermentation brings aromas and flavors along with it. The distillation process filters and concentrates those aromas and flavors. Barrel aging again filters, but it also adds a great deal to the liquid, including the appealing color. Then alcohol carries all those aromas and flavors to your senses and — let's be honest — provides a unique blend of psychic and physical effects that, in moderation, have enlivened and fascinated humans for millennia.

It all comes together in a single, delicious package. To quote Brillat-Savarin again: "Alcohol carries the pleasures of the palate to their highest degree." Smart guy, that Brillat-Savarin.

NO EASY WAY OUT

YOU'RE NOW TASTING whiskey; you've done the work of getting past The Wall. Congratulations! You're here, the mouth/nose combination is clicking, and you're ready to embark on the lifelong work and pleasure of tasting whiskey. The first thing to learn about the work and the pleasure is this: there are no shortcuts; there is no One Best Whiskey.

That's not the usual statement. There are books full of whiskey tasting notes, with ratings in numbers or stars of every whiskey

SHOTS! SHOTS! SHOTS!

Sip it? Or slam it? What do you think I'm going to say? If you slam back your drink of whiskey all at once, "doing a shot," it's *gone*. You enjoy one drink, you gasp for air a bit, and it's done, except for the finish, and you're one drink closer to oblivion.

Honesty is important: whiskey is a potent drink. Taking too many, too quickly is, frankly, dangerous. No matter how good it tastes, you must respect that, and take things slowly, and safely.

It isn't just dangerous to drink too fast; it blunts your appreciation of the whiskey, and quickly. "Taste" five whiskeys in 90 minutes, and you won't be tasting the last one, maybe even the last two. Sipping paces your enjoyment and ensures that you'll still be getting a full measure of flavor and feel out of the last one.

With all that said, there is something to be said for the occasional restorative gulp of whiskey. A quick dram can brace the nerves, if only in the fashion of a slap in the face; it shocks you, focuses you, hits the reset button. Just don't make it a habit!

---

the writer could find, buy, or get a sample of, and you can find the same in magazines and on whiskey websites. I write some of those reviews myself. You'll find "top 10" lists, "world's best" lists, and an ever-growing array of awards, medals, and ribbons. If that's not enough, there's someone in every whiskey bar and liquor store out there with an opinion on what the best whiskey is, often expressed like this: "I drink only X whiskey," which implies that you should, too.

I get it. It's an appealingly easy idea. There are a lot of choices, and as whiskey becomes more popular, there are more choices hitting the shelves every month. It's intimidating, and it can be expensive. Instead of spending a lot of money on whiskeys, and taking time to taste whiskeys, and doing all that thinking about them as you taste them, why not simply look at one of these guides and then go on your way rejoicing, drinking "the best" whiskey?

If you do that, you'll not only be cheating yourself out of a lot of fun, and a lot of good whiskey, you'll be stunting your education before it begins and maybe even condemning yourself to some serious dissatisfaction. I don't want you to become one of the people who will take me aside when I'm talking about whiskey or doing a tasting and ask, with clear confidence that there is some secret, single answer, "But which one is the *best*?" Because that's the one whiskey and the only whiskey they want to buy — *the best* — whether from a desire to save decision time, or to bask in the relieving knowledge that they bought the best, or to be able to tell their friends that they have the best whiskey.

Myself, I like to go to the liquor store or the bar and take a look at all my options. Do I want something tried and true, do I want to splurge a bit on a small upgrade from my usual, or do I really want to lay out the coin for something truly rare and wonderful this time?

2012 TOTAL WORLD SALES *

Whiskey Sales Worldwide

100

99.5

75

50

42.8

25

22

10

6.2

MILLIONS OF CASES

SCOTCH (BLENDS, SINGLE MALTS)

AMERICAN (BOURBON, TENNESSEE, RYE, BLENDED)

CANADIAN

JAPANESE

IRISH

*Measured in industry-standard 9-liter case equivalents

I've never yet made a decision that I've really regretted, because it's almost always been good, and it's been educational every time. There was one truly terrible blended whisky at the airport bar in Frankfurt . . . but even that made a good story: no one should ever taste a whisky named "Glob Kitty," even on a dare.

Barry Schwartz, in his book *The Paradox of Choice*, calls people who use these approaches to dealing with a proliferation of choices "maximizers" and "satisficers." Maximizers look to get the best possible results from their decisions, every time. Satisficers are looking for "good enough" results. As a confirmed satisficer, I'm hoping for a *little* better than merely "good enough," but you get the point. Maximizers generally have a harder time making a decision; they spend more time

researching it and asking what other people are buying and often wind up less satisfied with their decisions.

They're also going to pay more . . . a lot more. High-end whiskey is often rare whiskey, and that kind of rarity costs. A bottle of 40-year-old single malt can cost $1,000 or more; a bottle of the coveted Pappy Van Winkle 20-year-old bourbon will run you over $800, if you can manage to find one. There is not enough of what people call the best to go around, and looking for it can be maddening.

If someone's that fixated on getting only *the best whiskey*, it's possible that he doesn't even like whiskey that much. If he did, he'd be in it for the enjoyment the rest of us experience: drinking the whiskey, not owning it. These are people who are buying labels and

EVOLUTION OF FLAVOR AS A WHISKEY AGES

Bourbon

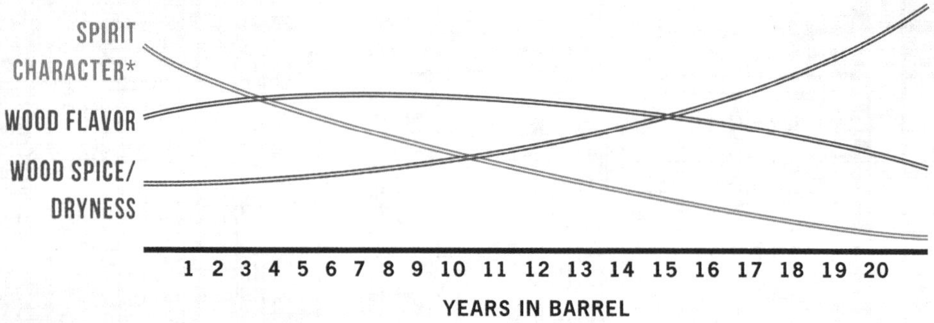

SPIRIT CHARACTER*

WOOD FLAVOR

WOOD SPICE/ DRYNESS

1 2 3 4 5 6 7 8 9 10 11 12 13 14 15 16 17 18 19 20

YEARS IN BARREL

Scotch

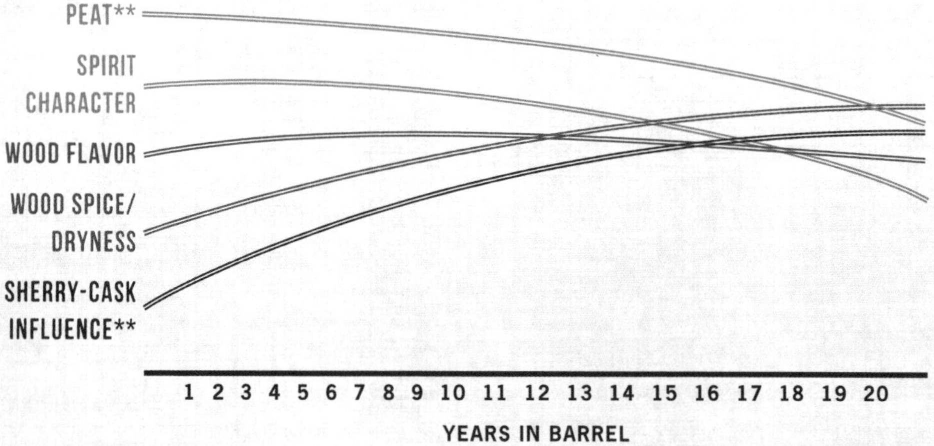

PEAT**

SPIRIT CHARACTER

WOOD FLAVOR

WOOD SPICE/ DRYNESS

SHERRY-CASK INFLUENCE**

1 2 3 4 5 6 7 8 9 10 11 12 13 14 15 16 17 18 19 20

YEARS IN BARREL

*"Spirit character" defines the nature of the new, unaged spirit — Glenmorangie's light and elegant sweetness, Glenfarclas's beefy and oily weight, Maker's Mark's clean corn, and all the many different shapes of peat. It starts out as the dominant flavor and quickly combines with everything else, the wood being first.

**Peat and Sherry are optional.

bottles, not whiskey. Let them buy the rare and expensive; when the bubble bursts, maybe you can pick them up at auction.

Then there are people who are just as focused, but on one particular whiskey or brand: Maker's Mark, Macallan, Jameson, Gentleman Jack, Johnnie Walker Blue, whatever. They'll drink only that whiskey, they'll let you know it's the best whiskey, they'll have a beer or wine rather than drink a different whiskey if their favorite isn't available.

No matter what whiskey they're drinking, they're wrong: it's not the *only* best whiskey for everyone. But for whatever reason, it's working for them, and they like it, and I doubt they're ever going to read this, so they'll stay happy drinking their whiskey of choice.

The folks you really have to watch out for are the category snobs. You can see them pop up anytime a story on whiskey runs on a national news website, because they can't resist the chance to tell everyone else they're drinking the wrong whiskey. The only true whiskey is sour mash, they'll say; you should be drinking single malt or you're not really drinking whiskey; Irish whiskey is the first whiskey; and so on.

They've made a singular mistake, and you shouldn't let them influence your choices. Because just like there is no One Best Whiskey, there is no One Best Type of Whiskey, either. It's fine for someone to say, "I like Scotch whisky the most," or "Bourbon's harsh on my palate, so I drink Irish whiskey," or "I think single malts have more flavor than blends." Those are personal preferences. But to confuse personal preferences for world truths is no way to go through life. (And that's true whether you're talking about whiskey or any other subject under the sun.)

Let's take this apart right now. Scotch whisky sells more than any other type, worldwide (with the exception of the "whiskies" of

southern Asia, most of which are not considered traditional whiskies at all because they're not grain based). Part of that success stems from the success of export marketing, some of it is left over from the once-wide influence of the British empire, and some of it is from the business and political failures that interrupted the growth of American and Irish whiskey.

Some of it, of course, is because Scotch whisky is an excellent product . . . but it has no exclusive hold on that claim. The other major whiskeys — bourbon, rye, Irish, Canadian, Japanese — are also excellent products, and well liked by their fans. I've had very nice examples of each of them, whiskeys I'd happily drink again and proudly offer to my best friends. You won't be able to find what you like by drinking only one type of whiskey.

So what do you pick when you go to the store? Is there a guide to picking the best whiskey? There is one, but let's have a look at which guides *don't* work first.

"OLDER IS BETTER." Older is certainly older, and older is usually more expensive. Better? Sometimes, sometimes not. Keep in mind, higher price does not always mean better whiskey; mostly it means rarer whiskey, and that's a different prospect. Young whiskey costs less because it's been held less time, but it also costs less because there's a lot more of it. There is always going to be more young whiskey than old whiskey because of the evaporative "angel's share" process we talked about in the previous chapter. Whiskey simply disappears in the aging process. Distillers put the same amount of money — grain, energy, labor, barrels, and the physical space for aging — into the barrel of 8-year-old whiskey as they did for the barrel of 20-year-old, and there's a lot less of the 20-year-old. If there's less whiskey, it's more expensive, so the older stuff is going to cost more. They have to sell it for more to make the same profit per bottle.

It is therefore in the whiskey makers' interest for us to believe that older, more expensive whiskey is necessarily better. It always tastes different, but "better" is more subjective. For example, bourbons that are 15 years old and older are enjoying strong popularity these days, led by the hard-to-find Van Winkle wheated bourbons. They score high in ratings, they win clutches of awards, and collectors hoard them jealously. But for me the sweet spot for bourbons is between 7 and 12 years old. That's when they've left behind the green and fiery days of their youth, and they aren't dominated by the drying, not-quite-astringent wood character of old age (sorry, "maturity"; I have to remind myself that I'm getting close to that era myself). There are exceptions, and there always will be — older bourbons that because of an exceptional barrel or warehouse placement retain more of the freshness of youth — but in my mind, at least, older is not always better. Rye whiskeys are even more variable on this angle; there are some spectacular young ryes. It's a matter of personal appreciation.

What about Scotch, though? That's where you'll find the truly stratospheric prices and the older-than-you-are whiskies that feed into this type of thinking. The older blends command higher prices, and once single malts get over about 15 years of age, their prices climb steeply. Surely that 30-year-old is more refined, more majestic, recognizably better than the same distillery's callow 15-year-old? Again, it depends on what you're looking for, what taste it is that you love. Distillery character can be as bold and roaring as the peat of an Islay or as light and loving as the malt of a Lowland. Yet the bold can be done in by aging too long in the wrong wood, or by a clumsily selected finish, and the delicate can

be enhanced greatly by skillful aging, perhaps in older refill casks that don't overwhelm.

You can learn what you like, the age you find most likely to please, only by tasting whiskeys. It's your best defense against paying a huge amount for a whiskey that may be disappointing.

"HIGHER PROOF IS BETTER." The idea here is that the standard minimum legal 80 proof (40 percent ABV) is "watered down." Therefore, higher-proof bottlings are better, not because you're getting more alcohol — though some folks do feel that way — but because you're getting more flavor and more stuff, and more of the whiskey's character comes through when you blend it into a cocktail, or add water or ice.

I've been guilty of this one myself; I'm a big fan of cask-strength whiskeys (bottled without dilution to a standard proof) and bottled-in-bond bourbons ("bonded" bourbon is legally required to be 100 proof). I like being able to cut back on the proof to my liking, and I like to know that there's as much flavor there as there can be. High-proof bottlings are often good values, too, particularly the bonded ones still on the market, because some consumers either don't know what they are or are intimidated by them. Heaven Hill has a 6-year-old bonded bourbon that just oozes with lusty young bourbon flavor and packs an authoritative 100-proof punch.

But what about one of my favorite summertime whiskeys, the standard "Yellow Label" Four Roses bourbon? For me it's perfect at 40 percent ABV when we've got one of our hot and humid summer days going; throw a handful of ice cubes in a squat, solid tumbler, drown them with Yellow, and drink at will. Just as I like a solidly overproof rye in a Manhattan, I prefer standard-proof whiskey in tall drinks for summer.

THE PEAT RACE

*P*eat freaks love to compare peaty whiskies, and they look to ppm (parts per million) of phenols, the smoky compounds from peat smoke, as an objective measure. Phenols are easily measured in malt . . . but that doesn't necessarily mean they all get into the bottle. Lagavulin distillery manager Georgie Crawford told me that phenols in malt are about three times what they are in the spirit. Don't get wrapped up in the numbers; peatiness is, after all, only part of a whisky's whole. Still, it's kind of fun to compare ppms. Here's the phenol content for some distillers and a few particularly peaty whiskies — but note that ppm can vary between bottlings. Also note that even unpeated malt, like Glenlivet, has some natural phenol content. (If you're wondering where Highland Park is, the distillery smokes some of its own malt to "between 35 and 50 ppm" and then mixes that in a 1:4 ratio with unpeated malt; the result is pleasingly variable.)

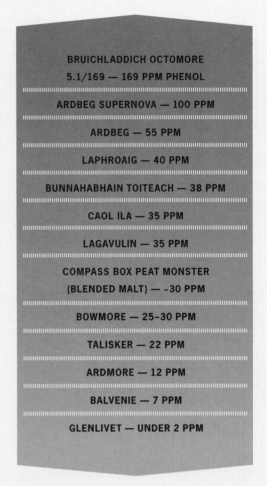

BRUICHLADDICH OCTOMORE
5.1/169 — 169 PPM PHENOL

ARDBEG SUPERNOVA — 100 PPM

ARDBEG — 55 PPM

LAPHROAIG — 40 PPM

BUNNAHABHAIN TOITEACH — 38 PPM

CAOL ILA — 35 PPM

LAGAVULIN — 35 PPM

COMPASS BOX PEAT MONSTER
(BLENDED MALT) — ~30 PPM

BOWMORE — 25–30 PPM

TALISKER — 22 PPM

ARDMORE — 12 PPM

BALVENIE — 7 PPM

GLENLIVET — UNDER 2 PPM

Then there are the whiskeys, lots of them, that simply aren't available at higher proof; most Canadian and Irish whiskeys, for example, and most Scotch blends. Do you just write them off? Of course not. Once again, you have to taste them — and in this case, taste them in different settings, neat, iced, or in cocktails — to know what you like.

"SMOKIER IS BETTER!" Obviously we're talking about Scotch whisky here, though there are some American craft whiskeys that are doing interesting things with smoke. The same misconception applies to them all: If smoke is good, *more smoke* must be better.

This reminds me directly of the 20-year arc of hoppiness in American craft beers: hoppy, hoppier, hoppiest . . . no, *hoppier still!* Because 25 years ago, you could scarcely

ALL YEARS ARE NOT EQUAL

*W*hiskeys also age differently. Bourbons age more quickly in their newly charred barrels in the hot warehouses of Kentucky than Scotch does in used barrels in the cooler, wetter climate of the Hebrides. Canadian whisky can face a wide variety of climate (the temperatures in the Hiram Walker warehouses near Windsor, Ontario, for example, are surprisingly similar to those in Kentucky), with concomitant variable effects on aging, while the tropical-climate whiskies of India and Taiwan age very quickly indeed. A 30-year-old single malt can be amazing; a 30-year-old bourbon would most likely be too nasty to taste, assuming there was even any left in the barrel. Don't judge different whiskeys by the same standards when it comes to age.

---

give away peaty whiskies like Lagavulin or Talisker. Port Ellen was closed, Ardbeg was closed, Bruichladdich would soon close, and peaty whisky was a thing for odd aficionados and for spicing up blends.

But as single malts gained popularity, the popularity of peat rose even more steeply, and peat aficionados were no longer so odd. Ardbeg and Bruichladdich reopened, sales and production increased, and we saw bottlings named Peat Monster, Big Peat, and The Big Smoke, along with highly peated distillery bottlings like Bruichladdich Octomore and Ardbeg Supernova. It seemed that what we really wanted was so much peat in the whisky that it would rise right out of the glass and smack us.

Which is great; if you really like peat, more smoke is better, up to a point. But if you're one of the whisky drinkers who honestly don't like it, or who like the richness and depth that a little smoke brings, *more* is definitely not better for you. Again, you can learn what you like only by tasting whiskeys, not by being told.

"CRAFT/SMALL MAKER IS BETTER." I like small producers. Meeting the brewers at a brewpub and talking about their beer is a great experience. You can learn a lot speaking to artisanal cheesemakers, bakers, and butchers. You'll learn why things are done the way they are, where the flavors come from, what makes their products different.

That's true of small whiskey makers as well. They do things differently, it's usually easier to meet them and talk to them about what makes their products different, and you can often walk right into where they make and age their whiskey. You can even shake their hands. That's great!

It doesn't necessarily make their whiskey better, though, does it? Think about it; my local craft distiller is a two-man operation, and they occasionally bring in a couple of volunteers to help bottle. They make a tiny amount of whiskey, and it's good stuff. Then there's Glenlivet, the second-best-selling single malt Scotch whisky in the world. Its distillers made 10.5 million liters of whisky in 2012. It's a global brand, but if you go to the distillery (and it's way out in the country, down narrow roads, where it's been for almost 200 years), you'll find that every drop is made by only 10 people. They're assisted by automation to some degree, but still . . . 10 people. It's good stuff, too; some of it is amazingly good.

Craft whiskey gets a halo from its association with craft brewing. Craft brewing brought real variety and beers with much greater flavor to the marketplace and competed against a very small number of huge brewers that made very similar beers with very little flavor. That's not what's going on in craft whiskey. In this industry the big distillers make great whiskeys, hundreds of them, that are clearly different; think Jameson vs. Knob Creek vs. Macallan 18 vs. Dickel Barrel Select.

The "big" distillers aren't even all that big; Glenfarclas and Heaven Hill, for instance, are large, but they're still independent and family owned. Big distillers are quite capable of being innovative, and they've often already looked at some of the stuff the craft distillers are trying, like small barrels, forced aging, and different grains. They've also got a lot more older whiskey — and usually lower prices, too, exactly because they have a lot more whiskey.

That's not to say there are not good craft whiskeys on the market; there are. But whether they're "better" or not is for you to say, not for someone to tell you.

THE BEST WHISKEY

I PROMISED YOU A GUIDE to picking the best whiskey, and now that we've gone through some of the wrong guides, it's time. You can probably guess by now what it is. *You have to try lots of whiskeys and then decide which ones are the best for your tastes.* Then you'll know how to pick the best whiskey, at that particular moment, for you. Even better, you'll probably know enough by then that you'll keep trying lots of whiskeys in case something new and different turns out to be just what you were looking for.

I'm not telling you to ignore whiskey reviews and ratings. They can be valuable guides in shopping for what is an increasingly pricey drink. But people who make flat statements like the ones above, that one type or brand of whiskey is the best, or that you simply shouldn't ever drink another type . . . yeah, them you should ignore; politely, if you can.

Good reviewers will rarely tell you that you simply shouldn't buy or drink a particular whiskey (and if a regular reviewer does say that, you ought to strongly consider it). What they will say is that the whiskey has a rough finish, or maybe that it isn't integrated well, with sharp flavors that poke out rather than roll into a smooth whole. They might note some off-flavors, they might say that some influences are overdone (such as a Scotch aged in sherry barrels that picked up too much sherry character). They may also note that the whiskey seems to be priced too high for what it delivers. Take all that into account when you decide whether to take this shortcut.

When I consider the different whiskeys of the world, I'm reminded of something the Scottish distillers say a lot when discussing their various bottlings, from popular-priced blends to loftily rare single malts: "It's horses for courses." You don't race the same horse on a steeplechase course as you do on a dirt racetrack or a turf course; you don't pour the same whiskey for your "I'm home from work" relaxation as you do to commemorate the birth of your first child — or your first grandchild.

Keep your mind open when you taste whiskey. I'm happy to move freely among the whiskeys of the world, enjoying all of them. I don't consider myself better than other people because I like more than one kind of whiskey; I count myself *lucky*. In the next chapter we'll take a look at how whiskeys get their different character. Keep in mind that "different" means just that: different, not better or worse!

CHAPTER No. 5

TASTING:

TAPPING INTO YOUR YEARS OF EXPERIENCE

Remember how I told you about the first time I got through The Wall and tasted fudge? If you were wondering how or why I tasted fudge in whiskey, you're asking a good question. Read enough tasting notes from whiskey reviewers, and you'll see them talking about smelling and tasting such things as orange, cinnamon, tarry rope, mint, fig, brine, leafy bonfires, oil, almond, medicine, grass, crushed ants . . . and I can guarantee that none of those things go into whiskey.

Longtime Heaven Hill master distiller Parker Beam doesn't hold with the idea that you can even taste those things in whiskey. He's tasted much more than his share over six decades in the business, and he's pretty emphatic that all you should taste in whiskey is what goes into it. "People say they taste mangos and leather," he told me. "I don't put mangos or leather in the whiskey. I put in corn, and I age it in oak barrels, and that's what I taste: *corn and oak!*"

I respect Parker deeply, but I have to disagree with him here. As we discussed in the previous chapter, there are many flavor compounds that are in the oak, there are more in the grains (the corn, malt, rye, wheat, and so on), more developed in fermentation and distillation, and even more created by the chemical interaction of the whiskey, the oak, and the air that the semipermeable wood allows to enter the barrel. Perhaps Parker meant just that: he tastes only things that come *from* the corn and the oak.

So if you want to taste those things — to taste the fudge, the mango, the tarry rope — you're going to have to think about what you're tasting, and what it makes you think about or remember. Don't worry; you've been studying this all your life. I call it the Karate Kid Method.

THE KARATE KID METHOD: FINDING SCENT MEMORIES

THE "WAX ON, WAX OFF" scene from the 1984 film *The Karate Kid* is an iconic movie moment. Danny LaRusso begs to learn karate from Mr. Miyagi, who agrees to teach him, and then sets him to waxing his cars, sanding a deck, and painting a fence. Danny's frustration builds until Miyagi reveals that the circular "wax on, wax off" motions he insisted Danny use, over and over, were training the boy's muscles to reflexive karate moves.

You're like Danny, but you've already waxed the cars. You're past The Wall, and you have the tools to start tasting whiskey; you've been training to be a whiskey taster all your life. You just didn't realize it. Every day of our lives, we eat, we drink, and we smell the world around us, but most of us never really think about what we're tasting. We might say it's "good," or "spicy," or "rich." Yet every one of us could be blindfolded and pick out a banana, a roast chicken, or pine needles by their smell.

Scent memory is powerful, and you can learn to harness it. Sometimes when I slice into a crisp green pepper, an old girlfriend comes to mind, because the perfume she wore — Alliage — had hints of that same fresh scent. Let such associations flow freely when you taste whiskey — make those wax-on, wax-off moves — and you'll be the Whiskey Kid.

GETTING SET TO TASTE

LET'S SET YOUR whiskey-tasting stage. Ideally, you'll want a quiet place with few distractions; the longer you can focus on the whiskey without interruption, the more likely it is that you'll start to make the sense associations that will frame the whiskey for you. Keep it quiet, or play music if that helps shut out the world for you.

Turn off any visual distractions, like your television and phone. Naturally you don't want to be tasting whiskey with any strong aromas around; don't taste while cooking or eating, and wash your hands with an unscented soap,

EVALUATING COLOR

EVALUATING COLOR CAN BE TRICKY. Bourbon picks up color quickly because of the new charred barrels, so it gets fairly dark quickly, and craft whiskey that is aged in small barrels, with proportionally more of the whiskey in direct contact with the wood, picks up color even more quickly. Scotch whisky can vary a lot in how quickly it picks up color: aging in a first-fill sherry barrel will give a whisky color much more quickly than aging in a second- or third-fill barrel, where the whisky will remain quite pale and delicate in color for years. Scotch, Irish, Canadian, and Japanese distillers are allowed to add color in the form of "spirit caramel," a caramel coloring made from heating sugars or syrups, so it's not always easy to tell how much color in their whiskies came from the wood. Some countries (Germany, for one) require labeling when coloring is added, and distillers often choose not to add coloring (and will usually state that on the label). American straight whiskeys are not allowed to add color, by federal regulation.

A spirit with pale straw or gold color will tend to have more distillery character, the aromas and flavors emblematic of that distillery's new make.

If your whiskey is tending toward mahogany or molasses in color, you've got a very old Scotch or a mature bourbon . . . or someone's been coloring your whiskey.

Unaged spirit is clear or "white."

Amber, deep copper, and tawny colors exemplify a middle-aged Scotch whisky, 15 years old or more (or a colored one), or a young American straight whiskey. Irish doesn't often get past this color, and it's common for Canadian.

If the whiskey is this dark, it's either colored or very, very old, and in either case I'd advise you to avoid it.

The colors of wood maturation: a sampling shows whiskey at zero, two, and four years of age, with concomitant deepening of the color from white to copper to mahogany.

rinsing well. Pick a comfortable seat, or stand if you prefer.

Set up some kind of vertical white background — something as simple as a plain piece of paper — so you can comfortably hold up a glass in front of it to examine the color. The light should be white and even, not too bright.

You'll want a large glass for water so you can rinse your mouth between sips, especially if you're tasting multiple whiskeys. Go with spring water, though if you've got great tap water, feel free to use that. At home I just put our tap water through a Brita filter, which works fine. You may be adding small amounts of water to the whiskey; you can pour from the water glass or from a smaller cruet; some use an eyedropper or a form of pipette for more exact measuring. If you want something to chew to refresh your palate, stick to a plain bread or plain crackers, like saltines or oyster crackers.

On the topic of refreshing your senses, I did learn one trick from a professional taster, someone who does olfactory analysis of food and drink every day. I was judging beers with him at a competition, and I noticed that every so often he would bend his right arm slightly, place his face in the crook of his elbow, against the sleeve of his shirt, and inhale sharply through his nose.

After the judging round was over, I asked him what he was doing. He said that he was, essentially, smelling himself, the base aroma of his own skin, the familiar smell of his clothing. That familiar set of aromas, always around him as a background, a baseline, served to reset his nose. I've tried it, and once you get over being self-conscious, it works well.

Finally, if you're going to take any notes on your tasting, get set with a notebook and pen, or your phone or your tablet. There are a few apps specifically for taking whiskey-tasting notes, but they're still evolving at this point and often force you to do notes their way. Instead, I use a more generic note-taking app (with a search function) and put down my thoughts freehand.

You certainly don't have to take notes, especially if you're not tasting by yourself. If you're tasting whiskey to learn more about it, and about what you like, taking notes lets you easily and confidently compare and contrast different whiskeys. You can also go back and look at what you thought of a whiskey months or years ago and think about whether the whiskey's changed or your own palate has evolved.

In a more general way, I've found that taking notes focuses you more on the tasting. There's more of a tendency to take things seriously, to find that right descriptor. I've had several friends (my wife, too) laugh about what hard work it is "tasting whiskey," only to have them change their tune once they sat in on a serious tasting with a comparison of notes.

Don't get hung up on it. Have fun with your notes if you'd like; they're your notes, after all. Whatever value they have is likely to be for you alone. I wrote notes for myself for years before sharing them with anyone else. It's simply another thing you can use to enhance the experience — or not.

Everything ready? Check the scene. It's peaceful, free from distractions of sound and smell, and comfortably lit, with your white background in place for color checks. You've got clean glassware, and your hands (and moustache, if you have one!) are scent-free. There's cool water handy for drinking and diluting, with maybe some crackers or bread. If you're taking notes, the means are at hand. And you have the whiskey you're tasting.

Now you're ready. Let's taste.

GLENCAIRN GLASS   OLD-FASHIONED GLASS   SHERRY GLASS

GLASSWARE

WHAT KIND OF GLASS should you use for tasting whiskey? There's a whole industry waiting on your answer! It's not just money or show, either. The type of glass really does have an effect on how your whiskey will smell and taste. Too wide a bowl, and the whiskey may oxidize more quickly, giving you only a quick shot at the initial aromas. Too wide a neck and opening, and the aromas can escape too quickly. Too thick, and you can't hand-heat the whiskey; too thin, and a thick-fingered guy like me can get nervous about breaking it.

When I taste whiskey for reviews, I use a Glencairn glass, a glass designed specifically for tasting whiskey. It has a tapered, chimney-like neck to focus and funnel the aroma while still being easy to drink from, unlike a snifter. The onion-like swell of the body allows for examination of the color, and for some hand-warming, if desired (I don't, generally). The small but solid base allows an easy grip without obscuring the drink, and the glass itself is sturdy without being clunky. It's a very good glass for whiskey.

TASTING HOW THE OTHER HALF LIVES

*O*ne of the more useful and fun tasting exercises I've taken part in was one I did with the publisher of *Whisky Advocate*, John Hansell. He and I were in Scotland, in the heart of the Speyside distilling area, the most dense concentration of whisky distilleries anywhere. We were taking a break from touring after a fine lunch at the Mash Tun in Aberlour, a small town right along the River Spey, about a mile and a half upstream from the Macallan distillery.

We walked down to the Spey Larder, a specialty grocer with all kinds of goodies. I got a coffee — I was flagging a bit and needed a reviver — and John started picking up little goodies: Dundee cake, orange marmalade, Scottish fudge, and more, about eight things in all, and a bottle of water. We walked down to the Spey and sat down on a bench; there was a fellow fly-fishing in the river just across from us.

John got out his purchases and started opening things up. As he did, he explained why he'd chosen them. These were all things that Scottish whisky writers and distillery tasters mentioned frequently when describing whiskies, and he thought I should know what they tasted like. It was like a Rosetta Stone for a whisky flavor code.

The Dundee cake was a rich fruitcake topped with almonds. The orange marmalade was intense, with a depth of sweet orange character. The fudge was quite different from what I thought of as fudge — more granular, and much more about sugar and caramel than cream. I savored each different bite and thought of whiskies.

When we were done, we drove down the road to the Highlander Inn in Craigellachie, and I got a chance to attach my new tasting memories to some fine Speyside drams. It was a grand afternoon.

Honestly, though, I mainly use the Glencairn glass because I have about a dozen of them from various whiskey events I've attended. The important point is that I use the same *type* of glass every time I do serious whiskey tasting — even for something like maple-flavored whiskey — to avoid the possibility of different glassware influencing my perceptions.

You'll want to use the same type of glass for all your serious whiskey tasting, and you'll want several of that type. They don't have to be expensive; you can pick up boxes of suitable glasses for a reasonable price at kitchenware stores. Get enough to taste several whiskeys at one sitting; then double that, to be able to do it with a friend. It's more fun with a friend.

Basically, whatever style of glass you decide on, it should be:

- Of clear, uncolored glass so you can see the color of the whiskey. (Master blenders sometimes use deeply colored glass to avoid being distracted by the color; their needs are different from ours.)
- Of sufficient, but not too generous, width and height. Don't use a short, narrow glass, such as a shot glass; you'll want enough room over the surface of the whiskey for the aromas to pool and concentrate, and you'll want enough height to be able to gently swirl the whiskey to stir up more aromas as you taste. Don't go too wide, either, or the aromas will quickly dissipate.

- Made with a solid base or a stem, so you can hold it without warming the whiskey if you choose. A small white wine glass or a sherry glass works fine; so does a classically solid old-fashioned glass (also known as a "rocks glass").
- Clean and well rinsed to wash away any cleanser residue. I wash mine by hand, rinse them with very hot water, and let them drip dry. The only thing that should be in the glass when you begin your pour is whiskey and air.

RELAX WITH THE WHISKEY

YOU'RE GOING TO ENJOY a whiskey, and you're going to learn about a whiskey. That's true of your first tasting, and it can be true every time you have a whiskey from now on, even if it's a whiskey you've had many times before. Stay sharp, and have fun.

Open the bottle: a new whiskey, a familiar whiskey, any whiskey, it doesn't matter. Pour about half an ounce (15 ml) into your glass. Now lift the glass to your nose. Don't stuff your nose into the glass, or you'll be overwhelmed by alcohol. Bring it gently up to your nose till you start to smell the whiskey, and hold it there.

Close your eyes . . . just drift a bit. Think of what the smell evokes, what memory it pulls up. Cookies? Sun-warmed grass? Golden raisins? Spices? Fingernail polish remover (acetone)? Smoke? Just-cut lumber? Honey on fresh bread? Gently sniff until you find an aroma that reminds you of something you've smelled before. Write it down, if you're taking notes. Wait for other notes to pop out; take a few breaths away from the whiskey and return to it. Swirl the glass a bit to stir up fresh aromas and smell some more.

Now take a sip, slowly. Close your mouth, and let the whiskey flow across your tongue. Hold it on your tongue for as long as it's comfortable, then breathe easily and swallow. It's quite likely that you'll taste different things as the whiskey first hits your tongue, then spreads, then vaporizes, and then other things, possibly quite different, as you swallow and the whiskey finishes.

What do you taste? Is it hot? Bitter? Sweet? What do you smell now? Is it the same as what you smelled from the whiskey before drinking it? It often is . . . and sometimes it isn't. Again, is there anything familiar? When a connection occurs to you, don't judge it, or be afraid to write it down, or say it out loud.

Now take another sip, and this time, work it a bit. You want to get the whiskey all through your entire mouth cavity. Don't swish it like mouthwash; that's too quick, and random. Slow chewing motions work well, and pull in small amounts of air as you do it; not too much, or you risk inhaling whiskey.

What you're trying to do at this point is get more airflow into your mouth and up the "chimney" of your nose, to carry the aromas of the whiskey to your sense of smell. You don't have to be obvious or ostentatious about it, and you don't have to work at pushing it up to your nose. If you chew and bring air in, it will happen.

Again, smell, taste, and think about what else smells and tastes like this. Do the aromas and flavors change as you breathe? Do new ones appear or change in intensity as you swallow and breathe over the thin layer of spirit still in your mouth, the moment known as the finish? Take more notes, if you're doing that.

Then comes the important part: do you like how this tastes, or not? What do you like or not like about it? As you think about that and make your judgments, you'll be doing what a friend of mine called "writing the Book of Your Taste," a book you'll be able to consult

WHERE WHISKEY GETS ITS FLAVOR

As a whole, each type of whiskey exhibits a common, recognizable range of flavors (though of course individual whiskeys may exhibit flavors outside that range). Flavors come from two major sources: the spirit side, which stems largely from the grain and the effects of a distiller's unique fermentation and distillation regimens; and the barrel side, the effect of the type of barrel and the aging environment. In most whiskeys, one or the other gets an advantage. In bourbon, for instance, the barrel contributes the majority of the flavor; in rye, it's the spirit. Here's how the flavor ranges break down.

Scotch

FROM THE SPIRIT: sweet malt, nuts, fudge, cake, peat (smoke, brine, tar), berries, honey, citrus, spice.
FROM THE BARREL: coconut, dried fruit, rich wine, oak bite, vanilla, drying wood.
ADVANTAGE: spirit in peated Scotch; barrel in sherried Scotch.

Irish

FROM THE SPIRIT: sugar cookie, assorted fruits, toffee, fresh grain.
FROM THE BARREL: dried fruit, wax, coconut, vanilla.
SLIGHT ADVANTAGE: spirit.

Bourbon

FROM THE SPIRIT: corn, mint, cinnamon, grass, rye.
FROM THE BARREL: coconut, maple, vanilla, smoke, spice, leather, dryness, caramel.
ADVANTAGE: barrel.

Rye

FROM THE SPIRIT: dry mint, anise, hard candy, flowers, meadow grass, bitter rye oil.
FROM THE BARREL: spice, leather, dryness, caramel.
ADVANTAGE: spirit.

Canadian

FROM THE SPIRIT: spice (pepper, ginger), rye, sweet cereal, dark fruits.
FROM THE BARREL: wood (oak, cedar), vanilla, caramel.
ADVANTAGE: spirit.

Japanese

FROM THE SPIRIT: fruits (plum, light citrus, apple), peat (smoke, seaweed, coal), grass, spice.
FROM THE BARREL: coconut, cedar, vanilla, oak, spices.
ADVANTAGE: even split.

with increasing confidence as you taste more whiskeys. You may rewrite it in the future as you taste more whiskeys and your tastes evolve, and that's okay, too.

As you're tasting you'll also want to consider how the whiskey fits together. Is it well integrated, or is it unbalanced? Does one taste overwhelm everything, a one-note song that deafens you to any other harmony? That might be the case when a whiskey is finished in a cask that's unfortunately inappropriate to its character, or in a young, smoky whiskey whose flavors haven't had a chance to meld properly.

Perhaps you have a whiskey that has a shy nose, that doesn't really open up until it's on your tongue, robbing you of half the fun. At the other end, a whiskey's finish may either drop off abruptly or turn in a significantly less pleasant direction than the main taste.

Age can unbalance a whiskey as well. Young whiskeys may be too fiery and rough, or "green" and spirity, not smoothed out enough by the barrel. Older whiskeys may be

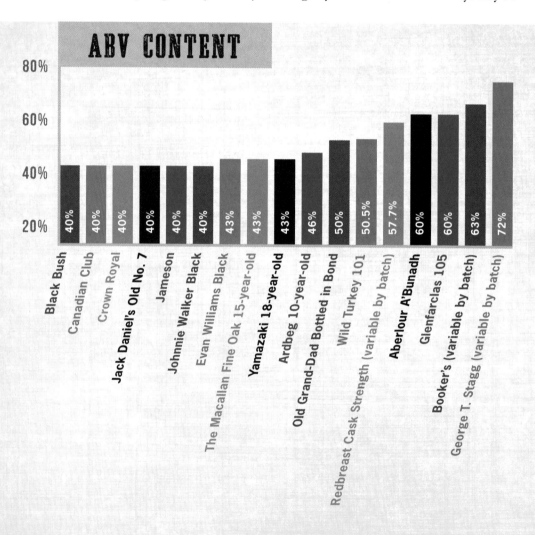

ABV CONTENT

Whiskey	ABV
Black Bush	40%
Canadian Club	40%
Crown Royal	40%
Jack Daniel's Old No. 7	40%
Jameson	40%
Johnnie Walker Black	40%
Evan Williams Black	43%
The Macallan Fine Oak 15-year-old	43%
Yamazaki 18-year-old	43%
Ardbeg 10-year-old	46%
Old Grand-Dad Bottled in Bond	50%
Wild Turkey 101	50.5%
Redbreast Cask Strength (variable by batch)	57.7%
Aberlour A'Bunadh	60%
Glenfarclas 105	60%
Booker's (variable by batch)	63%
George T. Stagg (variable by batch)	72%

overwhelmed by wood and evaporation to the point of being astringent, dry, with no life, no zest.

Any of these could be seen as a flaw compared to the experience of a whiskey that presents a rounded whole. Ideally, a whiskey should give you a smooth progression from initial aromas, through the flavors on the tongue, to the lingering flavors and sensations of the finish. There may be surprises along the way as flavors intensify on the palate or appear at the finish as more air mixes with the whiskey, but they are pleasing rather than a jolt.

"Integrated" isn't a code word for restrained or overly refined, either. A whiskey may well be a roaring giant of flavor, and some of the best of them are. But the good giants don't have two heads or three legs, or carry a flimsy reed instead of a club; they're balanced and strong all around.

WATERING THE WATER OF LIFE

TIME FOR HONESTY NOW. Is the whiskey simply too hot (too alcoholic) for your palate? That's what the water's for. Don't even think about being shy about this, or embarrassed; we all do it. Writers, reviewers, and certainly distillers and blenders: anyone who's serious about whiskey will taste it with water added. We'll talk more about this in chapter 13, but for now let's focus on the nuts and bolts of why water isn't really forbidden in whiskey.

First, a basic truth: whiskey doesn't come out of the barrel at exactly 40 percent (or 43 percent, or 45 percent, or 50.5 percent, or whatever your preferred bottling proofs out at). It comes out of the barrel at anywhere between 40 percent (the legal minimum in

most whiskey-producing countries) and as much as 70 percent.

The distillers blend together a number of carefully selected barrels to make a bottling batch, and then, unless this is for one of the relatively small number of barrel-strength bottlings, they add just the right amount of water to bring the batch to that label's bottling proof. It's "just the right amount" because excise taxes are usually based on alcohol, and governments are quite picky about how much alcohol is actually in the bottle so they're not losing a penny of taxes. Distillers don't really want to lose any whiskey, either; that stuff's valuable.

So all you're really doing when you add water is adding *more* water. Not a big deal.

Adding water to whiskey works for two different reasons. One's pretty simple: by lowering the proof, you're dropping The Wall again, to a new, even lower level. Don't drown the whiskey, but do a bit of quick math. Whiskey writer Chuck Cowdery makes it easy with this whiskey-dilution formula he worked out and put in his book *Bourbon, Straight*:

$$\text{Whi} \times ((bP/dP) - 1) = Wa$$
Whi = amount of whiskey
bP = bottle proof (or ABV)
dP = desired proof (or ABV)
Wa = amount of water to add to
achieve desired proof

Say, for instance, you want to drop half an ounce (about 15 ml) of 45 percent whiskey to a gentler 30 percent. The formula works like this: $0.5 \times ((45/30) - 1) = 0.25$. You'd add a quarter of an ounce (about 7 ml) of water. Spring or distilled water is best; tap water can come with unwanted flavors. You can pay a lot for fancy water, but a supermarket bottled water will work fine.

You'll want to experiment with how much or little water to add, and where the proof is comfortable for you, but once you've tried it, you'll be sure to keep at it. Most professional "noses," the skilled people who pick the barrels for blending at distilleries, will cut samples to 20 percent. It's a long day when you're nosing as many as a hundred barrel samples, and even cut to 40 percent, they'll numb your nose pretty quickly.

Water also frees some aromas and flavors. These aromatic compounds, mostly the fruity, zesty esters, are "locked up" when there is an abundance of ethanol in the solution; the ethanol molecules close in around them. When water is added, it splits open these ethanol straitjackets and the esters are released to your nose. Think of the differences your nose senses after rainfall: the fresh scents of plants, the distinctive aroma of wet pavement. Water has broken loose those aromas from chemical bonds and released them into the air.

Perversely, water brings out the sulfury compounds found in the heavier Scotch whiskies, leading to the release of unpleasant rubbery, "meaty" aromas. It will also subdue the presence of some desirable aromatics, particularly the smoky phenolic scents of peat and pleasant cereal notes.

Given the irrevocable changes water makes in a whiskey, it's always best to nose the whiskey neat (undiluted) first. It's easy enough to put water in, but it's the devil's own work to take it out; just ask a distiller.

There's one more trick you'll want to learn: waiting. If you let a whiskey sit, the flavors will change. Some things oxidize and transform; some things simply dissipate and vanish. In some cases this will help the whiskey, while in others it could make it bland or unpleasant. There are no guidelines or ways to guess this, but it is an interesting variation on the taste of your whiskey.

BLIND JUSTICE

SOMETHING YOU MAY begin to notice as you develop more familiarity with whiskey is distillery character. A distillery's whiskeys often show a similarity that an experienced taster will recognize and, to a certain extent, expect.

This can stem from the stills: Glenmorangie's uniquely tall pot stills make for a light, refined spirit, while Glenfarclas's squatter, broader stills deliver a heavier, almost oily character. It can come from the grain: Alberta Distillers Ltd. uses 100-percent rye in its whiskies, and it shows; the unmalted barley in Irish Distillers' single pot still whiskeys is distinctive. Consistent barrel selection, warehouse construction and position, water source, peat source, yeast, or the guidance of a longtime distiller or blender: all of these can build a unique, recognizable character in a distillery's whiskeys.

Distillery character is the basis of people's cleaving to a particular distillery's whiskeys above all others. They find that character, and they love it, and nothing else will do for them. When they see a new expression from that distillery, they expect that character, and they know they're going to like it.

That's just one of the things that can throw off your perception when you taste whiskey, but it's a key to a whole group of them: expectations. It's how your brain can trip up your tongue before you even taste a whiskey.

Your eyes have input on tasting; they see the label on the bottle. When I know that I'm tasting a Buffalo Trace whiskey, for example, I'm already in a receptive frame of mind. I *like* Buffalo Trace whiskeys, I've learned to expect them to be pleasurable, and that inescapably colors my perception.

You can try to be objective, you can say you're tasting with your tongue and nose only, you can claim that no prejudice exists in your mind . . . but you're just fooling yourself. You can only go so far. At the back of your mind, working on you in ways you won't or can't admit, gnawing at the solid, sturdy taproot of your senses, are all the memories and opinions you have of the producer and its other products, the place you got the drink, the way the bottle looked, what other people have said about it, your developed opinion of the general style of the whiskey — all that, tearing away at your objectivity.

You can restore your objectivity with a blindfold and an assistant. It's not a magic trick; it's blind tasting. If you want to find out what you truly think about a whiskey, taste it blind with two other similar whiskeys. Have your assistant pour in another room (my daughter usually helps me out here), and have her either mark the glasses or write down the order to ensure that she knows which one is which — and you don't.

Is it a lot of work? You bet. If you're just a casual drinker, it makes no sense to go to all this trouble. But there is no better way to learn about whiskey. Blind tasting makes you think. It's hard work. There are no shortcuts, no "yeah, there's that house character," because you don't know whose house you're in! When you have none of those aids, you have to really think about what you're tasting, to try to pick up what the important components are, how it fits together, how it progresses on your palate. It will make you think deeply about taste, about mouthfeel, about finish. It is the only way to do honest, unbiased tasting.

If you really want to get serious, you can do triangle tasting. That's blind tasting with a trick question. Take three somewhat similar whiskeys — for instance, similarly

Seiichi Koshimizu, revered Chief Blender at Suntory Yamazaki whisky distillery, Japan

aged expressions of peated single malts, such as Laphroaig, Talisker, and Caol Ila. Then have your assistant pour three whiskies — *any* three whiskies — without your knowing which whiskies they are. Your assistant could pour two Taliskers and a Caol Ila, or one of each, or maybe even three Laphroaigs, but you won't know. This really focuses your senses, because you'll have to be looking hard for similarities — which might not be there at all.

Blind tasting opens your eyes. Try it, and see what you learn. But if you'd like to do something that's a lot less hassle (and a lot easier to do on your own), try open-label tasting with two similar whiskeys.

Side-by-side tasting reveals differences with the bright light of comparison and can help you home in on just what it is you like or don't about a whiskey. Pour tastes of the standard bottlings of the three Kildalton distilleries on the southeast coast of Islay, for instance: Laphroaig, Lagavulin, and Ardbeg. As you address the sweet smoky natures of each, you'll come to realize that although all three are powerfully peaty, there are clear differences, and those differences will teach you about the individual whiskies, their homes, and peated whiskies in general.

When you're done — single, blind, or side by side — relax and reflect, while finishing up whatever's left of the whiskeys you've poured. You've written another entry in "Your Taste," that book you'll be consulting as you move further into the widening landscape of whiskey.

SHARING THE FUN

YOU'VE DISCOVERED HOW enjoyable really *tasting* your whiskey can be. There's a lot to be said for simply drinking and enjoying it, to be sure, but tasting is a different thing,

with rewards of its own. If you want to share that pleasure with friends or relations, it's easy enough; you'll mostly need more glasses, and the right approach.

The tricky part of sharing whiskey tasting with friends isn't the material part: the whiskey, the glasses, the water, or note pads. It's the attitude, both yours and theirs . . .but mostly yours. The thing to remember is that you want your friends to have a good time, to enjoy tasting the whiskey. It's not about showing off your whiskey collection or your whiskey knowledge; it's about sharing the pleasure you get from good whiskey.

Pick your guest list. You'll want to keep it small the first time around, two or three friends. Sound them out to see if they're even interested; I wouldn't really be interested in a tequila tasting, myself. After you get a few of these tastings under your belt, you can expand them, maybe do a dinner with whiskey, which can be a great night. (However you make your guest list, think ahead about your friends getting home safely. If they're not walking or taking public transportation, they should have a non-tasting friend along to drive back.)

Once you've got your friends set, decide what it's going to be about. Do you want to taste a few single malts, try some bourbons, experiment with Irish, or maybe one of each? Tasting, as you've discovered, is a great way to point up the real differences among various whiskeys of the same type, or to characterize the differences of the major divisions.

Keeping it simple at this point is probably best. Three is a good number. Select examples of one type, or examples of the major whiskeys: a bourbon, a Scotch, and an Irish. That brings up the question of what to pick. You have to draw a somewhat fine line here. Go too ordinary, and your guests may think you're insulting them; go extraordinary, and your guests may feel intimidated.

Triangle Tastings

THEME	WHISKEYS
Flagship peated whiskies, with quite different peat characters	Caol Ila 12-year-old, Lagavulin 16-year-old, Talisker 10-year-old
The Kidalton distilleries, with more subtle peat differences	Ardbeg 10-year-old, Lagavulin 16-year-old, Laphroaig 10-year-old
Sherried single malts, a comparison of the dried fruit character sherry aging brings	GlenDronach 12-year-old, Glenfarclas 12-year-old, The Macallan 12-year-old
Verticality, a comparison of house character at different ages	Glenfarclas 10-year-old, 12-year-old, and 17-year-old
Blends, evaluating what each blend aims for, and looking for the "creamy" feel of the grain	Dewar's, Famous Grouse, Johnnie Walker Red
High-rye bourbons, a comparison of rye character	Basil Hayden, Bulleit, Old Grand-Dad; for fun, consider throwing an actual rye like Old Overholt into the mix
Wheated bourbons, a comparison of that smoother "whisper of wheat"	Larceny, Maker's Mark, W. L. Weller Special Reserve; add a 15-year-old Van Winkle if you can find it
Older bourbons, showing how the flavor shifts to drier, spicier oakiness	Bulleit 10-year-old, Elijah Craig 12-year-old, Jim Beam Signature Craft 12-year-old
Different Irish single malts	Bushmills 10-year-old single malt, Tullamore Dew 10-year-old single malt, Tyrconnell single malt
Irish single pot still character, in young, older, and blended whiskies	Green Spot, Jameson 18-year-old, Redbreast
Canadian flagships with varying rye character	Alberta Premium, Black Velvet, Canadian Club

I'd advise you to err on the side of egalitarianism and pour flagship bottles, rather than pull out the treasures of your collection. Think about it. If you start by pouring the three highest-end whiskeys you have, where do you go from there? If one of your friends decides he really likes a truly rare whiskey, he doesn't want to hear, "Oh, you can't get that one anymore, and if you did find a bottle, it would probably cost you over $500." Or what's worse, what if they don't like any of them? You may feel like a boob, or you may think your friends are tasteless idiots, and neither is much fun (or likely to lead to more tastings).

Instead, go with something approachable, not bold and intimidating, and maybe a small step above the basic bottlings in the category. For example, you could pour Johnnie Walker Black, a tasty blended Scotch whisky with a bit more oomph than the standard Red label. If you want a single malt, you're already a step above: start with a solid Speyside 12-year-old, like Glenfiddich or Glenlivet. You could let them taste Black Bush, a Bushmills with some added depth from sherry-cask aging. For a bourbon, maybe Maker's Mark, with its smooth wheated character, or surprise them and pull out a rye, like Rittenhouse.

The idea is to keep it interesting without raising the stakes. Because with whiskey, there's always the temptation to go right to your favorites, and push people to enjoy them as much as you do, and that's just not how it works sometimes.

Realize that sharing the fun means being with the people you're tasting whiskey with, in the same room, at the same table. I do online tastings sometimes, and it's better than being alone, but it's nowhere near as good, as spontaneous, as valuable as being with the people and their whiskeys. You can't hear laughter or see faces in a chat room; you can't pull out another bottle to share during a video chat.

That means you'll need to get your nose out of this book, and your fingers off the keyboard. You'll need to clean up your kitchen a bit, buy some bread, some cheese, maybe some smoked salmon or a cut-vegetable plate. Get more glasses if you need them, and bottled water, and a small pitcher.

Set up your tasting area for however many you are, maybe going a bit less insistent on the "no distractions" part. It's probably best to put aside the note taking at this point.

When they arrive, offer them a drink, but don't have more than one before the tasting. The more you have to drink or eat, the less sensitive the palate is, and you want to give the whiskeys a fair chance.

Pour the first whiskey. Remember: chances are your friends won't be past The Wall yet, so concentrate on gentle nosing at first. Start with something simple; nose the first whiskey and open up with whatever you're smelling. It's best if you take it slow; you want to guide the tasting, not lead it or take it over. Try to get some conversation going on what they're smelling, and don't just say, "No, I don't smell that." Don't get too picky, don't be too firm, don't tell your friends how they *must* do this. Instead, suggest to them that what you've been doing is working pretty well, and they can try it.

When it comes time to taste, encourage them to sip slowly, and to save some of the whiskey to compare with the other two. Be quick to suggest adding water if someone gets that painful "hot hot hot!" look on his face, and add some to your own glass as well. This is an inclusive process, and you don't want him to feel left out.

After you've tasted the three whiskeys, talk about which ones they liked and, maybe, didn't like. Now's the time for talking, and maybe having some more whiskey; the ones you've tasted, or something else, if they'd

WHAT YOU'RE TASTING

Just like any other work of human art — a cathedral, a novel, a painting, or a fine meal — whiskey is built from a variety of elements. Grain, water, yeast, and oak aging, yes, but what I'm talking about are the congeners, or the elements — literally, the chemical elements — that assemble to create the scent, taste, and flavor of a whiskey. Here are those building blocks.

Grains

The flavors of the grains come through fermentation and distillation (if the final proof is not too high) and are one of the major components of what you taste in some whiskies. Malt whiskies get a sweetness and a nutty, warm cereal character. Corn yields sweetness and the recognizable flavor of . . . well, corn. Rye is somewhat bitter, herbal, grassy, and minty and can add those characters even in relatively small amounts.

Esters

Esters are fruity, aromatic by-products of fermentation and can be carried over through distillation. Various esters have different aromas (e.g., isoamyl acetate smells like bananas, and ethyl caproate like apples), and the degree of reflux and how the cuts are done determine how much will be in the spirit. Esters are also formed in the barrel by the breakdown of lignins and have yet more aromas. For example, ethyl syringate smells of tobacco and fig; ethyl ferulate, spicy/cinnamon; and ethyl vanillate, a smoky, burnt aroma.

Lactones

Lactones are found in oak and come into whiskey during the aging. Bourbons, being aged in new barrels, pick up more lactones than whiskeys aged in used barrels. Two isomers of oak lactones are typically found in whiskey: cis-lactone gives the whiskey a sweet vanilla-coconut character; trans-lactone yields a spicier blend of cloves and coconut but is weaker.

Phenols

Phenols are the main smoky aromas in peat-smoked malt, measured (and touted) in parts per million. Their utilization can vary depending on the fermentation and distillation process; numbers don't mean everything.

Alcohols

Ethanol is not the only alcohol created during fermentation and may not be the only alcohol carried over in distillation. It is not highly flavored, with a mostly clean and just a tiny bit sweet essence. The other alcohols may be collectively called fusel alcohols, and they are undesirable, yielding oily flavors in high concentrations.

Methyl Salicylate

Methyl salicylate is present in low levels in some white oak; it gives a minty aroma to young whiskeys.

Vanillin

Oak yields vanillin in a number of ways, including the breakdown of its lignin. Its vanilla character is most notable in bourbon.

Aldehydes

Aldehydes have their own aromas — floral, lemon, or solvent — and can also react with oak lignin to create esters.

Tasting individual casks can be a quiet and intense moment in the warehouse.

like. It's up to you now; the whiskey will have broken the ice, and you can go on to talk more about the whiskey . . . or about anything else your friends care to.

There's the cleanup afterward, and yes, maybe some of your friends might want to stay longer than you'd like. It's whiskey; make allowances.

In the end, all the work you put into tasting whiskey is worth it for the good times, and the good tastes, and what you'll learn from the experience. It doesn't stop there, either. Opening your mind to tasting what's in your whiskey will bring you to think more about what you're tasting every day. You'll taste new things in your food, in your other drinks, and smell new things on the breeze. Your world of pleasures will expand.

It's not all about whiskey, after all. Karate training aside, Mr. Miyagi still got his cars waxed.

TABLE WHISKEY: THE HOUSE BOTTLE

I HAVE SOME WHISKEYS that I always keep in the house. Blended Scotch: Johnnie Walker Black or Compass Box Great King Street, sometimes Dewar's. Bourbon: Jim Beam Black, Evan Williams, or some Very Old Barton if I've been to Kentucky recently. Irish: usually Powers. Canadian: Canadian Club or VO. And in the summer I'll pick up a handle — a 1.75-liter big-boy bottle — of Pikesville rye for highballs.

I've got hundreds — literally — of other bottles, some rare and some wonderful, that I've picked up in the past 20 years. They're the ones I'll pull out when something special comes around: a birthday, a major holiday, a promotion, an unexpectedly welcome guest. There are other mid-level bottles that I'll savor more often. But most days, when I'm having a whiskey before dinner, or making a cocktail, or keeping my thirst quenched while grilling, I'm going to that stable you see above, the ones I call my table whiskeys.

When it comes to "advanced" whiskey drinkers, though, I'm feeling out of touch because of that. I've encountered a growing amount of whiskey snobbery from people who won't drink a whiskey unless it's rare, or "rated above 90," or single malt/single cask. I almost wonder if they like drinking whiskey, or just like people knowing that they drink expensive whiskey.

Table whiskey isn't rare, or expensive, but it's pretty down to earth. Imagine if whiskey were cars, and you and I were hosts on *Top Gear*, the popular BBC series in which the hosts drive some new supercar every week. The only times we'd drive "ordinary" cars — table cars — would be to make light of them, or after we've made bizarre modifications.

I love watching *Top Gear*. It's funny, it's interesting, and who knows, it's possible I'll get to drive a car like that someday. Once. But meanwhile, I drive a table car every day. That's real life.

In real life there are people who can drink very rare whiskey every time, because they have enough money to not care, or because they've made other sacrifices. That's great! But the simple facts of the equation are that if enough of us start doing that, rare whiskeys will become even harder to get, and even more expensive, and even more frustrating.

So I'd encourage you to put some effort into finding some reasonably priced, readily available table whiskeys you like. That way you'll always have drinking whiskey available when friends show up, or when you want a quick highball with dinner, or when you feel like a cocktail but don't really want to put a $250 bourbon in there.

I like whiskey, and I like beer. Both drinks offer me options for different occasions — thoughtful sipping, grinning glassfuls — and both offer good value all along the price spectrum. I guess I also like them because they're egalitarian, without a lot of the baggage wine has. If we want to maintain that, we ought to talk up the virtues of table whiskey.

MAPPING WHISKEY STYLES

There's a temptingly interesting concept about what Europeans drink (and what drinks they make) that's referred to as the "grape/grain divide." Before the days of cheap transportation of goods and people, before the days of international brands and refrigerated storage, the wine and beer regions of Europe grew naturally from what people had to work with.

In the warmer south, the theory goes, grapes thrive, and the people made wine. In the cooler north it's all about wide expanses of grain rather than grapes, so the people brewed beer. It's an attractive theory: Italians make wine, Spaniards and Greeks drink wine, and Germans, Dutch, Scandinavians, and the British brew beer. In France the line runs roughly through the country in the northeast, slicing off Nord–Pas de Calais, Alsace, and Lorraine, where the wine-loving tendencies of the French drop off in favor of bière de garde, saison, and pilsner. Champagne is up there too, of course, but it's not a sharp line.

Germany may seem a bit difficult to sort out. Here brewing overlaps with the substantial wine production in the upper Rhine and Mosel valleys. That seeming conflict dates back to the Roman era. The Romans didn't care for beer — the upper classes, at least (Emperor Julian said of the drink, "You smell like a goat") — and they brought winemaking

with them to ensure a ready supply. It stuck; there's even a wine tent at the famously beery Munich Oktoberfest.

Add in the strong pockets of apple-based booze in Spain, Normandy, western Germany, and England, and you realize it's quite a fuzzy line when you're used to boldly drawn ones . . . but the concept still holds up. It's not surprising, really. At a time when people rarely traveled more than 10 miles from their birthplace, they usually ate and drank what grew plentifully in that area.

THE GRAPE / GRAIN DIVIDE

ONCE KNOWLEDGE OF distillation and the necessary metallurgical arts spread into Europe, the southerners made brandy, or grappa, and the cooler northerners made

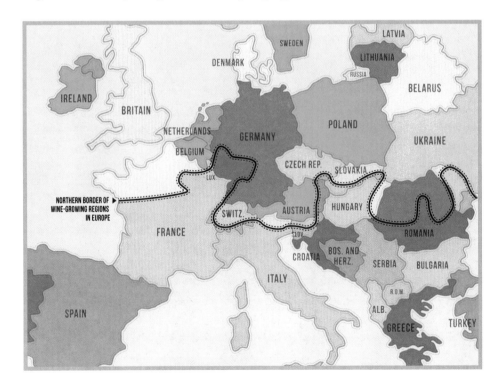

vodka — and whiskey. While beer is distilled into schnapps even today in Germany, in almost every case whiskey is made from grain that is malted and fermented for that specific purpose (as is vodka, originally made from grain, not potatoes; the New World tuber was introduced to Europe through Spain in the 1500s). When distillation was introduced to northern Europe, sometime around 1400, unaged grain spirit was soon being made for medicinal purposes, for perfumes and essences, and for drinking. Drinking quickly became the primary use, and the rough, clear spirit was variously known as *vodka*, *korn*, and *uisce beatha*, the last being the Gaelic for "water of life" (*aqua vitae* in Latin), as spirits were known in the late Middle Ages.

Grape and grain divided and conquered Europe. It was now up to the Irish and Scots to stake their distinctive claims in their own offshore corners of the continent.

TRANSPORTATION LIMITS

IF YOU TAKE THE IDEA of the grape/grain divide further, expanding it out of Europe into the whiskey regions of North America, you can apply it to the different whiskeys that have grown up and prospered, and learn why they are what they are. The grape/grain divide addressed broad swathes of regions and agriculture, but things are more compartmentalized than that. It's not just about grains that thrive in an area; it's down to particular grains and the fact that when whiskey was first being made distillers were usually farmers, and they didn't have a lot of choices.

Let's look at a modern idea that hearkens back to those early days and reveals a lot about why whiskeys are what they are. Locavores are a growing movement of people who reject the idea of shipping food and drink thousands of miles. They want to get their food and drink — as much as possible — from local sources, optimally within 100 miles.

That obviously limits what fresh fruits and vegetables are available to them, what cheeses and sweeteners they can eat. There's no frozen lamb from across the world for them, no out-of-season fruits and vegetables from another hemisphere, and no exotic flavors from other climates. They celebrate the local harvests and preserve them in any way they can to eat through the winter (or pay handsomely for what others have preserved).

Farm-to-table restaurants have reinvented this idea, working with local suppliers, preserving foods, and using every bit of the plant or animal. But when you're limiting yourself to the local foods and you're in, say, Chicago, recipes will change. You won't have olive oil, for instance, or Tabasco sauce, and even things as common today as black pepper are off the menu. You have to use what you have.

Where does that leave whiskey? How much being a locavore cuts into what whiskey you can comfortably drink depends on definitions. Is a whiskey local if it's distilled within 100 miles, or does the grain the whiskey is distilled from have to be grown nearby? That depends on the locavore, and on the strength of his or her taste for whiskey.

But back in the days when whiskey was just getting started (in the late Middle Ages in Ireland and Scotland, and in the 1700s in America), there was no such waffling about the meaning of "local." "Local" meant grown within 5 or 10 miles at most, and local grain, whatever it was, was what you used to make your whiskey; there was simply no other economical way to do it.

That's because transportation costs were astronomical, relative to today's. Goods traveled by water, powered by wind or river current (subject to the whims of the first and the one-way direction of the second), or on land, carried solely by human or animal muscle. The only significant improvements in transportation since the Roman Empire were on the ocean, where more sophisticated sailing ships allowed faster travel, with fewer crew and larger cargos. Even these newer ships were still largely grounded during winter's harsher weather.

Where grain was transported by water, it mostly traveled down rivers from the interior, and then from one port to another. And for the most part, transport of grain wasn't possible unless a farm was close to water, because the low ratio of bulk to price made even short overland hauling prohibitively expensive. The relative costs of such ground transport are staggering to modern minds. In the late 1700s, for example, the cost of shipping a ton of freight over 3,000 miles from England to Philadelphia, the largest and best-connected port in the American colonies, was the same as hauling that ton of freight a mere 30 miles over land, a distance that barely gets you out of the city's suburbs today. You can imagine what transportation costs were like in the rough ridges of the Scottish highlands, or across the Irish hills and bogs, before canals and railroads.

The effect this had on whiskey was profound. Until the Industrial Revolution changed the equation completely in manufacturing and transportation, distilling was diffuse and small scale, done by farmers and their relatives to create whiskey that could be bartered for necessities through the year. Whiskey was just another farm-made product, like cheese, butter, cider, or bacon.

It's easy to see why farmers distilled grain from their surplus grain crop rather than selling the grain. Getting 40 bushels of barley to market meant moving around 1,200 pounds of grain, or about eight mule loads. Mashed, fermented, and distilled during the quiet months after the harvest, 40 bushels yielded about 20 gallons of whiskey. Even with the added weight of stoneware jugs or wooden barrels, 20 gallons of whiskey could be slung on the back of a single mule and traded at a higher return than what the grain would bring.

These are the kinds of factors that shaped how whiskey was made in the four traditional whiskey-producing areas: Scotland, Ireland, the United States, and Canada. Whiskey making in Scotland and the United States was largely set in place before the transportation revolutions of the nineteenth century; railroads, canals, and steam power would have a place in the shape of Irish and Canadian whiskeys. Japan, a fifth area — colonized, if you will, from Scotland's whisky traditions — would be a product of twentieth-century technology, using peated malts imported from Scotland by steamship. Here's how it happened.

SCOTLAND: BACK IN THE GLENS

FOR THE MOST PART (excepting the Lowlands of the south), Scotland's geography encompasses a series of barriers: ridges, steep ravines, rivers, long estuaries, and the ocean-moated islands. It almost seems designed to keep people from trading.

It's also cool, and the soil is often rocky. Barley grew well here, and still does; it was often made into whisky here, and still is. Barley is a grain that a farmer can use in a number of ways: it is a good animal feed and remains so even after it has been used to make beer and whisky; fermentation takes the sugars, leaving cellulose and proteins behind, and cattle make good use of them. Although it is not a particularly useful grain for baking because it has a low gluten content, it makes a sustaining and satisfying meal as porridge or soup.

But it is uniquely suited to brewing. It is easily malted, much more so than some grains, like corn. That low gluten content makes for a much less sticky mashing when the malt is heated to convert the starches to sugars, and it doesn't foam like rye does (and rye does, so much so that it's actually a problem in brewing). Barley grows inside a husk that acts as a natural filter after brewing, giving a relatively clear beer, which makes distilling much easier.

Barley was a Scottish farmer's friend, even after the English tried to squash home distilling beginning in the 1780s. The English government was looking for revenue (a hunt that would eventually lead to the Boston Tea Party and the Revolutionary War in America), and one of the places it looked was in drinking. Malt was taxed, stills were taxed, sales were taxed. Until 1781, home and farm distilling was legal so long as the product wasn't sold. When the commercial product was sold, with the taxes figured in, you can guess that there was a price difference. Farm distillers were quick to realize that the differential was in their favor, if they were willing to risk smuggling small kegs of whisky over the hills on ponies or their own backs.

The benefit was enough — often the difference between survival and calamity for a tenant family working a small holding, known as a "croft" — that the substantial risk was taken by literally thousands of crofters. The topography that hindered trade was a boon for illicit distilling, with abundant small streams for cooling and water supply, high hilltops for observation of approaching strangers, plentiful

The Blair Athol Distillery in Pitlochry, Scotland, founded in 1798

Most of the barley used in Scotch whisky is grown right in Scotland.

The spirit that came out of those small farm stills was not what we think of as Scotch whisky today. It was unaged, though it may have spent a month or so in wood during the storing and transport. It was often spiced or flavored with fruits. But it was spirit, distilled from malt, often with a smoky "reek" from the malt having been dried over a peat fire, and when it *was* aged, it was aged in barrels that had been used before, with the oaky tannins largely leached out of the wood. Scotch whisky had developed its basic DNA.

Two major steps in the evolution of Scotch whisky took place after the Excise Act of 1823 brought Scottish distilling into the light. First, the act made it much more attractive for farm distillers to "go legal," sometimes on the same spots where they had illegally distilled before. Duty was lowered, the regulations and tax structures were changed to make the Highland style of all-malt, slower distilling more profitable for legal distillers, and, importantly, enforcement was significantly increased.

As the Highland-style whisky became more widely available, merchants bought it and offered it for sale. Through another evolutionary process guided by changing government policy, customer preference, and canny business sense, this straight distillery spirit became aged spirit, then a blend of malts. After the invention of the continuous still and a change in government policy that allowed the previously illegal blending of malt and grain whisky, the blended Scotch whisky we are familiar with today emerged. Blended whisky was consistent, and it was less assertive than straight malt whisky, and thus more attractive to a larger number of consumers, who willingly took to it in the millions, in the UK and around the world.

The other innovation was simple economics that turned out to have wonderfully

peat to fire the still, and bogs and glens to hide the activity.

There was also a preference for the home-distilled spirit, illegal or no, that spread all the way to London. The way the taxes were imposed often led the Lowland commercial distillers to make spirit in ways that were more concerned with price than quality. A tax on the size of stills, for instance, rather than on their output, led to broad, shallow stills that ran faster, hotter, and harder to focus on quick output. The Lowlanders would also immediately take to Aeneas Coffey's continuous still, the column still used today for grain whisky. The farm distillers ran on the "sma' still," the small pot still that was easier to heat and manage, more adapted to the small scale of farm distilling, and easier to conceal when the government excise men came looking for illicit distillers.

In earlier centuries, the green and gloomy glens of Scotland sheltered legions of illicit "sma' still" distilling operations, progenitors of the eventually legal Scotch we know and love today.

synergistic effects. Great Britain had long been one of the major markets for sherry, the Spanish fortified wine (and still is, even though consumption has dropped off significantly). In the nineteenth century it was still the custom to ship sherry in barrels, and Scottish distillers saw these used sherry barrels as a cheap source of cooperage.

The flavor of the whisky was changed by interaction with the leftover wine and the Spanish oak; happily, it was a delicious change, and sherry wood aging became part of some distillers' regular program. The same thing would happen when America's bourbon industry expanded to the point at which its cast-off barrels — allowed to be used only once for bourbon — would become plentiful enough to age Scotch whisky; they now account for about 90 percent of the barrels in Scotch warehouses.

Though it was the lack of effective, economical transportation that shaped Scotch whisky, the nineteenth-century revolution in industrial transportation and manufacturing, combined with the inexhaustible energy of the pioneers of Scotch whisky, would gain it a huge global market.

THE UNITED STATES: DOWN IN THE HOLLER

AMERICAN WHISKEY WAS shaped by a similar set of circumstances. Two sets of circumstances, actually: American rye whiskey grew up in the ridges and valleys of Pennsylvania's Appalachian and Allegheny Mountains, then floated down the Ohio River and decided to become bourbon. Both, again, were products of their geography and time.

American rye (as distinguished from Canadian rye whisky) was a creation of central European immigrants who came to Pennsylvania in the eighteenth and nineteenth centuries. Moravians and Germans in particular, often fleeing religious persecution, came to the area and commenced brewing and distilling, spreading west across the colony. The whiskey from these distillers kept the soldiers of the Continental Army warmed at the Valley Forge encampment in 1776.

Why rye? It was familiar to them; rye was the main bread grain in their homelands. It also has agricultural advantages; rye grows easily in marginal soils, with a dense root structure that holds loose soil and prevents erosion, and it will control weeds with its expansive growth. And while it can foam quite dramatically as it ferments, rye gives an excellent amount of spicy flavor to the spirit (as it does in rye bread).

It was a good time for farm distillers in the Pennsylvania colony. They grew their rye, brewed their beer and distilled their whiskey, and hauled it over the low but imposingly steep ridges to markets where they could trade for manufactured goods, tea, sugar, and gunpowder. The unaged whiskey was flavored by allowing fruit (most often cherries), herbs, or hot peppers to steep in it.

After the Revolutionary War was over and won, however, the newly created federal government had a problem: a huge war debt, owed largely to European banks. One of the ways they came up with to retire it was an excise tax on spirits, collected from distillers. The farm distillers in western Pennsylvania were incensed by this tax. They felt that it unfairly targeted them, since they thought they weren't getting much benefit from the federal government anyway. It was also hard for them to pay the tax, which had to be paid in cash, not goods. The frontier economy was largely barter based; there wasn't much currency in circulation in "Westsylvania," as the area centered on Pittsburgh was called.

The farmers refused to pay the tax, and in July of 1794 they burned the home of the inspector of revenue for southwest Pennsylvania, John Neville. It was the start of the Whiskey Rebellion, the first major challenge to the new federal government. After negotiations failed, President George Washington reluctantly called out the state militias to quash the uprising. Washington inspected and briefly rode with the troops during the march west, the only time a sitting president would lead troops in the field as commander-in-chief.

The ploy worked; the rebels faded away, a small number were arrested, and two men were sentenced to hang but then pardoned by Washington. The upshot of it all was mixed. The tax was never fully collected and was repealed in 1801. Rye whiskey continued to be the dominant spirit in western Pennsylvania and Maryland well into the twentieth century. After a steep decline that left American rye whiskey at death's door by 1990, the spirit has made a handsome comeback, in the form of such products as Wigle Whiskey, a Pittsburgh craft-distilled rye named for one of the leaders of the Whiskey Rebellion.

In the wake of the suppression of the Whiskey Rebellion, many of the rebels took to the Ohio River and floated downstream to escape what they saw as the reversal of the liberties promised by the American Revolution; they mostly settled in Louisiana. But some probably stopped to farm the dark, rich soil of Kentucky, where a native North

American grass was already being turned into whiskey: corn.

Corn whiskey and its more refined cousin bourbon are the most American of spirits, made from this native grain with European distilling techniques. The question of who first turned corn into whiskey is a contentious one, with several claimants. The earliest, and least likely, is George Thorpe, at the Berkeley Plantation near Williamsburg, Virginia, all the way back in 1622! Thorpe wrote in a letter to his backers in England, "We have found a way to make so good a drink of Indian corn as I protest I have divers times refused to drink good strong English beer and chosen to drink that." It seems almost certain that this was a corn beer; there is no other evidence of distilling at Berkeley at the time.

The most frequently mentioned name is that of Evan Williams, namesake of the well-known Heaven Hill bourbon brand. Bourbon historian Michael R. Veach neatly disposes of this claim by noting that when Williams was supposed to be distilling the first whiskey from corn, he had not yet reached America; Veach cites "the existence of a receipt for Williams's

After the American Revolutionary War, when the new government taxed distillers to pay off war debt, angry citizens faced off against federal tax collectors, leading to the Whiskey Rebellion.

passage from London to Philadelphia on the ship *Pigoe* dated May 1, 1784" (*Kentucky Bourbon Whiskey*, 2013).

Veach then notes several other candidates who were probably distilling in Kentucky in 1779: Jacob Myers and the brothers Joseph and Samuel Davis. That these men were distilling or had the wherewithal to distill in 1779 is a matter of record, but as Veach points out, there were no government records at this time, which predated liquor taxation in Kentucky. It is likely that we will never know with certainty the first person to distill corn into whiskey, and why should we? We don't know who first distilled barley into whiskey in Ireland or Scotland, either.

What we do know is that corn grew well in Kentucky, and still does; today there are fields of corn all through the bourbon heartland, which stretches from Louisville south to Loretto and east to near Lexington. Corn is easily stored, and the stalks make excellent cattle feed. It is the basis of cheap and filling food for people: mush, cornbread, fritters, the simple hoecake, and the ubiquitous Southern breakfast staple, grits. It is hard to malt but is abundant in convertible starch; add some barley malt to the cooked corn mash, and the chemistry will bring the corn right along.

Again, the farmer-distillers who made the spirit, sometimes on very primitive equipment indeed, used what was locally plentiful, mixing it with barley malt for the chemistry and a bit of rye or wheat for flavor. They bartered spirit for goods (keeping some for themselves), and they began trading their whiskey farther from home. The success of that trading and the way the reputation of Kentucky whiskey grew leads to another pair of mysteries about bourbon: who first aged it in charred oak barrels (and why), and why do we call it "bourbon"? Again, theories abound.

The most common one you'll hear on why barrels were charred is that it was done so they could be reused; the charring, the explanation goes, would take the smell of the previous contents out of the wood. Fish is often given as the example of "previous contents" (though you have to wonder if even charring would get the smell of smoked or salted fish out of a barrel).

As to why the whiskey was aged, you will likely be told that as the whiskey was floated downriver to New Orleans on flatboats it aged in the barrels, and the boatmen noticed that it was much better for it. The downriver trip only took about a month, though, so it's unlikely that much significant aging would take place.

Veach's research again has turned up evidence that the barrels were deliberately charred to affect the flavor of the whiskey. He quotes an 1826 letter from a merchant in Lexington, Kentucky, to the Bourbon County distiller John Corlis about barrels of whiskey to be purchased, suggesting that if Corlis could burn the barrels on the inside to the depth of "say only a 16th of an inch, that it will much improve it."

This burning, Veach points out, emulated the aging process used for French brandy and cognac, which were popular imports in New Orleans. He speculates that this popularity may well have led merchants to try this charred barrel aging with Kentucky whiskey. That would be when folks started calling it one of my favorite nicknames for bourbon: "red liquor," for that hint of ruby in the brown that notes a good bottling.

Finally, why "bourbon"? Was it from an association with Bourbon County in Kentucky? That seems a bit of a stretch, as bourbon was made in several other places. Or was it that the "good stuff," the aged whiskey, was available on Bourbon Street in

New Orleans? Or was it, as Veach suggests, a marketing idea to make it appeal to the French expatriates in New Orleans? The best answer is the simple one: we don't know. There is no solid proof for a definitive answer to any of these questions. We'll simply have to be satisfied with drinking the whiskey.

Bourbon would change again, going from a largely pot-stilled spirit to one that is almost exclusively made using column stills (though a pot still–like "doubler" is often used for the second distillation). It was more efficient, and — unlike Scotch — very little of bourbon's flavor and character comes from the size and shape of the still. It's the corn and the charred oak that do it.

The other major change in bourbon's character was in the late 1800s, when there was a reaction to the sharp and sometimes less than ethical economic practices that had led to the rise of the "rectifiers." Like the meatpackers in Upton Sinclair's muckraking classic, *The Jungle*, many whiskey sellers were running a business in which what was represented on the label sometimes bore little resemblance to what was actually in the bottle. These blenders would mix neutral spirit with flavorings and colorings — caramel, creosote, wintergreen, and glycerin were popular — to create "whiskey," which infuriated the straight distillers; genuine aged bourbon cost a lot more to make than flavored spirit, which was often only days old at the time of bottling.

The distillers took their fury to Washington, where it resulted in two pieces of legislation. The first was the Bottled-in-Bond Act of 1897. The "bond" referred to government oversight and regulation, particularly the bonded warehouses established in the wake of the Whiskey Ring scandal of 1875 (a

Sour mash ferments in cypress tubs at Maker's Mark.

conspiracy of government officials and distillers to evade excise taxes on whiskey).

To comply with the act and be labeled "bottled in bond," whiskey had to be at least 4 years old, bottled at 100 proof, have no additives other than pure water, and be the product of only one distillery. Clearly this meant that almost all rectifiers' whiskeys were not going to make the cut, and distillers moved to make sure that drinkers knew that bottled-in-bond whiskey was "the good stuff." The rectifiers were unimpressed and continued to sell their product simply as "whiskey" or even "Old Bourbon," with no legal restraint. What's more, bottlers of good-quality whiskeys blended from authentic bourbons felt that they were harmed by the law.

Another form of regulation would be needed to straighten out the mess, and it came with the Pure Food and Drug Act of 1906, which was prompted in part by public disgust generated by the portrayal of the meatpacking industry in Upton Sinclair's *The Jungle*. Back in these pre-Prohibition days, bourbon was still held in high regard by the nation in general, and along with meat, and milk, and medicine, whiskey was something the public wanted to be wholesome.

It wasn't easy — it took 3 years of additional wrangling to settle the whiskey issue, and eventually President Taft had to provide the final opinion — but in 1909 whiskey got the protection it deserved. The definitions that had been so long fought over boiled down to something fairly simple:

- Whiskey had to be made from grain.
- A product that was all aged grain spirits was to be labeled "straight whiskey."
- If high-proof unaged grain distillate ("neutral spirits") was flavored to create a whiskey, it had to be labeled as "blended."

It was a decision that has shaped the flavor and character of bourbon and rye (and all types of whiskey made in America) ever since. There have been changes, but the basic identity — which hearkened back directly to those early barrel-aged whiskeys of the 1830s — has remained safe and stable.

WHISKEY, MADE IN IRELAND

UNLIKE THE STORIES of Scotch, American rye, and bourbon whiskey, Irish whiskey is not one of largely unplanned chance. It did start out that same way, back in the mists of the early days of monastic culture in Ireland. But the Irish whiskey we know today is a different spirit from that unaged essence, changed by currents of history, business, and politics that, in the end, are perhaps not so different from unplanned chance, despite the appearance of purpose.

The question of how Irish whiskey evolved is further complicated by a basic identity crisis. There are currently only three major Irish distilleries — Midleton, Bushmills, and Cooley — and a large Tullamore Dew distillery under construction, but they have a number of different brands, and they are different enough that we can't even agree on what Irish whiskey *is*. All of the following might be what Irish whiskey is . . . except it isn't.

- Irish whiskey is triple distilled . . . but only if the Irish whiskey you're talking about is from the Midleton or Bushmills distilleries.
- Irish whiskey is unpeated . . . unless it's Cooley's peated Connemara whiskey.

A huge old copper pot still rests on the grounds outside the Old Midleton Distillery in County Cork, Ireland.

- Irish whiskey is made with unmalted barley . . . but only if it's made from the single pot still spirit from Midleton.
- Irish whiskey is blended . . . unless you're drinking a Bushmills or Tullamore Dew single malt, or an unblended pot-still whiskey from Midleton, such as Redbreast.

Knock your head against it long enough, and you'll realize that the glib answer is the correct one: Irish whiskey is whiskey that's made in Ireland. Still, most Irish whiskeys share a smooth, luscious approachability (which is likely why Irish whiskey is so often enjoyed neat) that is the result of that evolution, and perhaps, more than the other whiskeys of the world, Irish has not so much a common formula as a common character.

That's not how it started out, though, and it started out a long, long time ago, probably the longest time ago. Any serious student of distilling history recognizes that grain-based distillation probably began in Ireland, led by the eclectic interests of Irish monks. The Irish monastic culture was a rich one, a lighthouse of learning far on the western edge of Christendom that attracted scholars from across Europe.

One of the secrets the monks brought back from their own travels was that of distillation, used to create perfumes, essences, and medicinal elixirs. Distillation had already been used to make wine-based beverages, and in Ireland's cooler climate it was a short step to distilling beer to make *usquebaugh,* also seen as *uisce beatha,* the Gaelic words for what was known in other places in Europe as *aqua vitae, eau-de-vie, akvavit:* the "water of life," or perhaps "lively water." (The monks may have been dabbling in alchemy; compare *aqua vitae* to other formulations of the alchemist: *aqua fortis,* "fortified water" or nitric acid, and *aqua regia,* "regal water" or nitrohydrochloric acid.)

An idea like this couldn't be kept bottled up, and usquebaugh soon crossed the narrow sea to Scotland. As more people made it, and drank it, and said it, usquebaugh, pronounced (roughly) "ish-ka b'ah," got shortened to just "ish-ka" and then twisted a bit to "whisky"; listening to anyone who's had a few too many drams makes it easy to understand how that could happen.

Back in Ireland, meanwhile, the monks and others concentrated on making the stuff rather than naming it. Irish whiskey was being made from malted barley and flavored with spices and fruits. Much like Scottish whisky, there were small farm distillers, legal or illegal depending on the changing laws (and the distiller's temperament), and large commercial distillers grew up in the towns: Dublin, Cork, Tullamore. Unlike the Lowland Scottish distillers, however, these distillers — with names such as Jameson, Powers, Tullamore Dew — would come out on top in the quality competition and keep the illegal distillers of the clear, unaged spirit still known today as *poitín* ("potcheen") in a minority position.

There were to be two major differences in how the Irish distillers did it. Where the Lowlanders addressed the volume issue of the small still by seizing on Coffey's continuous still for making whiskey 24 hours a day, as fast as you could pour fermented wash into the still, the Irish took a different, more direct path: they simply made the farmer's pot still

bigger. A lot bigger, as you can see by the monsters on display outside the Jameson/Irish Distillers Ltd. (IDL) distillery near Cork and the old Jameson distillery on Bow Street in Dublin (now a museum and tasting center).

The other difference was driven by a factor we've seen as a surprisingly major driver in whiskey character: tax law. In this case, it was the malt taxes imposed on brewers and distillers by the UK government. The tax was first imposed in the late seventeenth century and changed through the eighteenth century; it was a policy tool used to encourage and discourage distilling and brewing in different areas of the UK and so was constantly being tweaked by Parliament. At some point Irish distillers decided to include a substantial amount of unmalted raw barley in the mashbill of their whiskey, thereby dodging this heavy excise.

(At least, that's the common story. It's worth noting that this is also the common explanation of why Guinness Stout is brewed with unmalted roasted barley, and it turns out not to be true. Irish brewers were not allowed to use unmalted barley when these taxes were in place, and it's likely that Guinness was later brewed that way for the flavor. Whatever the reason, Irish distillers did put unmalted barley in their mash, and IDL still does.)

The Irish spirit, distilled in large copper pot stills from a mash of malted and raw barley, has a taste like no other, whether it is a serendipitous result of tax laws or a deliberate formulation. You only need enter the brewhouse at IDL's Midleton distillery to understand why. I've been in over a thousand brewhouses in breweries and distilleries in Europe and the Americas, and I've never smelled the fresh, intense aroma I smelled as soon as I walked in the door at Midleton. It was like fresh-cut grass and barely ripe fruit with a strong underlay of hot cereal, an incredibly appealing smell of burgeoning nature.

The whiskey that comes from this mash and these stills is called single pot still whiskey. But that's a new name, imposed on the industry by regulations that shied away from the old nomenclature: pure pot-still whiskey. Apparently "pure" is a word that is no longer allowed to be applied to whiskey.

Call it what you will, this whiskey is at the heart of IDL's blended whiskeys and is the heart and the whole of a few straight-up single pot still bottlings, such as Redbreast, the independently bottled Green Spot and Yellow Spot, and some new expressions from IDL such as Powers John's Lane and Barry Crockett Legacy (named for the long-time master distiller at Midleton). You can easily detect the fresh, fruity nature in these bottlings.

But Irish whiskey would change again after pure pot-still whiskey was developed; there were several changes, unfortunately brought on by external disaster. As Irish distillers went big in their delicious distillations, Scotch whisky was humming along with its accessibly blended bottlings, and both types were selling magnificently around the world. Then the roof fell in.

The Irish struggle for independence, from the Easter Rising of 1916 through the Irish Civil War, concluding in the establishment of the Republic of Ireland in 1948, had a throttling effect on Irish whiskey, which had developed a huge export market. Sales to the worldwide British Commonwealth dropped precipitously as relations deteriorated and essentially ceased during the Anglo-Irish trade war in the 1930s.

At the same time, American Prohibition crushed sales to the U.S. market. There was a small amount of illegal shipment from Ireland, but nowhere near what there had been before the victory of the temperance fanatics.

Bushmills would change in response to these problems. Once a double-distilled, lightly peated whiskey (but always malt; Bushmills never made pure pot still), in the 1930s Bushmills would move to a lighter, unpeated, triple-distilled whiskey. It survived, when others in the north would close.

But overall, the closure of Irish whiskey's two biggest markets and the general restriction of trade from the two world wars, combined with most Irish distillers' steadfast refusal to adopt the milder blended style of Scotch whisky, pushed Irish distilling to the brink in the 1960s. The remaining distillers in the Republic merged in 1966 to form Irish Distillers Ltd. They built a modern joint distillery in Midleton in 1975, and 11 years later they bought out Bushmills in the north. All Irish whiskey was now made by one company — one company, against the world.

And finally, under this tremendous pressure to survive, IDL turned to the lighter, blended whiskey that would lead, eventually, to the incredible growth Irish whiskey has experienced over the past 20 years. Jameson was reformulated as a lighter, blended, triple-distilled whiskey . . . but the center of it was still pure pot still.

When Cooley opened in 1989, it made a throwback double-distilled whiskey, a peated whiskey, and eventually bottle-aged grain whiskey. Bushmills now makes single malt whiskeys in various expressions, aged in varied woods. Midleton makes an increasingly dizzying array of whiskeys with four different versions of pure — excuse me, *single* — pot still spirit at the center of the blends and minglings of the pot still whiskeys in its bottlings.

Irish whiskey is a variety . . . which grew, oddly enough, out of a monopoly. It has changed, vitally, and relatively recently, and that change has put it on a rapid rise in global popularity that has distillers scrambling to keep up.

CANADA: THE SPLENDID BLENDED SPIRIT

LIKE THE OTHER MAJOR whiskey types, Canadian whisky began as a scattershot of small distilleries, with farmers and millers turning bulky, excess grain into raw spirit for barter and sale over the horizon (and as always, some personal use). The differences in Canada were related to the much greater distances and the much less dense population, which helped lead to a quicker consolidation.

Before we see where it came from, let's talk briefly about what it is. Canadian whisky is a bit difficult to get a handle on, though not as indefinable as Irish whiskey. Canadian whisky is, by and large, a blended whisky, with two major components. There is the base whisky, a spirit that has been distilled to a very high proof, around 94 percent alcohol. Then there is the flavoring whisky, a lower-proof distillate.

These whiskies are aged separately at some Canadian distilleries but as a blend at others; there are almost as many ways to do it as there are distillers. They use different grains; the predominant one is corn, but all use at least a small amount of rye, and Alberta Distillers uses almost all rye. A distiller may make and use several different types of base whisky, depending on the type of grain used. Proportions of aged base and flavoring whiskies vary and make up different expressions.

This is not "blended" in the American sense, meaning straight whiskey cut with grain neutral spirit. Canadian, like good Scotch whisky, is blended from a variety of aged whiskies of different character. In Canadian whisky's case, it has been more affected by political geography than physical geography. While the earliest small distillers set up shop on their farms, mills, or homes, they were relatively quickly put out of business by large distillers: Molson (at an early stage in its history it was Canada's largest distiller as well as a growing brewery), Gooderham and Worts, Corby, Hiram Walker, Seagram, and J. P. Wiser.

The large distillers were able to grow and thrive through export trade, historically the solid base of Canada's economy. They adapted the column still. In its earliest form, several large distillers used the "box of rocks" still: a wooden column filled with large, smooth stones that allowed for evaporation and reevaporation — reflux — of the spirit as steam passed upward through the box. The small distillers were not big enough to take advantage of the efficiencies of the column still and opportunities of the export markets, and they withered.

Large distillers, though, need large markets to sell to in volume. That's why Canadian whisky makers learned about blending at about the same time the Scots did: aging and blending a variety of whiskies made for a smoother, more palatable blend that was desired by more customers. The Canadians took a mix of pot-still and column-still whiskies, aged them all separately, and then blended the aged whiskies for different flavors. Blending worked, and worked so well that it became the template for Canadian whisky.

But they also studied the same German and Dutch distilling traditions that had informed American whiskey making, and from them they learned that even a small addition of rye to the mashbill makes for a big dose of flavor and aroma in the spirit. This little distilling secret would shape Canadian whisky as much as blending did. Rye grew just fine in the soils and climate of Canada, and even as the base grain shifted from wheat to full-on rye itself, and then largely to corn at present, rye has been a constant in Canadian whisky, adding spiciness to the sweet character.

That flavor sat well with Canadians, and with their export markets. Canadian whisky found a huge market in America, especially during the Civil War, when American distillers were largely shut down. It still sells strongly, and after years of slowly declining sales (with the exception of Crown Royal, which continued to grow), it is showing a turnaround. The sweet/spicy flavor makes it a favorite in cocktails and highballs.

Any discussion of Canadian whisky history has to address Prohibition (although Canadian distillers at the time largely chose not to; most destroyed their records from the period and denied participation in illegal exports). The conventional wisdom is that Canadian whisky is what it is because of Prohibition, that the lack of homemade whiskey in America for 13 years (and 10 months and 20 days, but who's counting?) created an easy market for an established whisky industry situated just across a long, relatively undefended border.

Hiram Walker's Canadian Club distillery was, after all, on the very banks of the Detroit River, right across from the Motor City, and there was a frequent passage of small boats. This illicit business made Canadian distillers millions and made their whisky huge. So we're told, and so we believe.

The fact is, Canadian whisky was already big business, and Prohibition made selling it openly illegal. Sales in an illegal market may be substantial for a distiller, but they come with obvious problems; for instance, the smuggler and the retailer get most of the profit, since they're running most of the risk. Yes, *Boardwalk Empire* shows huge piles of Canadian Club being unloaded for illegal distribution, but it's a television drama, not a documentary. Enforcement was tightening, and the freewheeling smugglers of the early 1920s found it increasingly harder to get the goods across the border. It's telling that Hiram Walker's sons sold their distillery and brands in 1926 for a price that barely covered the value of the aging whisky in the warehouses.

Canadian whisky seems to be on the verge of a resurgence as distillers are realizing the potential of the variety of aged stocks they have. If they lose a bit of that renowned Canadian modesty, the world may have another chance to learn about this splendid, blended spirit.

JAPAN: AN APT PUPIL

UNLIKE THE OTHER MAJOR whisky areas, we can pinpoint exactly when whisky started in Japan, and who was responsible, and exactly why it was done the way it was. When Japan was opened to the West in the mid-1800s after 200 years of isolation, one of the things that came to the islands was whisky.

It was accepted, and imports grew, but one Japanese whisky importer, Shinjiro Torii, wasn't satisfied. He wanted to make Japanese whisky. Torii had the connections and the money, but he needed a distiller. He found Masataka Taketsuru, a young man who had traveled to Scotland to study chemistry and wound up becoming very interested in whisky, distillation, and Scotland; he fell in love and married a Scottish woman, Rita Cowan. After working at Hazelburn and Longmorn, he returned to Japan with Rita. In 1923 he went

The Nikka Yoichi distillery lies on the island of Hokkaido. Its distinctive kiln towers blend traditional European-style stonework with a decidedly Japanese aesthetic.

to work for Torii at his new Suntory distillery in Yamazaki, between Osaka and Kyoto.

The whisky Taketsuru made for Torii was first launched in 1929. Shirofuda ("White Label") was unabashedly Scotch-like: big, bold, smoky with peat. It was too much for the market. Taketsuru left Suntory in 1934, and Torii switched course to a new, milder spirit he called Kakubin ("Square Bottle"). Kakubin was much more successful, and the blend is still made today. Taketsuru would open his own distillery, in Yoichi on the northern island of Hokkaido, where he would make his beloved smoky whisky.

Now, these whiskies, and the ones that would follow after, are malt whiskies. The base of the tree of Japanese whisky is firmly rooted in Taketsuru-san's Scottish education; indeed,

his Scottish family ties. Japanese whisky is made with malt imported from Scotland. It is a combination of blends and single malts. Is it simply Scotch whisky made in Japan?

Most definitely, it is not. Torii wanted to make Japanese whisky, and so he did. Former Suntory master distiller Mike Miyamoto tried to explain the difference to me. "Shinjiro Torii wanted to create whisky to appeal to the Japanese palate, a delicate palate," he said. "We like well-balanced, mild, and sophisticated whisky. We introduced the blending concept of single malts. Some say it's not single malt, but the rules say it is, if it's from one distillery. It makes a very balanced single malt."

Miyamoto is a bit vague there, but taste is somewhat subjective. He does put his finger on one thing that makes Japanese whisky quite different from Scotch: blending single malts. Scotch whisky comes from about 100 distilleries, and almost all of them trade spirit back and forth in cashless transactions for blending purposes: a smoky one here, an older fruity one there, some frisky young sweet stuff for the base. Japanese whisky makers, with only a bare handful of distilleries, don't have that option.

What they've done is use a more Irish philosophy, creating variants within their own walls. By creating a variety of blending stock with different stills, fermentations, malts, and barrels (some unique to Japan), Japanese whisky makers have learned to work their whisky to exactly where they want it.

As they reached that point, and took that whisky out to the world, whisky drinkers have recognized that this is a whisky area with a distinct personality. Indeed, in some recent competitions Japanese whiskies have been judged as best in the world. The student has joined the master.

AMERICAN CRAFT DISTILLERS: A WILD VARIETY

AMERICA'S CRAFT DISTILLERS don't really constitute a whiskey region, but they do represent a profusion of influences and outputs that appears to be headed for real significance in a relatively short period of time. They have exploded in number over the past few years. The number of distillers increases every day, and whiskey is a popular product: as I write this there are nearly three hundred distillers making whiskey in the United States. That's up from fewer than five only 20 years ago.

If those kinds of numbers sound familiar, it's because they track the same kind of growth curve we saw with craft breweries. When the first new American craft brewer, New Albion Brewing, opened in 1976, there were only about 35 breweries in the country. Now, less than 40 years later, there are over 2,500, and the growth is still soaring. It's hard to say how many will still be around in 20 years — brewers or distillers — but it's safe to assume that it will be closer to today's numbers than those of 20 years ago.

What's behind that? There's an element of interest in local businesses, a support of small companies over large ones, and some contrarian resistance to being "marketed to" by slick branding and ads, and that's all part of it. But the main appeals of craft brewers, and the new craft distillers, are variety and exclusivity.

Exclusivity is a heady thing to some consumers. If you've found a great small-batch whiskey, you know something most people don't, and you're enjoying something most people aren't even aware of. That's a special excitement that marketers call "discovery," and craft distillers, with their tiny output and limited distribution area, can deliver it in spades.

Even better, like the craft breweries, you can go to the distilleries and actually see whiskey being made and meet the people who make it. That's exclusivity: "I met the distiller." The big distillers may have visitors' centers and tours, but they can't offer anywhere near as intimate an experience.

But it's variety that makes the craft distillers interesting, and that's the basis of why they are what they are. It is literally impossible to assign a common character to craft distillers' whiskeys, even more so than with Irish whiskey. They make whiskey with myriad different types of stills, a full cornucopia of grains — malt, corn, *blue* corn, oats,

Balcones Distillery in Waco, Texas

wheat, rye, triticale, quinoa, buckwheat, spelt, millet, and more — barrels of varying size and char and toast, wildly different flavors, aged and unaged bottlings, a range of blends, and smoke from different sources. Some even make whiskey from different types of craft-brewed beer.

Where did that variety come from? From the pioneers: small winemakers and craft brewers. Small winemakers have tried new techniques, new science, and new blends of grapes; they've grasped new territories and made small production work profitably. Craft brewers have not only opened whole new areas of brewing; they've gone deep into the history books to re-create old styles. They're using new strains of hops and newly treated types of malt, varieties of different grains, barrel-aging their beers. . . .

Sounds familiar, right? Craft distillers are reaping the advantages of coming late to the small-scale booze-production party. They can see the kind of great reception innovation gets, and wholesalers and retailers already are convinced that small brands and producers can be worth higher prices and will sell. There are even fabricators ready to make small-scale equipment, thanks to the changes small wine-makers and brewers have made in the business of drinks.

Craft distilling continues to evolve, of course, and part of that is economics. When small distillers start out, they need something to sell, which is how we got a slew of "white whiskeys," unaged (or "lightly aged") spirit that folks took to out of enthusiasm and curiosity. Some are smooth and interesting, some are harsh and need mixing to be enjoyed, but all are interesting practice for tasting whiskey; you don't get many chances to try the unaged spirit. That's a great opportunity to see exactly what barrel aging does for whiskey.

Another trick craft distillers use to speed up cash flow is using smaller barrels — which increases the ratio of surface area that's in contact with the spirit — or by hotter warehousing, which drives the spirit deeper into the wood. Both methods increase the rate of loss to evaporation, but they do accelerate aging, kind of. These methods will "color up" a whiskey quickly, but it's not the same as maturation in a standard-size barrel. That's okay for some distillers; they're looking for that difference. Still, many craft distillers move to standard barrels as they get some experience (and money) in hand. It continues to change.

We haven't seen what craft distilling's whiskeys will look like yet. Corsair Distillery founder Darek Bell likes to call the current period of this industry Craft Distilling 1.0 and sees new things coming in version 2.0. Almost certainly, though, Craft Distilling 2.0 will continue to surprise us with even more variety, and even more stretching of the definitions and parameters of "whiskey."

GLOBALISM: WHISKEY AROUND THE WORLD

THERE ARE MORE DISTILLERIES than these, to be sure. Small whiskey distillers are popping up across Europe, in Sweden, France, Switzerland, England, and Germany; in Asia, where the tropical climate is driving interesting experiments in short-term aging at such distilleries as Amrut (India) and Kavalan (Taiwan); and in Australia and New Zealand, where distilling is coming back strongly from some setbacks after early trials.

Climate will play a large part in creating the character of these whiskeys, as will supply of grain. New woods hold promise, as do new ways of managing hot-climate and cold-climate aging. There is little consensus among the distillers as yet, no definable regional character.

And perhaps there will not be one. Maybe America's craft distillers are the vision of the future; variety, change, multiplicity. While established distillers will continue to craft their traditional, excellent whiskeys, true to their regional, historical roots — much like traditional brewers in Germany, Belgium, the UK, and eastern Europe do today — regional boundaries will mean nothing more to new distillers than a change in language and currency when they buy supplies and sell their whiskey.

The grape/grain divide is still there, in production and consumption, but it seems to blur more every year as populations shift, and climate changes, and cultures become less distinct. American craft distillers make malt whiskey, Australian distillers age whiskey in Australian port casks, Belgian distillers make whiskey from their country's distinctive beers. There is only so much you can learn about whiskey history without realizing that it's taking place right around you, slowly or quickly, all the time. Things change; they have since the Irish monks first distilled beer, and to think of whiskey only as a traditional, authentic, historic drink is to ignore reality. Whiskey is different from what it was when I began to drink it, 30 years ago, and I guarantee you that it will be different in 30 more years. That's whiskey; that's life.

SCOTCH:
HOW THE WORLD SAYS "WHISKY"

Just think about it: Scotland, tiny Scotland, shipped the equivalent of 1.19 *billion* bottles of whisky to the world in 2012. America exported a little less than a third as much whiskey. If you take out what they ship right across the border to Americans (which adds up to about one-fifth of total Scotch exports), Canadian exports are a drop in the bucket. Irish whiskey is growing tremendously fast, but even *total* sales are less than one-tenth of Scotch whisky exports. It's no wonder that when the world says "whisky," they mean Scotch.

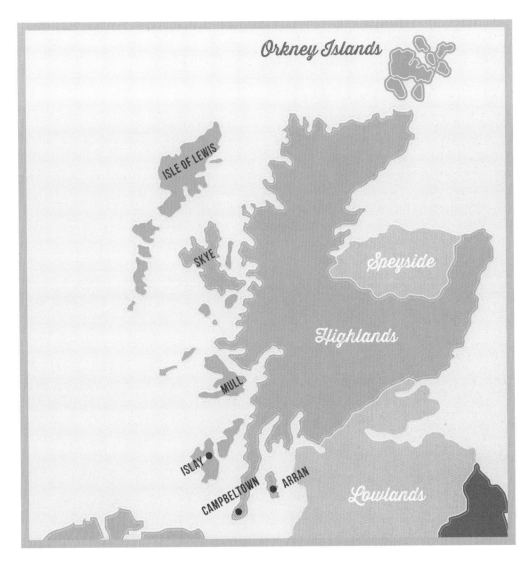

What they really mean is blended Scotch, not the single malts you hear so much about. For sheer volume it's brands like Johnnie Walker, Bell's, Ballantine's, Famous Grouse, William Grant, Dewar's, and Chivas Regal that rule the shelves in stores, bars, and homes. That's the way it's been for well over 100 years. The rise of single malt whiskies is a recent phenomenon; 30 years ago you'd have been hard pressed to find more than about five brands of single malts in even the best stores and bars. If you went to a specialty store, you may have found a few more, lovingly procured and packaged by independent bottlers.

What's since happened in those 30 years is revolutionary. Single malts have become a major market, equaling now almost 20 percent of Scotch whisky sales in the United States—an unthinkably large number 30 years ago. Faced with a glut of whisky in the early 1980s — the "Whisky Loch," driven by increased production to a growth curve that suddenly flattened as vodka exploded in popularity — more and more whisky makers bottled malts from

HOW DO YOU SAY THAT?

When I said that Scotch is how the world says whisky, I didn't say they said it *right*. While the names of the blends are all pretty easy to say (for obvious reasons), you'll hear the names of single malts pronounced in all kinds of ways by retailers, bartenders, and drinkers. There's no shame in that: there are some that the Scots can't even agree on (and if as an American you think that's funny or quaint, just ask folks from across America how they pronounce "Louisville").

I don't have the room or the authority to tell you how to pronounce all of them. There are two good sources on the Web, though. *Esquire* hired Shakespearean actor Brian Cox to pronounce the names of over 30 of the most popular (and some of the most difficult) online at its *Eat Like a*

Man blog (get there by going to Esquire.com and searching for "Brian Cox Scotch"); they're mostly like I've heard them pronounced by Scots in the industry. There's a more complete list, intoned by Pip Hills, founder of the august Scotch Malt Whisky Society, that sounds more authentic to me (find it by searching for "Pip Hills whisky pronunciation guide").

I'll give you a couple of the most often mispronounced ones. First, Islay is "EYE-luh," not "IS-lay." The odd-looking anCnoc is "uhn-NUCK." Bruichladdich is *close* to "bruek-LAD-ee," though there's a real lilt and roll to the first "ich." And my favorite is Glen Garioch: it's pronounced "glen GEE-ree," with two hard "G"s. I've no idea why.

The Glenmorangie distillery in Tain, in the Highlands region of Scotland, was founded in 1843.

their own distilleries, creating single distillery blendings of malts of varied age (the age on the label is always that of the youngest whisky in the mix), with no grain whisky. When they did, they discovered an aficionado market of previously unknown proportions.

The success of single malt bottlings changed the industry. It's made drinking Scotch whisky a much more interesting, even intriguing pastime, one with heightened demands and rewards, along the lines of getting very involved with drinking fine wine. Where there may be 10 blended Scotches generally available (though that's growing as well), there are single malts for sale from around a hundred distillers, each with its own story, unique characteristics, and fans (and detractors). Most good American bars will have at least three single malt choices these days.

When I say that the success of single malt bottlings changed the industry, though, I don't mean just the Scotch whisky industry; the effects were much more far reaching. The success of the single malts led to a similar specialization in bourbon, where small-batch and single-barrel bottlings and a trend to older whiskeys helped turn around a long decline. Irish whiskey made similar changes, adding upgrade steps to portfolios with age statements and the triumphant return of single pot still whiskey. Canadian whisky has been making moves toward premiumization with special releases of much older whiskies and barrel finishes.

But when you look further, you see that the influence is even broader. Trends that might be traced back to the success of single malt Scotch whisky include the increase in sales of aged rum, new emphasis on unique blends of botanicals for gin (and a tiny increase in long-forgotten genever), estate-bottled tequilas, even new bottlings and interest in apple brandy. I'd argue that although it's not a frequent cocktail ingredient, the connoisseur's acceptance of single malt Scotch led to a perceived opening for high-end spirits in classic cocktails, which has created a huge new niche in high-end bars.

It's been nothing short of revolutionary, truly. What makes it even more amazing is that these revolutionary whiskies are the product of solidly traditional concerns that have rejected change as anathema, where "because that's the way it's *done*" is not only carved in stone, it was carved in stone hundreds of years ago, and you'd better not think about touching those stones, lad!

The slightly younger Glenfiddich distillery in Dufftown, in the Speyside region, was founded in 1887.

THE SCOTCH WHISKY ASSOCIATION

*A*s a trade group the Scotch Whisky Association (SWA) has been tremendously successful. They essentially wrote the rules on what is and is not Scotch whisky; the latest iteration, promulgated by the UK government, is called the Scotch Whisky Regulations 2009. (The name "Scotch whisky" is itself a protected geographical indication under European Union regulations.) They literally lay down the law, and they defend it overseas. The SWA's legal affairs department has prosecuted Scotch whisky knockoffs around the world, often with great success.

It took a while to grow to such effectiveness. The SWA recently celebrated their centenary (with an exhibit hosted by the Scottish Parliament and a nice memento bottling I was lucky enough to get some of; a blend, naturally, and tasty stuff). They started as a trade association against price cutting, and until the 1970s they regulated Scotch whisky prices. They're still concerned about prices, but these days it's the government's continuing flirtation with minimum pricing and the ever-present battle with excise tax increases that catches their attention in that area.

The SWA is an effective group that vigorously defends the traditional image and definition of Scotch whisky. That can be a double-edged sword as other countries' whisky industries continue to experiment with variation and innovation.

DEFINING SCOTCH

SOME DISTILLERS AND independent bottlers were plucking around the edges of Scotch manufacturing traditions as the market grew in the past 15 years or so, and the industry reacted by clarifying the rules of what is and is not Scotch whisky, and then split that definition into five subcategories. Let's have a look.

According to the Scotch Whisky Regulations 2009, anything labeled "Scotch whisky" must:

- Be mashed, fermented, distilled, and matured entirely in Scotland
- Be made from water and malted barley, "to which only whole grains of other cereals may be added"
- Be converted using only the enzymes in the grain

- Be fermented by the addition of only yeast
- Be distilled to no more than 94.8 percent alcohol by volume
- Be matured in oak casks (no larger than 700 liters) in an excise warehouse "or a permitted place" for no less than 3 years
- Retain the color, aroma, and taste derived from the raw materials, process, and maturation
- Have nothing added to it other than water and/or "plain caramel coloring"
- Have a minimum ABV of 40 percent

There are five types of Scotch whisky by regulation. Two are the "singles":

- *Single malt Scotch whisky* is distilled in one or more batches at a single distillery, but from only malted barley, and in pot stills. (These are the familiar single malts.)

FIVE TYPES OF SCOTCH

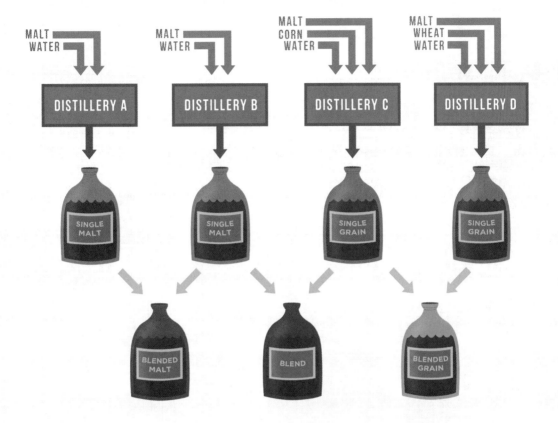

- *Single grain Scotch whisky* is a Scotch whisky that has been distilled in one or batches at a single distillery, from, at least in part, cereal grains like wheat or corn.

There are three types of blended Scotch whisky:

- *Blended malt Scotch whisky* is a blend of two or more single malt Scotch whiskies that have been distilled at different distilleries. These were formerly called "vatted Scotch whiskies," which is arguably

either less or more confusing to the consumer, depending on whom you ask. There weren't a lot of them, but there are some more emerging lately, such as William Grant's Monkey Shoulder, and several from Compass Box, including Flaming Heart and Peat Monster.

- *Blended Scotch whisky* is a blend of one or more single malt Scotch whiskies with one or more single grain Scotch whiskies. This is the familiar, large category of blends.

Visitors to Glenfiddich often find themselves ending their tour at the Malt Barn, the distillery's on-site restaurant and bar, where samples of otherwise unavailable bottlings can be savored.

- *Blended grain Scotch whisky* is a blend of two or more single grain Scotch whiskies that have been distilled at different distilleries. These are not common; Compass Box Hedonism comes to mind.

The regulations seem quite restrictive, especially for single malts: must take place entirely in Scotland, only water and malt, no added enzymes, must be distilled in pot stills, only oak casks, no additional flavors, just a bit of caramel coloring. But really, much like the standards of identity for bourbon are today (see chapter 9), these regulations are not so much restrictive as a recognition of the status quo.

This is the way the distillers want it, for the most part. They've stretched things a bit in the past, and the labeling got a bit loose in the mid-2000s, which is what triggered these new regulations. Now everyone is restricted the same way.

INDEPENDENT BOTTLERS

*N*ot all whiskies are bottled by the distillers. Many of the great blends, like Johnnie Walker and Dewar's, started out being made and marketed by men who were either grocers or wine merchants. They would buy whisky from distillers, sometimes age it themselves, blend it, then sell it to customers and eventually to agents in other areas and countries.

Independent bottlers also brought some of the first single malts to the market. They would buy barrels of whisky from brokers or direct from distilleries. The brokers made their living by facilitating the trading of aged whiskies that the different blenders needed to create their whiskies. They would buy lots from different distillers and swap them. Sometimes barrels were left over; these would be sold to the independent bottlers. And in the lean times of the industry, there were always distillers who were willing to sell entire casks, aged or new, to independent bottlers for a quick shot of cash.

The bottlers — firms like Gordon & MacPhail, Signatory, Cadenhead's, Berry Bros. & Rudd — would gather these casks, age them (sometimes leaving them in the distillers' warehouses, marked as theirs, and sometimes moving them to their own warehouses), and bottle them as either continuing brands or as-we-have-it runs. Depending on the terms of the sale, the malt may or may not have been identified on the label. Back before the current days of single malt ascendancy, an independent bottler was often the only way to get a taste of a distillery's malt.

The whisky market is tougher these days, as supply is being squeezed by demand, and rare whiskies command high prices at auction. But the bottlers have years of connections to fall back on, and they continue to make some very good whisky available.

PUTTING THINGS TOGETHER

FOLLOWING THE RULES isn't the straitjacket it might seem. The distillers can still vary lots of things: the type of yeast and the speed of the fermentation affects the estery fruitiness of the spirit; the shape and size of the stills and the type of condenser affect the weight; the timing of the heads and tails cuts greatly affects the flavor and "cleanness" of the spirit; and then there's the choice of wood for aging, the type of warehouse and its location, and how long the whisky stays in the wood.

(Compare this, just to be mean, to America's biggest-selling spirit, vodka. The distillers can use grain, potatoes, grapes, whatever; they can distill it once or — literally — 199 times, each time removing more flavor; they can filter it, and of course, dump a trendy new flavor into it, making all the preceding choices essentially null and void. And flavored or not, none of it makes one bit of difference once the vodka's inevitably poured into a glass with Red Bull or tomato juice.)

The master whisky blenders know their home distillery's choices on those factors deep in their hearts and use them when they create expressions of single malt. Once an expression is created, the blender's job is to use what

WHAT ARE GRAIN WHISKIES?

*Y*ou'll hear about blended Scotch being a mix of malt whiskies and grain whiskies. We know what malt whiskies are; those are all the single malts with the richly Scottish names. And grain whiskies, those are the whiskies made from grain — is malt a grain? What are grain whiskies, anyway?

Grain whiskies are distilled from a variety of grains (usually whatever's good and cheap; currently, that's often wheat) to a very high proof on continuous, or column, stills. That part was explained at the beginning of this book. It's not vodka, any more than Canadian blending whisky is vodka, because part of spirit is intent. This spirit is intended to be whisky, so different things will happen to it than filtration, dilution, fancy packaging, and forceful marketing.

The high-proof whisky is aged in casks (most often former bourbon casks) for at least 3 years to smooth the rawness, giving it a creamy mouthfeel and notes of vanilla and coconut from the oak (and to make it legally "whisky"). Some grain whiskies are aged longer, of course. And some are bottled as just grain whiskies, with no malt whisky. They're good enough to stand on their own; lighter in character, but still whisky.

Most grain whisky goes into blended Scotch. Snobs may tell you that it's used just to add cheap bulk and to dumb down the flavor. That may be the case in cheap blends, but in the flagships and the premium blends, the grain is as important as the malts, adding that mouthfeel and balancing the prickliness or thickness of the malts. If it were "just" grain whisky, blenders would just open the spigot on the tank and add it. But they blend in several different grain whiskies: different ages, different distillery sources. It's whisky, true and solid. Respect it.

stocks are available to maintain that expression, consistently.

Remember, the age of an expression is not the age of every whisky in the bottle, or an average; it is merely the age of the youngest whisky in the bottle. With that baseline age, blenders can range upward and use what they need to keep the whisky tasting the same, every time. It's a job that requires a keen, well-trained nose and a mind for detail and organization: how much stock do they have, of all ages, in what barrels, in which warehouses? How much should they be telling the distillers they need in 5 years, 12 years, 20 years? It's a guess at best as the times get longer, but it has to be an informed guess.

That's just for single malts, at one distillery. Expand that job to making and maintaining the gigantic volumes of blended whisky that leave Scotland every week, and consider: now the blenders are faced with knowing other whiskies' characteristics, how much is needed to get just the right note, what those stocks might be, and how they can be replaced in case of problems with supply, because after all, a lot of times the whiskies going into a company's blends are made at distilleries owned by other companies. They're traded back and forth in a complex system of equalities known generally as "reciprocity."

Don't think the blends are simple matters of "throw some 3-year-old grain whisky in with 8-year-old malt from this distillery for sweetness and a little bit of 10-year-old from this distillery for a touch of smoke." Blends can be quite complex, with several different aged grain whiskies and malts from 20 or more distilleries, carefully proportioned and married, and adjusted as needed when supplies vary.

Blends have been successful — wildly successful — for a simple reason. They fill a need, a desire, for a drink with a certain amount of a certain kind of flavor. They are not as intensely focused as single malts; they're not meant to be. Blenders look at blending as the ability to make a whisky taste the way they want it to, not the one way a distillery produces it.

Just as there are different kinds of cars for different budgets and needs, there are different blends for different price points and palates. Need to get around but don't have much money? Small used car; that is, a store-brand blend, or bargain label, meant to be mixed with seltzer or soft drinks. Want something a bit more luxurious, something a bit more pricey? Trade up to a new compact, or a "preowned" better line; try something with a bit more character, a bit more malt, and get to know your tastes for peat or sherry wood aging. Need something for commuting or running about town? A small, comfortable sedan or hatchback, fun but reasonable; or in other words, a good bottling for rocks or Scotch and soda and relaxation. Got that professional job, and you're looking for something that's really enjoyable? Sport sedan, highway cruiser, crossover: look at some blended malts or age-statement blends.

And if you've hit it big, then you can really drive (drink) anything you'd like. While you may think that means single malts, there are blends at that level, too: the Johnnie Walker Blue Label (perhaps even the King George V

The single malt whiskey produced by the Aberfeldy distillery in Perthshire, founded in 1896 in the Highlands of Scotland, is a major component of Dewar's blended whisky.

bottling), the Chivas Royal Salute Stone of Destiny, and the Black Bull 30 Year Old Deluxe, for example, are all excellent whiskies. We'll talk about it more in subsequent chapters on Irish and Canadian whiskies, but just know this: blends can be simply excellent whiskies. The idea that they're cheap, and not as good, is a relatively new one, and largely an outgrowth of single malt snobbery and a proliferation of lighter blends that started during Prohibition and kept on right up through the 1970s.

Blends are circling back to what they used to be: a spectrum of choices, "flavor packages," to use a phrase in vogue in the industry. Malts, on the other hand, have stubbornly stayed the same, even when they weren't being sold on their own; blends have driven that trend, too, of course, because the blenders wanted and needed those consistent flavors.

Now the consumers want those flavors, straight up in single malts. They want them so much that stocks are under pressure and prices have gone up and up. Some people predict that the price increases will bring drinkers back to more robust blends (though the "more robust blends" are often similar in price to entry-level single malts), but so far the sales of single malts continue to rise. Let's take a look at how those flavors are kept consistent.

MAINTAINING MALT CONSISTENCY

IF YOU TOUR MORE THAN three or four Scottish distilleries, you're going to pick up some common themes. Frequently you'll hear a distiller proclaim, "Our whisky can only be made in this particular spot"; this usually has to do with the water source or climate. You will also hear, "While other distillers may do things another way, here at this distillery we continue to do it this way"; this usually reflects a sensible refusal to mess with success. The one I particularly like is when a distiller points out the geometry or size of the stills; this, you're told, "is what makes our whisky here unique," with the strong implication that the stills were made to the order of some distilling genius.

Well, yes and no. Yes, if you moved the distillery somewhere else, or you built a copy of it in another spot, the spirit would almost certainly be different; it's been tried, it doesn't work. It's almost like an indefinable manufacturing equivalent of *terroir*, a combination of humidity, sunlight, water, wind, and other factors that bend a spirit in ways science can't encompass. It sounds romantic, but it's really quite scientific — chaos theory, as applied to distillery design — and alternately frustrating and wonderful, depending on who's concerned. And certainly yes in the case of the stills, because the shape of a still has a direct bearing on reflux, which in turn directly affects the character of the spirit and ultimately the character of the whisky.

However, talk to enough people in the industry, and you begin to realize that many of these logistical arrangements came about "just because," not from any great plan of the original distiller or the master planner. You learn that stills were bought because they were affordable, often secondhand from a distiller who had gone out of business. Glenmorangie's famously tall stills (at almost 17 feet, the tallest in Scotland), which make the whisky light in character and quite elegant, were famously bought secondhand from a gin distillery; rather than have them changed to fit the norm, Glenmorangie simply put them into service.

After hearing so many similar stories, I was standing in the new expansion stillhouse at Glenlivet, looking at the stills and wondering, Why are they shaped in that particular way? I had the opportunity, so I asked Richard Clark, the brewer, exactly that question. He answered, with a bit of a grin, "That's the way we've always done it."

Then he got quite earnest and continued, "But that's really what it is. Do it the same way, whatever that way is. Because whatever reason they were made that way *doesn't matter*. That's how your spirit is made, and that's how your spirit is. You'd never want to change it."

FINISHING

One way to add a new character to Scotch whisky was pioneered by Dr. Bill Lumsden at Glenmorangie and Balvenie malt master David Stewart in the 1990s, a technique that's come to be called "finishing." As a whisky comes to maturity, it is dumped from its bourbon or sherry cask into a different cask. These subsequent casks often were previously used for aging wines, such as Madeira, port, sauternes, or Malaga, or for aging rum or other spirits.

Finishing falls within whisky-making regulations because the casks are oak, and they are drained before being refilled with the whisky, so nothing is being physically added to the spirit. What is added is flavor, aroma, and synergistic effects between the new barrel character and the old. Carefully done, finishing can create something new and quite good.

But finishing can also ruin good whisky. Pick the wrong barrel for a whisky, and the contrasts can ruin it. Leave it in the finishing barrel too long, and the finishing effects will overpower the whisky. I've had whiskies that suffered from too-long finishes; one was finished in a port cask, a wood that can be delightful if used skillfully, but one that can be dreadfully sweet and fruity if used too long.

Finishing was quite the vogue for a while. It's not as widely used as it was, but the blenders who continue to use it are, generally, the ones who have mastered it.

Casks mature in the warehouse of the Glenmorangie distillery in Tain, Scotland. The wooden mallet is a "bung starter," sharply hit on the sides of the bung to pop it out.

Glenlivet's global brand ambassador, Ian Logan, took it from there (not the everyday tour guide, I'll admit), when we started talking about how the distillery had expanded. They'd installed this second set of stills, built to the same ratios and proportions as the first. But these were fully automated: computer-actuated valves, temperature probes everywhere, and enabled to make every batch just like the one before.

"It's a balance, between tradition and expansion," Logan said. "Is it about quality? Or consistency? We've bet on consistency. You may not get that rare amazing run every now and then, but the overall level of quality, every day, every run, is much higher than before. We're retrofitting the same equipment on the old stillhouse."

"Still," he said, "the automation doesn't work without the people. Ten people make the second biggest production single malt whisky in the world; ten people make all of it. People make whisky."

The funny thing is, a day later I was in the stillroom at Dalmore, where things are manually controlled — barely. The stillhouse is a madhouse, with some very odd stills indeed: the wash stills with a cutoff flat top (the lore is that they were originally cut off to fit under the ceiling), the spirit stills with cold-water jackets around the necks to cool the copper for more reflux. There are two sets of stills, the newer one with the exact same quirks but on a much larger scale, and when everything comes together . . .

"It's an unbalanced distilling system," stillman Mark Hallas noted. "The spirit's different coming off the different stills, but over 24 hours of distilling, it balances." He grinned. "Automate it all you want, the most important part is the meat in the machine." He grinned again and tapped the side of his head. As Logan said, people make whisky.

Twin "pagoda" kiln towers at the Strathisla Distillery in Keith, the oldest continuously operating distillery in Scotland

Sometimes, also, a person makes whisky. There is much said about the team, the cooperation necessary in the industry to make a whisky, and there are many factors that go into Dalmore other than the stills: the array of different types of casks they use, the multi-pathed blending of the casks to make the different whiskies. But right there in my notes from my visit to Dalmore it says: "The aroma in [the warehouse] is unique: salt, stemmy grape, malt, earth. What makes Dalmore what it is: eccentric stills, varied casks, careful selection and blending. And Richard Paterson."

Paterson has long been the master blender for Whyte & Mackay, the parent company of Dalmore, and a legend in the industry. He is The Nose, trained in blending by his father,

SCOTCH: FLAVOR PROFILE FOR ICONIC BOTTLINGS

This chart rates five core characteristics on a scale of 1 to 5, with 1 = faint to absent, and 5 = powerful and fully present.

Whiskey	PEAT	SHERRY	AMERICAN OAK	MALT	MOUTHFEEL
SINGLE MALTS					
ARDBEG 10-YEAR-OLD	5	1	2	3	3
GLENFARCLAS 15-YEAR-OLD	1	4	2	3	4
GLENFARCLAS 12-YEAR-OLD	1	2	2	4	3
GLENLIVET 12-YEAR-OLD	1	1	3	4	2
GLENMORANGIE ORIGINAL	1	1	4	2	2
HIGHLAND PARK 12-YEAR-OLD	4	3	1	3	3
LAGAVULIN 16-YEAR-OLD	5	1	1	3	4
MACALLAN 18-YEAR-OLD (SHERRY OAK)	1	5	1	2	5
BLENDS					
CHIVAS REGAL	1	1	2	2	2
DEWAR'S WHITE LABEL	1	1	2	3	2
JOHNNIE WALKER BLACK	2	3	2	2	3

said to have been the youngest man to become a master blender. Like David Stewart at Balvenie, Dr. Bill Lumsden at Glenmorangie, and many, many others, he has put his stamp on the whiskies from this distillery (and on the blends from Whyte & Mackay) for now and likely for years to come after his inevitable retirement. A single person in this position, with the right talents and a fairly free hand,

can be enormously influential on how the whiskies are made at a distillery, how they are aged and blended.

There is, of course, another factor at play in blends, and that's inertia. Even a master blender has a hard time turning an established blend; you've got the flavor of the blend to preserve, of course, and the sales, and you don't want to react to every twitch of the

ISLAY AND THE ISLANDS

Scotch whisky is traditionally divided into regions, one of them being the Islands. These include the Orkneys and the Isles of Skye, Mull, Lewis, Jura, Arran, and, of course, Islay.

Islay is home to eight distilleries: clockwise, from the northeast, there's Bunnahabhain, Caol Ila, Ardbeg, Lagavulin, Laphroaig, Bowmore, Bruichladdich, and the youngest addition, Kilchoman. There are some iconic whiskies in there; at least, they're iconic now. Thirty years ago you could barely give the stuff away; it was considered too smoky, too rough, too singleminded.

Now, of course, that last sentence is answered with, "Yes, you're damned right it is; bring me another!" Peat is king, and Islay is the seat of power. You must visit Islay, you'll be told, if you're serious about Scotch whisky.

If you approach Islay from the air, you see an island, separated from even its nearest neighbor, Jura, by rough, open water. It looks separate, distinct. But if you approach Islay by sea, you realize how easy it is to slip from island to island to shore to cove, and how everything links together. Once you've had some of Bunnahabhain's unpeated whisky, or tasted the peaty mainland smoke of Ardmore, the continuity of it all comes home. This is about Scotch whisky, not just Islay whisky, or Highland whisky.

There's debate about whether Scotch whisky has *terroir*, the characteristic donated by the land that is so much touted for French wine. The question is muddled. The malt may be Scottish grown, but it may also be European; the water is usually local, but it may be from city mains; warehouses may be beside the distillery or miles away.

If there is *terroir*, it is a minor factor compared to the character that comes from the individual distillery and the generational continuity of the people who work there. On Islay the somewhat idiosyncratic distilleries are staffed by people who

1	ARDBEG		
2	BOWMORE	**7**	GLENGYLE
3	BRUICHLADDICH	**8**	JURA
4	BUNNAHABHAIN	**9**	KILCHOMAN
5	CAOL ILA	**10**	LAGAVULIN
6	GLEN SCOTIA	**11**	LAPHROAIG
		12	SPRINGBANK

either are from Islay (Ileachs, they call themselves) or have come there and settled in. With about a third of the people on the island directly or indirectly employed in the whisky business, it makes a difference.

I asked Laphroaig distillery manager John Campbell — an Ileach himself — what makes Islay whisky different. He didn't hesitate: "Peat," he said. "Islay whisky has flavors from the earth, versus flavors from a cask. It has a depth of flavor." The heavy use of peat on Islay brings all four of the ancient mystic elements together: water and earth create peat and barley, water then steeps the barley to make malt, and the earth (peat) is burned (fire) to create smoke (air) that permeates and dries the malt. The whisky is a whole.

The aficionados are right: you should go to Islay if you can. The small towns have friendly pubs with good beer, the climate is bracing, and the people are solid. And the whisky's pretty good, too.

SPEYSIDE

Speyside is the region alongside the River Spey. It is a sparkling river, the second longest in Scotland at 98 miles, but not too big, certainly no Mississippi or Hudson. With the heavy density of distilleries in the area, it's hard to believe the river has stayed clean, but it is quite healthy and protected. You're likely to see fly fishers in the water during the season.

The density of distilleries is nearly cheek by jowl in spots such as Rothes and Dufftown. Good water flowing over good stone will attract a distillery, and the Spey has done just that. In turn, the clusters of distilleries have spawned subsidiary industries. The Speyside Cooperage is here, banging away on hoops and staves. Forsyths builds the stills and condensers for most of the industry in Rothes (partly on the site of the previous Caperdonich distillery). There is also a "dark grains" processing plant in Rothes that takes distillery waste (spent grain, pot ale) and makes it into animal feed. That's only fitting: Speyside is also where much of Scotland's barley is grown to begin with.

But we're here for the whisky, and there's plenty to be found. The Speyside character, generally, is an unpeated one. Generalizations are trite, but there you are. Speyside distillers have experimented with peat in recent years as smokeheads have demanded more, more, *more*, but the region is home to some beautiful examples of what Scotch whisky can be without peat.

Speyside distillers listen to their casks, the wood telling them what can be done with extraction and age. Here's where you'll find Macallan running its devoted Spanish oak program, paying to build sherry casks for producers, then getting sherry producers to age their wine in them for

2 years so the distillery can dump them and take them back to Scotland. It's costly — each cask costs about $1,000 — but there's no other way to get the flavors Macallan wants, which are the flavors we want.

This is a region of complicated topography, filled with valleys, hills, the great ridge of Ben Rinnes, and tributaries to the Spey. It was home to illicit distillers, and to Glenlivet, the first to go legitimate under the rules of the 1823 Excise Act. Founder George Smith, the first to get a license, so enraged his scofflaw neighbors that he carried a pair of pistols for defense in the early years.

You can wander among distilleries for days here; there are over 30 of them. Stop in the small towns along the river, sample whiskies at the Craigellachie Hotel, maybe even try the fishing. It's whisky country, where there's a distillery around almost every corner.

market's palate when what's old may become new at the speed of social media. There's also the weight and impact of tens of thousands of barrels of whisky, all made the same way, and often in the same proportions; you can't aim it in a different direction very easily. Changing a whisky has to be done very carefully, and with great deliberation.

HOW TO CHOOSE

HAVING LEARNED SOME of what goes into the putting-it-together side of Scotch whisky, how do you make a choice on what you're going to drink? Much depends on your own tastes. I'd advise you to start with blends or flagship single malt bottlings, the 10- and 12-year-old (or 16-year-old, in the case of Lagavulin) malts that are the bread and butter of a range.

The blends are going to be a less expensive way to learn what you like from among the general camps of Scotch whisky. You may find you like the restrained smoke of Johnnie Walker (less restrained in the Double Black bottling); consider trying Black Bottle or Teacher's, a smoky single malt such as Talisker, or one of the Islays. Maybe you like the sherried richness of the Famous Grouse; you could find similar character in the Macallan, or try it with a hint of peat in Highland Park. Find a taste for Chivas Regal? Step up to the 18-year-old bottling, or slide over to the single malt side to try the Glenlivet or anCnoc. If the honeyed notes of Dewar's do it for you, get more with the 12-year-old, or get at the heart of it with Aberfeldy. Remember, blends are built from malts, but they often arise from a multiplicity of inputs.

It's in single malts that you're going to see the distillery character most clearly, unblended. The flagship bottlings are younger, so the

"Nosing" a cask sample at the Glenfiddich distillery

influence of the cask is at its least. With these bottlings you can see what a distillery is about.

If you don't want to shell out the money for bottles, you can find a good whisky bar to try all these. You can also make it to a whisky-tasting event or festival to get the chance to sample multiple whiskys, usually with some expert, enthusiastic commentary.

"GONE SILENT"

SCOTCH WHISKY HAS SUCH a long, long lead time that a lot of things are thought about differently in the industry. It's nothing to see a warehouseman rolling along a barrel that's older than he is. In 2007 Glenfarclas brought out a brilliant series, the Family Casks, that was a bottling of their selected malt whiskies from every "vintage" from 1952 to 1994, an amazing tour de force from their deep stocks of aging malts.

Then there are whiskies from distilleries that no longer exist. They're not re-creations, or fantasies; they're carefully guarded legacies. Most distilleries are owned by companies that have more than just the one. Diageo owns 28, for instance. When they deem that they have enough stock from one for their foreseeable purposes (or sometimes when they've bought a redundant one from a competitor), they may decide to mothball it, carefully close down the workings with an eye toward preserving it for future use while saving money on operations. Such a distillery is said to have "gone silent."

Malts from these distillers are used in blends, or they may be bottled as single malts; Diageo has a series of them that they call the Rare Malts. But we always hope that they will come back. Ardbeg did, after all; Bruichladdich did; Glenglassaugh and Glen Keith did.

Those that don't, and won't, such as Brora, Port Ellen, Glenury, and Rosebank, those that are demolished, or gutted and turned into fashionable apartments, are gone to us. But their whisky lingers on, like a marvelously vibrant and living echo. I had a Brora 30-year-old last year that was simply phenomenal. While it angers you that the fortunes of business, the boom-and-bust cycle of whisky, led to its loss, you still just have to cheer that, thanks to careful warehousing, the whisky is still around.

Enjoy these whiskies while we have them. And yes, these are probably ones you don't want to pour over ice if there's a Scot nearby.

As you make your way through Scotch whisky, learning what you like, what you don't, and what you love, keep in mind that this is a more complex road than tasting the other whiskies of the world. That's not favoritism; it's just facts. There are many more Scotch whisky distillers than there are bourbon or Canadian whisky distillers (and the Irish and Japanese aren't even in the running). Sure, there are more craft distillers, but let's see how they're doing in a hundred years. Scotch whisky is lovingly varied, and there's always — always — more to learn.

Don't stop learning, don't stop tasting. Sample, read, visit, discuss, repeat. Every cycle you'll learn more, and the whisky only gets better as you do.

IRISH:

SINGLE, DOUBLE, TRIPLE

According to tradition, St. Patrick used the three leaves of the shamrock to explain the persons of the Christian Trinity to the people of Ireland. One leaf was the Father, one the Son, the third the Holy Spirit, and together they made one plant. Similarly, the state of Irish whiskey can be directly tied to the *four*-leaf clover. The four leaves represent the different whiskeys that the major distillers produce and the places where they make them.

1 BUSHMILLS
2 COOLEY
3 KILBEGGAN
4 MIDLETON
5 TULLAMORE DEW (UNDER CONSTRUCTION)

Ireland

ONE is the single pot still whiskey at the heart of Irish Distillers' whiskeys, a unique type of whiskey made only in Ireland.

TWO is the double-distillation method used by Cooley, a throwback to pre-1960s Irish distilling.

THREE is the triple-distilled whiskeys that are made at Midleton (Jameson) and Bushmills, a process that makes these whiskeys light and approachable.

FOUR is the number of major distilleries: Midleton, Bushmills, Cooley, and Kilbeggan, the last one being generous, because while Kilbeggan is a large historic distillery, what's there currently is a mini distillery built inside it. However, William Grant & Sons has broken ground on a full-scale Tullamore Dew distillery in Tullamore, which should be online in 2014, at which time we can count that as four. There are other small distillers popping up, though, and former Cooley owner John Teeling is converting Diageo's former Dundalk brewery to a distillery, so happily, "four" won't be a significant number in Irish whiskey much longer.

That's the real story of Irish whiskey in the current era: growth. After the disastrous collapse of Irish whiskey, as noted in chapter 6, the industry has had to rebuild itself from the ground up. With the steady support of Irish around the world, the growing popularity of Irish-themed pubs — also around the world! — and the generally growing interest in whiskey, Irish is making a fantastic comeback.

STORIES

WE WERE DRINKING IN Chicago, and a good friend was leaving the next morning for Ireland, to work with Diageo on Bushmills. What could be more appropriate than toasting his new adventure with a glass of Bushmills 1608, their 400th-anniversary whiskey?

AT A WHISKEY AND SPIRITS show, it took me 45 minutes to get to the Jameson table, just in time to get the very last drops they had of the awesome Rarest Vintage Reserve — that's the kind of luck that makes me laugh.

TEN OF US, A BOISTEROUS late night in the Buena Vista Cafe in San Francisco, surrounded by rows of Tullamore Dew bottles on the walls. "Irish coffees all around?" I asked. No arguments, and wasn't that hot, sweet liquor delicious?

EIGHT OF US, HEADS DOWN against the evening's gusty wind and rain, walking half a mile to a small beer festival. "Here," I said, and passed my flask, full of warm, aromatic Redbreast. "Brilliant!" someone blurted, and the flask came back empty; mission accomplished.

*G*ood friends and good whiskey are a great thing, and they're all a bit different. When I think of nights drinking bourbon, I think of laughter and card playing. When I think of nights drinking Scotch, I think of music and, more often than not, talking about whisky. But when I think of the nights I've enjoyed Irish whiskey, what I think of are stories.

Can't say why. It might be the Irish tendency toward storytelling; it's been said that it's as hard to get a Scottish distiller to tell stories as it is to

get an Irish one to stop. (Not true, really, but it's a close contest.)

But it might be the accessibility of Irish whiskey: everyone will take part. Irish is smooth, a bit sweet, and flavorful, without the new-wood roar of bourbon, and — unless you're drinking Connemara, of course — without the "love me or hate me" polarity of a peated Scotch.

There's the complexity that multiple-cask aging and blending can bring, there may be that unique brightness of single pot still character, and there's the depth of malt and the creaminess of grain — but it's all welcoming. You're not asked to accept Irish whiskey; it's as if the whiskey takes a seat and accepts you.

Irish doesn't demand much, and it doesn't take itself too seriously. Which brings to mind another story: Bushmills master distiller Colum

Egan was in the midst of a very serious panel presentation on "Understanding Irish Whiskey," before hundreds of very serious whiskey aficionados. Egan was leading them through a tasting of Bushmills 21-year-old.

Don't just taste it, he urged; use all your senses. Smell the fruity, nutty aromas. Look at the beautiful amber color. Feel the slick, malty slide of a drop. (All very good advice, by the way.) Listen to your whiskey, he said, very seriously, and held the glass up to his ear, furrows of concentration on his face. Leaning into the microphone, he whispered, "It said," then in a quavering comic falsetto, "'Drink me!'" The audience broke into laughter, and he had them in the palm of his hand.

Whiskey, stout, cider, and *craic* — the classic fare of a lively Irish pub

The United States is the largest market for Irish whiskey. Sales have increased by about 20 percent each year for the past 20 years, an amazing stretch of growth, albeit from a sadly small base to start. While Jameson's is the biggest brand by far, with a bit over two-thirds of the U.S. market, there's been lots of room for other names to succeed, and the past 10 years have seen a flood of new brands, the surest sign of growth. We've even seen the reentry of Tullamore Dew, now the second-largest Irish whiskey in global sales, but missing from the U.S. market for a while.

Astute readers will have noticed that I mentioned that a Tullamore Dew distillery was under construction and will no doubt be wondering where the whiskey's been coming from. Tullamore Dew comes from Midleton under a long-standing contracted agreement, a fairly common arrangement in the whiskey business, as you may be starting to understand. That kind of arrangement is where the slew of other Irish whiskey brands are coming from: Connemara, Tyrconnell, John L. Sullivan,

Michael Collins, Slane Castle, and others. Mostly they come from Cooley (the first two are Cooley house brands), though that changed when Beam Global (yes, that Beam) bought Cooley in 2011 and soon announced they would be cutting off the supply of contracted whiskey that John Teeling had built Cooley's business on. These other brands have been scrambling for supply, which is exactly what Teeling hopes to give them with his new business in Dundalk, noted above.

MIDLETON: WHISKEY CENTRAL

BUT THERE ARE A LOT OF other Irish whiskeys: Midleton Very Rare, Powers, Jameson, Paddy, Crested Ten, Redbreast, Green Spot and Yellow Spot — they all come from Midleton. Or Irish Distillers Ltd. Or Jameson. It's all the same thing.

Allow me to explain. By 1966 Irish whiskey production in the Republic of Ireland was down to a sad total of three companies: John Jameson & Son, John Power & Son, and Cork Distilleries. They made a bold (or desperate) decision and consolidated into one company: Irish Distillers Ltd.

In the mid-1970s the company brought online a single modern facility in Midleton, alongside the old Cork Distilleries plant, and wound down and closed the other distilleries (including Jameson's Bow Street distillery in Dublin, which is now a rather fantastic tourist attraction, with a great tour for whiskey education, and tasting). All production would now take place in Midleton, and the surviving brands would all come from there. This big distillery is still run by Irish Distillers (as a subsidiary of French drinks giant Pernod Ricard), at Midleton, and is known for its

major brand, Jameson, and you may hear it called by any of those three names.

But the important thing about Midleton is what they do there, because it's bewildering. The distillation paths are complex, multi-branching, and resistant to simplification. It's not just that they have pot stills and column stills and may run whiskey through both; they also use different cut points (when the flows from the pot stills are diverted from the heads, heart, and tails) for different whiskeys, with different redistillation programs of the cuts, emerging as four distinct pot-still spirit streams (or maybe more, according to Dave Broom's *The World Atlas of Whisky*, referencing a "gentle quizzing" of now-retired master distiller Barry Crockett, who led much of the design of this system).

Before the spirit even gets to this hot coppery maze, it gets the addition that makes it unique: raw, unmalted barley in the

Welcome to the "Jameson experience" in Midleton, Ireland.

IRISH: FLAVOR PROFILE FOR ICONIC BOTTLINGS

This chart rates five core characteristics on a scale of 1 to 5, with 1 = faint to absent, and 5 = powerful and fully present.

Whiskey/Distillery	"PURE POT STILL"	SHERRY	AMERICAN OAK	MOUTHFEEL
BUSHMILLS BLACK BUSH	1	4	1	3
BUSHMILLS	1	2	4	2
BUSHMILLS 16-YEAR-OLD	1	3	2	5
COOLEY KILBEGGAN	1	1	2	2
TYRCONNEL	1	1	4	3
MIDLETON GREEN SPOT	5	2	4	3
JAMESON	2	2	3	2
JAMESON 18-YEAR-OLD	4	3	2	4
REDBREAST	5	3	3	4
TULLAMORE DEW	1	2	3	2

brewhouse. This is the oddity that defines single pot still Irish whiskey, what may well have been the product of a sly cost-saving method in the mid-1800s to duck the UK tax on malt by replacing part of the mash with unmalted barley.

These days the ratio is about 60:40 barley:malt, but it varies with what they're making. It makes for a headily fresh scent in the brewhouse, and a substantially different weight and mouthfeel in the spirit; the raw barley has different nonfermentable components that come through brewing and distillation as a pleasantly syrupy feel and a green, fruity aroma of apples, peaches, and pears.

That's the stuff that makes these Midleton whiskeys what they are, the very heart of it all.

To get it head-on, try some Redbreast. I had my first taste of it years ago when an Irish friend in Philadelphia, just back from a visit home, pulled a flask out of his pocket while we were at a formal dinner. "Try this," he whispered. I don't exaggerate when I say I was stunned, and then hooted in pleasure; an embarrassing moment, but I was struck by the wonderful freshness of it, the coiling soft mouth, and the vaporous flow of fruits and spice it left in my mouth as I breathed. What is it, I asked? He grinned. "Can't get it here." Now we can, and believe me, I do.

SEEING SPOTS

reen Spot was once a "white whale" of a whiskey, available in only one place: Mitchell & Son's shop in Dublin. They were whiskey bonders, merchants who would buy casks from distillers and then bottle them for their own sale. The name "Green Spot" represented how they would mark the barrels they had purchased: a daub of green paint on the end. There were Yellow, Red, and Blue Spots as well at one time, but over the years, only Green Spot remained: 100 percent single pot still whiskey, carefully selected from among the stocks at Midleton.

When I learned that Mitchell & Son had expanded availability of Green Spot to the duty-free shop at the Dublin airport, I grabbed a bottle on my next trip to Ireland. Mine! As fate had it, my wife picked me up at the airport, and we went directly to a party at a friend's house. An Irish friend. Well, we opened the bottle, and it was very well received indeed. Happily, by the next time I went to Ireland, Mitchell & Son had, among the burgeoning growth and growing acclaim for Irish whiskey, revived the Malaga wine–finished Yellow Spot, and this time I brought back a bottle of each. Rumor is strong as I write this that Red and Blue will be back soon; I guess my next trip will need a suitcase big enough to fit a rainbow.

Another component of Midleton's genius is their wood management. I tried Jameson for the first time in the '80s: not impressed. I was drinking Wild Turkey and Glenlivet at the time, and Jameson had neither the zest and fire of Wild Turkey nor the elegance of Glenlivet. It was fairly lifeless stuff. But when I tried it again in the late 1990s, in the spirit of fairness after a great experience with Black Bush, I was surprised to find it quite nice. Was it me, or had Midleton changed something?

Probably to some degree it was my own evolving tastes, but it was also Midleton. They'd invested heavily in their barrels and pioneered the idea of wood management:

tracking barrels through the warehouse and noting the quality of the whiskey that came out of them. Ger Buckley, the master cooper at Midleton, noted that the distillery greatly increased its use of bourbon barrels starting in the late 1970s. "Before that, we used wine casks, new casks, whatever we had," he said. "It was just a container."

Today's distillers recognize that a barrel only has so much to give a whiskey. Some flavor changes come from the slow breathing in the barrel, the exchange of oxygen, and the "angel's share" evaporative losses over the years in the warehouse. But a significant effect comes from the wood, and after a certain

Bushmills's Black Bush is lush with sherry cask influence.

number of uses, a barrel is simply played out. Hard as it is to believe, it took till the 1980s to figure that out, and Midleton's distillery staff were among the first to address it.

They don't use barrels till they're worn out anymore. The barrels they do use are — like everything else here, it seems — quite a variety: used bourbon, "new" bourbon (virgin oak casks built and charred to bourbon-type specifications), sherry, port, Madeira, Malaga, and refill casks.

The complexity of these components gave Midleton some of the range for blending that their Scotch whisky counterparts had with their multiplicity of fellow distillers. They have been using that range to create more new whiskeys, and it's gained them the attention they deserve. Jameson has exploded, and that means there is both room and desire for more complex, flavorful, and different versions. Midleton has obliged with the 12-year-old, 18-year-old, Gold, and Rarest Vintage Reserve, an excellent range of whiskeys that

GO WITH THE FLOW

No matter where we're looking at distillation, when we talk about "cuts," the diversion of heads (or foreshots) and tails (or feints), and the selection of the hearts, we don't mean "cut out." When the flow of spirit is cut, it is redirected. That redirection is not into a waste stream; it's usually into a holding vessel, where it will be redistilled. There's still alcohol in there, because distillation is not a precise process, and there are flavor elements in there the distiller wants.

The trick is in how you combine cuts with each other, with fresh wash, and with multiple charges from the same source, then redistill them, and how you redistill them. Which still you use to redistill makes a difference, as does how you drive the still (how hot and fast), and adjustments can be made on the still as well.

Eventually these redistillations reach a point where all that's left are compounds — flavors, aromas, sensations — that are not desirable. Some distillers dispose of them, some burn them, some sell them as chemical feedstock. Those are the only products that are truly "cut."

vary in age and blending complexity (and, in general, have an increasing ratio of single pot still whiskey).

They've also committed to increasing the number of straight single pot still whiskeys they bottle. We've already seen some of this with the Barry Crockett Legacy and Powers John's Lane bottlings and an increasing range of Redbreast expressions. It's a great time for Irish whiskey.

BUSHMILLS: BUILDING ON TRIPLE DISTILLATIONS

BUSHMILLS LOOKS LIKE A Scotch whisky distillery. There, I said it. There are two Charles Doig–designed pagoda malting chimneys (Bushmills used peated malt well into the twentieth century, before the Irish whiskey realignment), pot stills, and long stone buildings. If it weren't for the "Old Bushmills Distillery" sign on the roof, I might be able to fool a kidnapped whiskey drinker into thinking he was in Speyside.

It's not surprising. It sits just across the North Channel from southwest Scotland: 31 miles from Port Ellen on Islay, 39 miles from Campbeltown on the Kintyre Peninsula. Trifling distances. They do make malt whiskey here, and there are no column stills. There's no peat, either, but that's not peculiar. Even the triple distillation isn't unique; Auchentoshan keeps its Lowland lightness the same way.

It's what Bushmills does with that triple distillation that makes the difference. It's faced with the same problem as Midleton: a need and a desire to blend, but no friends to supply blending whiskeys. So like Midleton,

Bushmills has approached this as a problem to be solved internally. It does this by making "triple distillation" an understatement. Multiple cuts and redirections of spirit are made, and it's much more complicated than simply distilling wash, doing a heart cut, distilling that spirit, and then distilling the heart cut again to make it lighter and stronger. Once the distillers have run the spirit all through the stillhouse, working it like a boxing trainer, they turn it into a variety of wood, and a lot of that wood is young. Bushmills doesn't use any barrel longer than 25 years (when your oldest whiskey is 21 years old, that's not hard). Bushmills Original is aged primarily in bourbon wood and blended with Midleton-supplied grain whiskey (again, that contractual thing that keeps Irish whiskey going) that has been aged separately. Black Bush, which was my reintroduction to Irish whiskey, is a full 80 percent Bushmills malt whiskey, 70 percent of it aged in sherry casks. It's a much deeper set of fruit flavors, a bit heavier than the Original. I first tasted it at the rehearsal dinner for a friend's wedding, and I almost missed the ceremony.

The 16-year-old is a three-wood whiskey. It is all malt, aged in bourbon, sherry, and port wood, and it's a regular in my flask lineup for its rich, fruity, nutty depth. I wish I could find and afford the 21-year-old, but only 1,200 cases are released each year. It is further aged in Madeira wood, and my, oh, my, does that give it added heft and richness.

Bushmills was sold to Diageo by Pernod Ricard as part of a complex acquisition deal in 2005. While Pernod owned Bushmills (as part of Irish Distillers Ltd.), they were not really interested in promoting a competitor to Jameson, their global growth giant (it's only fair, then, that Diageo killed Bushmills Irish Cream Liqueur after they bought the distiller; why compete with their blockbuster, Baileys

Irish Cream?). Now Bushmills is a true competitor, and Diageo has been gearing up for increased bottling. The pipeline is filling, and a few new products have been introduced: Bushmills Irish Honey flavored whiskey, and the Bushmills 1608 400th-anniversary bottling, made with some crystal malt (a toe dipped into the wide variety of malts that brewers regularly use, and one that I hope is being expanded upon in other distilleries as you read this). So keep an eye on Northern Ireland for some fun.

COOLEY: MAKING A RUN

THE COOLEY DISTILLERY is the result of a conversation struck up in a Boston bar almost 50 years ago. That's where John Teeling, a risk taker and a true entrepreneur, started talking about the possibility of creating a real Irish-owned competitor to what was then a foreign-owned Irish whiskey monopoly. Once he got the idea, he stopped talking and started gathering money, while continuing to pursue his main career in commodities exploration and acquisition. By keeping the negotiations and capital sourcing well under wraps, eventually he was able to buy an industrial alcohol plant in Cooley, about 60 miles north of Dublin. The plant had column stills, and he bought the pot stills out of an old whiskey distillery. His Cooley distillery finally opened in 1989.

Teeling was bucking trends — whiskey was far from taking off in 1989, and Irish whiskey was definitely not a growth market yet — and he had a business plan that would turn out to be flawed, but when I asked him why he took such a bold move, he shrugged it off, noting the higher risks of his primary job: "The risk was high, but that is what we do — we explore for diamonds, gold, or oil, so whiskey was no worse." Put that way, whiskey looks like a walk in the park.

But Teeling was banking on being able to sell 200,000 cases of whiskey a year. When Pernod Ricard took over Irish Distillers just as he was about to open Cooley, the plan changed. With this one company now controlling almost 100 percent of Irish whiskey, distribution became a problem; no one wanted to get cut off from selling Jameson or Bushmills just because they agreed to sell Cooley's whiskey. Teeling would find a way to make money by selling bulk whiskey to other people with the same vision he had: bucking the Irish whiskey monopoly.

That was Teeling's part of the vision. The rest would come from Cooley's initial — Scottish — distiller, Gordon Mitchell, and his wry successor, Noel Sweeney. All involved are unapologetic about not following the triple-distillation gospel for Irish whiskey, and why shouldn't they be? "Historically there were multiple types and expressions," Teeling told me. "Peated [whiskey] was common, as there was no coal; Bushmills had peat in the 1960s. Double distilled was common; Jameson was double distilled in the early days. There were numerous pure single malt distillers, like Allman's, in Cork."

Sweeney put it more succinctly, with a sideways grin: "Making peated whiskey was a kick in the arse for Scotch. Look, 70 percent of whisky is Scotch; they must be doing something right."

The fact is that Cooley has had an absolutely outsized effect on Irish whiskey. Even with only about 1 percent of the total sales of the category, it is regularly considered as a major player. Beam Global bought Cooley (for $95 million, which may turn out to be a major bargain) in 2011 and began giving it the capital and promotion money it needed. Now that

Japanese whisky giant Suntory has bought Beam, little Cooley has true global reach.

The Cooley whiskeys are punching out of their weight class as well. Connemara, the iconoclastic peated Irish, is boldly smoky, balanced by a solid malt underpinning. Kilbeggan is a tasty blend, sweet and juicily fruity. The Tyrconnell, a double-distilled single malt (and doesn't that sound familiar), is quite Scotch-like indeed, and a series of cask finishes have reinforced the impression by skillful handling.

That's the big three — Midleton, Bushmills, and Cooley. With three of the world's biggest spirits producers each backing one, none can be discounted. Tullamore Dew is a major player as a brand, but we'll have to wait and see how the new distillery shapes the whiskey. It will be interesting to see what the whiskey will become when it is no longer dependent on the supply of another distillery.

But then there are interesting times ahead for every part of Irish whiskey as this category gets revved up to reclaim its place in the world market.

A warehouse at the Midleton distillery in County Cork. Note the bourbon barrels in use in the background, and the much larger sherry butts, or casks, featured in the foreground.

AMERICAN:
BOURBON, TENNESSEE, AND RYE

The term "American whiskey" covers three well-known types of whiskey that are relatively similar — bourbon, Tennessee whiskey, and rye whiskey — and a number of other, lesser-known types, like corn whiskey, wheat whiskey, blended whiskey, and spirit whiskey. (We'll talk about the multitudinous other types of whiskey being made by small American craft distillers in chapter 12.) They are the result of centuries of experiments, evolution, and commercial success or failure, honed down to these categories by making what Americans liked to drink.

They are also the result of a fairly detailed set of "standards of identity," set by the government in the Code of Federal Regulations, Title 27 (Alcohol, Tobacco Products, and Firearms), Part 5 (Labeling and Advertising of Distilled Spirits), Subpart C (Standards of Identity for Distilled Spirits), paragraph 22 (Standards of Identity), wherein Class 2 is all about "whisky." That's right: the American government calls it "whisky," with no "e," even though almost every American brand uses the "whiskey" spelling. (As I told you before, the spelling is not really that important, and I'm going to continue to use "whiskey" through this discussion.)

Legally, interpreting and enforcing these rules in their application to labeling is the job of the Alcohol and Tobacco Tax and Trade Bureau (ATTTB, or TTB), an agency that was spun off from the Bureau of Alcohol, Tobacco and Firearms (ATF) during the shuffling of law enforcement agencies in the wake of the 9/11 terrorist attacks. The ATF law enforcement duties (mostly smuggling interdiction, in the case of alcohol) were transferred to the Department of Justice and the agency was renamed the Bureau of Alcohol, Tobacco, Firearms and Explosives; the TTB took the taxation and labeling approval functions and stayed with the Department of the Treasury. The TTB is responsible for enforcing the standards of identity.

We need to pry them open to understand American whiskey. You may not think that a bunch of rules and government regulations are going to make interesting reading, and you'd be right. To tell the truth, reading them is like reading most regulations: painful and dull. But it also reveals a lot about why American whiskey is made the way it is, and tastes the way it does, and even something about why Scotch, tequila, and rum taste the way they

do. So I'm going to help you understand them. That's my job.

It's not easy. There are rules and identities wound within rules and identities here, and parsing them out is a frequent topic of discussion in the online whiskey discussion sites. Whiskey writer Chuck Cowdery has made something of a specialty of interpreting the rules and has on occasion brought inaccuracies to the attention of the TTB, resulting in label changes; one case involved a spirit made from potatoes that the TTB approved as "potato whiskey." That's definitely *not* in the standards. Let's have a look at what is.

GIVE IT TO ME STRAIGHT

TO BEGIN, THERE ARE three parts to the standards. The first identifies whiskey, the second delineates two classes of whiskey — corn whiskey is one, and the other contains bourbon, rye, wheat, malt, and rye malt whiskeys — and the third makes a further definition of "straight" whiskey.

PART 1: DEFINING WHISKEY

THE FIRST PART'S PRETTY basic stuff: whiskey is distilled from grain. Specifically, whiskey is a distillate made from a "fermented mash of grain." The final distillation must be to less than 190 proof (95 percent ABV, which is very high; above that, a distillate is considered "neutral spirits" or "alcohol" . . . or "fuel") "in such manner that the distillate possesses the taste, aroma, and characteristics generally attributed to whisky."

That's kind of odd, because the definition goes on to say that the distillate has to be "stored in oak containers" (unless it is corn whiskey). But it has to taste and smell and

The old Wild Turkey distillery, now replaced by a much larger, modern plant, in Lawrenceburg, Kentucky

fermentation flavor left. Wild Turkey master distiller Jimmy Russell explained that to me this way: "How do you like a steak?" he asked. Rare, I told him, and he nodded. "There's more flavor of the meat in it that way. Same way, we run the spirit off at a lower proof, and put it in the barrel at a lower proof, so there's more good flavor in there."

In addition to those proof requirements, bourbon must be made from a mash that is at least 51 percent corn, rye from a mash that is at least 51 percent rye, and so on, similarly, for wheat, malt, and rye malt whiskeys. These types of whiskey must also be aged in "charred new oak containers." You can age your whiskey in used barrels, but then the label must call it "whiskey distilled from bourbon mash" (or rye, wheat, etc.). It doesn't have to be in big letters, but it has to be there.

The niche definition for corn whiskey, such as Heaven Hill's Mellow Corn and Georgia Moon, in contrast, *specifies* that if the whiskey is aged — for which there's no requirement — it be aged in "used or uncharred new oak" containers and not "subjected in any manner to treatment with charred wood." Corn whiskey should taste like *corn*, not oak.

have the "characteristics generally attributed to whisky" when it comes off the still? It's the storage in oak containers, not the fermentation and distillation, that gives whiskey its flavors, aromas, and colors. Like I said: it's not easy understanding these rules! Finally, to be labeled "whiskey," it must be bottled at no less than 80 proof.

PART 2: DEFINING WHISKEY CLASSES

THE NEXT PART OF THE standards is more particular. The final distillation must be under 160 proof. If the whiskey is aged in oak, it must go into the barrel at no more than 125 proof, or what distillers call the "entry proof."

The lower proof, compared to the initial definition, means there's more of the grain and

PART 3: DEFINING STRAIGHT WHISKEY

THE THIRD PART OF THE standards, the part about straight whiskey, talks about age. If a whiskey has conformed to the standards explained above and was stored in the oak containers for at least 2 years, it is "straight whiskey": straight bourbon whiskey, straight rye whiskey, and so on.

The TTB labeling regulations also say that if the youngest whiskey in the bottle is under 4 years old, the label must state exactly how old it is; once it hits 4 years of age, no age statement is needed. If an age statement is used — as with Knob Creek's "aged nine years" — all whiskey in the bottle must be at least that old.

Keep in mind that unless a straight whiskey is labeled as a "single barrel" bottling, it is a blend of at least two barrels (and usually over a thousand at the larger distilleries), though some distillers prefer to call it "mingled" or "married" rather than "blended." They don't want any confusion: American "blended whiskey" is not a blend of aged whiskeys like blended Scotch; it's a blend of straight whiskey and cheap, unaged grain neutral spirit, a product aimed at the low end of the market. There aren't many of these left.

There's one more part to the definition, and that has to do with purity. The addition of "harmless coloring, flavoring, and blending materials," which is allowed in other spirits, is specifically prohibited in the case of straight whiskey; no such material whatsoever is allowed. Bourbon and rye are not allowed to be colored, flavored, or adulterated with anything but enough pure water to bring them to bottling proof. The flavored whiskeys you've seen recently are all labeled as "bourbon flavored with . . . ," a little bit of government-required honesty.

TO SUM UP

THOSE ARE THE REQUIREMENTS. American whiskey — bourbon, rye, and the others — is:

- Distilled from a fermented grain mash of at least 51 percent corn (or rye, or wheat, etc., and most have a larger proportion of the main grain)
- Distilled to a proof no higher than 159 (79.5 percent ABV)
- Aged, at a starting strength no higher than 125 proof, in a charred, new oak barrel (used barrels *may* be used, but the labeling is different)

- Bottled at no less than 80 proof, with no coloring or flavoring added

Further, if it is aged for more than 2 years in the oak, it is "straight whiskey"; if it is aged less than 4 years, it must have an age statement on the label.

It's also interesting to consider what the regulations *don't* require. Despite what people might tell you — although most of it *is* — bourbon does not have to be:

- Made in Kentucky
- Made from corn and *only two* other grains
- Aged in white oak barrels
- Aged in *American* oak barrels

You might also want to compare straight bourbon whiskey to single malt Scotch whisky. Consider this: A single malt is all aged malt whisky from one distiller, at least 3 years old (usually older). Straight bourbon whiskey is all aged whiskey from one distiller, at least 2 years old (almost always at least 4 years old). Neither bourbon nor single malt are blended with neutral or grain spirits. Yet while you'll find only a couple of good single malts for less than $40 these days — Bowmore Legend and Glenmorangie Original come to mind — you can still buy a bottle of good, flavor-packed bourbon — Evan Williams, Very Old Barton, Old Heaven Hill Bonded, all around 6 years old — for under $15!

STRICTER THAN SINGLE MALT

IF YOU WANT TO GET BOURBON that is held to even tighter standards of origin than single malt, track down some bottled-in-bond bourbon. It's not that hard; the Old Grand-Dad Bottled in Bond is pretty easy to find, Very Old Barton Bond is widespread in Kentucky and surrounding states, and Heaven Hill has two bonded versions of its Heaven Hill brand (you want the white label) and also Old Fitzgerald, a rare wheated bond. They're good whiskeys, with that 100-proof power that makes them stand out in a cocktail, but they don't get a lot of love from their company's marketing departments, or from bourbon drinkers in general, and that puzzles me.

What's so special about bottled-in-bond whiskey? If people know about it at all, they most likely think it means that it's 100 proof. It's a lot more than that; it has to meet the requirements of the Bottled in Bond Act of 1897. That means all the whiskey in the bottle has to be:

- At least 4 years old
- Bottled at no more or less than 100 proof
- Have no additives other than pure water
- Be labeled as the product of the distillery where it was made and, if different, the distillery where it was bottled
- Be the product of only one distillery, and made by the same master distiller, in one distilling season of a single year

Think about that last one. All the whiskey in the bond is guaranteed to be made by the same person, at the same distillery, in one season. Makes single malt's "all from one distillery" look a bit less exacting.

But bonds today are not exclusive whiskeys. To tell the truth, they're usually pretty cheap; the ones I list above can mostly be had for under $20 a bottle. "A lot of the brands are older labels that maybe at some point were exclusively bonds," Heaven Hill's long-time communications director Larry Kass explains. "You'll have small brands that are bonds, but not big brands. They never had marketing support, so there's not that cost."

Bond is a term that's not well understood among bourbon drinkers, a little historical quirk that doesn't really mean much. For the taster, though, these can be a bonanza, with or without a few drops of water. Old Grand-Dad's high-rye formula sings clearest at 100 proof, a fruity, spicy bourbon with a solid body. Heaven Hill 6 Year Old is a favorite: a bold, raunchy beauty, rich with notes of warehouse reek, that sweet smell of bourbon slowly drooling from the seams of the barrels, caramelizing in the hot Kentucky summer as it oozes down over oaken staves. They'd be great whiskeys at twice the price.

It's not just bourbon, either. You can get bottled-in-bond rye; Rittenhouse Rye bonded is spectacular stuff, and probably the hottest-selling bonded whiskey right now, thanks to critical acclaim and the love of mixologists for its classic taste in classic cocktails. Mellow Corn corn whiskey is bottled in bond and aged 4 years in used bourbon barrels; if you

Oak barrels at the Jack Daniel's warehouse in Tennessee

Bourbon

- AT LEAST 51% CORN, PLUS RYE / WHEAT AND BARLEY
- NEW CHARRED OAK BARRELS
- MADE AND AGED IN THE U.S.

TRADITIONAL BOURBONS

- Made with corn, rye, and barley
- Spicy (cinnamon, pepper, mint), fiery, powerful flavor

GOOD BUYS
(UNDER $30, *at a traditional volume*)
Buffalo Trace
Bulleit
Eagle Rare 10-Year-Old
Elijah Craig 12-Year-Old
Evan Williams Single Barrel
Evan Williams Black
Four Roses Yellow
Jim Beam Black
Jim Beam White
Old Forester
Old Grand-Dad 100
Very Old Barton Bottled in Bond
Wild Turkey 101

PREMIUM BOTTLINGS
($30–$100)
Angel's Envy
Baker's
Black Maple Hill
Blanton's
Booker's

PREMIUM BOTTLINGS
($30–$100) CONTINUED
E. H. Taylor, Jr.
Elijah Craig 18-Year-Old
Elmer T. Lee
Four Roses Single Barrel
Four Roses Small Batch
George T. Stagg
John J. Bowman
Knob Creek
Parker's Heritage Collection
Wild Turkey Kentucky Spirit
Wild Turkey Rare Breed
Woodford Reserve

SUPERPREMIUM BOTTLINGS
($100+)
A. H. Hirsch Reserve 16-Year-Old
Elijah Craig 21-Year-Old Single Barrel
Jefferson's Presidential Select
Jim Beam Distiller's Masterpiece
Michter's 20-Year-Old
Wild Turkey Tradition
Willett Family Reserve

WHEATED BOURBONS

- Made with corn, wheat, and barley
- Smoother, softer, less spicy flavor; ages well

GOOD BUYS
(UNDER $30, *at a traditional volume*)
Larceny
Maker's Mark
Old Fitzgerald Bottled in Bond
Old Weller Antique

PREMIUM BOTTLINGS
($30–$100)
Maker's 46
William Larue Weller

**SUPERPREMIUM BOTTLINGS
($100+)**
Pappy Van Winkle's Family Reserve
    15-Year-Old
Pappy Van Winkle's Family Reserve
    20-Year-Old
Pappy Van Winkle's Family Reserve
    23-Year-Old
Van Winkle Special Reserve

Tennessee Whiskey

- MADE WITH CORN, RYE, AND BARLEY;
  EMPLOYS LINCOLN COUNTY PROCESS
  (PRE-AGING CHARCOAL "MELLOWING")
- SWEET, SMOOTH FLAVOR WITH BIG
  CORN CHARACTER

**GOOD BUYS
(UNDER $30,** *at a traditional volume***)**
Gentleman Jack
George Dickel No. 12
George Dickel No. 8
Jack Daniel's Old No. 7

**PREMIUM BOTTLINGS
(UNDER $30)**
George Dickel Barrel Select
Jack Daniel's Single Barrel

Rye

- JUST LIKE BOURBON, BUT 51% RYE
- SPICY, HERBAL, GRASSY FLAVORS, WITH
  A BIG KICK; FIERY WHEN YOUNG

**GOOD BUYS
(UNDER $30,** *at a traditional volume***)**
Bulleit Rye
Jim Beam Rye
Old Overholt Rye
Rittenhouse Rye Bonded
Wild Turkey Rye 81

**PREMIUM BOTTLINGS
(UNDER $30–$100)**
(ri)1 (from Jim Beam)
Dad's Hat
FEW Rye
Jefferson's Rye
Knob Creek Rye
McKenzie Rye
Michter's US1
Rendezvous Rye
Sazerac 6-Year-Old
Sazerac 18-Year-Old
Templeton
Thomas H. Handy
Wild Turkey Rye 101
Willett Family Estate Rye

**SUPERPREMIUM BOTTLINGS
($100+)**
Jefferson's Presidential Select
    21-Year-Old Rye
Van Winkle Family Reserve Rye

thought bourbon smelled like corn, Mellow Corn smells like sweet, oily-rich corn — corn eau-de-vie.

Finally, it's not whiskey, but you can also get Laird's Straight Apple Brandy — real New Jersey–style applejack, from a company whose distilling roots go back to 1780 — in a genuine bonded version, and it's worth looking for. Made under all the same requirements as bonded whiskey, aged in charred oak barrels for at least 4 years, it's rich with apple and vanilla aroma and has a smooth but potent punch of flavor; the apple on the finish as you breathe across the drying spirit is inspiring. I've been in Laird's warehouse in New Jersey and was struck by how much it smelled and felt like a bourbon warehouse.

Bonded whiskey (and apple brandy) is still "the good stuff," even though it's often overlooked. Find some, and see what history tastes like.

INNOVATIONS IN BOURBON

THE STRICT RULES about how American whiskey can be made are a double-edged sword. They assure the consumer of a quality product, unadulterated by cheap neutral spirits, colorings, or flavors — the bane of the rectifiers banished for good — and ostensibly guarantee that bourbon and rye will maintain a consistent style.

But that's not quite true, actually. Old-timers confirm that bourbon *has* changed somewhat over the past 60 years, and it is for the better. Corn is more uniformly high quality, and we've learned a lot about the chemistry of stills, warehouse construction, and wood management, from the science of forestry to new ways of heat-treating barrels.

"You're probably old enough to remember tasting some musty bottles of bourbon," Dave Scheurich mentioned to me when we were talking about this. Dave was the distillery

---

THE 53-GALLON BARREL

*W*hile we're talking about strict rules, why are all American whiskey barrels 53 gallons? Like much of whiskey making, that's a standard that came about through common usage, rather than because of a consideration of the benefits, and it's not a legal standard. Old-timers will tell you that the barrels used to be 48 gallons and were easier to move around, and significantly, that's what all the ricks in the warehouses were built to accommodate. During World War II a study was done to see how much bigger the barrels could be built to save seasoned oak wood without having to change the ricks: 53 gallons was the size. The change was made, and it's become the de facto standard. Every major American distiller uses 53-gallon barrels.

BOURBON FLAVOR GRAPH

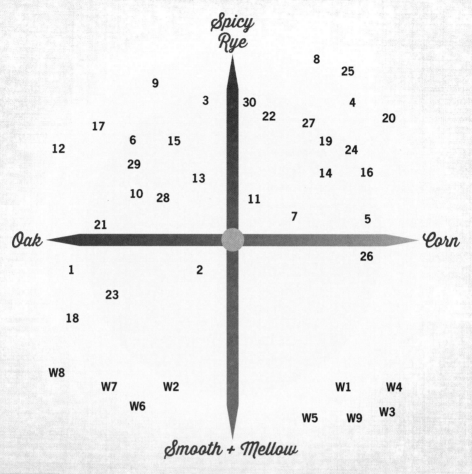

KEY

WHEAT

W1	Larceny
W2	Maker's 46
W3	Maker's Mark
W4	Old Fitzgerald Bottled in Bond
W5	Old Weller Antique
W6	Pappy Van Winkle's Family Reserve 15-Year-Old
W7	Pappy Van Winkle's Family Reserve 20-Year-Old
W8	Pappy Van Winkle's Family Reserve 23-Year-Old
W9	William Larue Weller

TRADITIONAL

1	A. H. Hirsch Reserve 16-Year-Old
2	Angel's Envy
3	Baker's
4	Basil Hayden
5	Blanton's
6	Booker's
7	Buffalo Trace
8	Bulleit
9	E. H. Taylor, Jr.
10	Eagle Rare 10-Year-Old
11	Elijah Craig 12-Year-Old
12	Elijah Craig 18-Year-Old
13	Elmer T. Lee
14	Evan Williams Black
15	Four Roses Small Batch

16	Four Roses Yellow
17	George T. Stagg
18	Jefferson's Presidential
19	Jim Beam Black
20	Jim Beam White
21	John J. Bowman
22	Knob Creek
23	Michter's 20-Year-Old
24	Old Forester
25	Old Grand-Dad 100
26	Very Old Barton Bottled in Bond
27	Wild Turkey 101
28	Wild Turkey Kentucky Spirit
29	Wild Turkey Rare Breed
30	Woodford Reserve

manager at Woodford Reserve at the time. "You don't get those any more. And you know there aren't as many distillers around, either. The reason's the same: it was a tough business in the 1970s and '80s, and the guys who made bad whiskey aren't around now."

The flip side of the regulations is that they seem to force these whiskeys into what could be a stultifying similarity: all made with a majority of one grain, all distilled to roughly the same proof, all aged in the same new charred oak barrels, all chivvied into the same rough age groups, and no fiddling with color or flavor. That's exactly the complaint you'll hear from those who reject the category (usually Scotch drinkers): "Bourbons all taste the same: oaky, vanilla-sweet, hot, and rough," or some variation of that.

THE MASHBILL

STARTING AT THE BEGINNING, there are the ratios in the mash. Increase the base grain, and bourbon becomes sweeter, while rye becomes spicier, more forward. Or tweak the small grains: increase the rye, as in Bulleit, and you get a bourbon that can pass for a rye whiskey in a blind tasting (maybe that's why Bulleit Rye is made with a 95 percent rye mashbill, for a clear difference). Use wheat instead of rye, as is done with Maker's Mark, the Van Winkles, W. L. Weller, and Old Fitzgerald, and you get a much smoother, mellower bourbon, even when young.

A distiller may have more than one mashbill for bourbons, another for rye, maybe another for a run of wheated bourbon. Beam, for instance, uses a high-rye mashbill — at 30 percent rye, it's quite high — for Old Grand-Dad and Basil Hayden's, and a more traditional proportion for its other whiskeys.

A bourbon drinker has to admit that there's maybe something to it. Scotch distillers work with stills of varying geometry and

Anatomy of a Mashbill

 CORN

 RYE

 MALT

 RED WINTER WHEAT

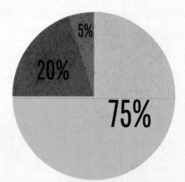

5%
35%
60%

Four Roses bourbon
(High Rye)

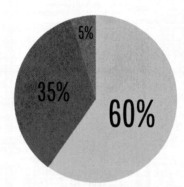

5%
20%
75%

Four Roses bourbon
(Low Rye)

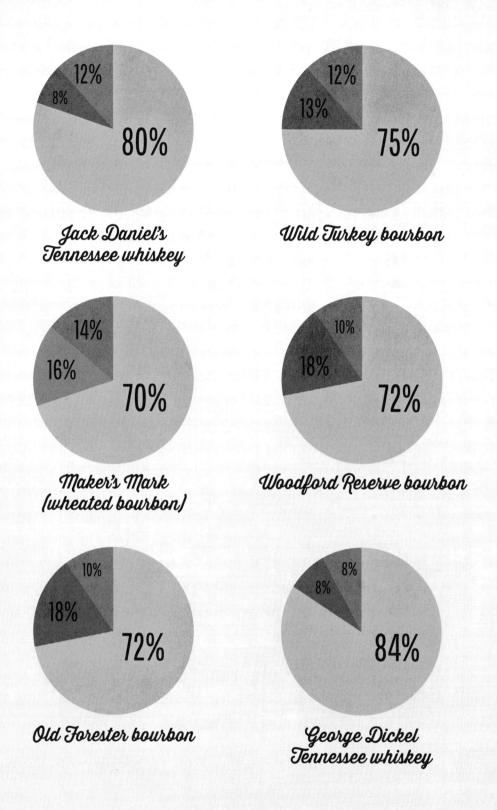

Jack Daniel's Tennessee whiskey
80% 12% 8%

Wild Turkey bourbon
75% 12% 13%

Maker's Mark (wheated bourbon)
70% 14% 16%

Woodford Reserve bourbon
72% 10% 18%

Old Forester bourbon
72% 10% 18%

George Dickel Tennessee whiskey
84% 8% 8%

construction, they can play with the cuts and redistill, they have the option of peating their malt from a bare whisper to a roar, and they can play their barrel types like a huge console organ. Irish distillers have even more options, with their combination of pot and column stills, double or triple distilling, and raw barley additions. The Canadians use any kind of still they want, about any grain they want, and blend as they see fit. American distillers, in comparison, work within a relative straitjacket of regulations, which traditional practice only pulls tighter.

But don't pity the American distillers. They have their own methods of innovation.

THE YEAST

USE A DIFFERENT YEAST, or run it at a different temperature, and you get variations in the esters from fermentation. Bourbon distillers can be quite particular about their yeasts and carefully preserve the strains. Vary the amount of backset — sour mash — in the fermenter, and you've made another change.

THE BARREL

AS NOTED EARLIER, THE column stills are pretty uniform, but what comes after distillation is anything but. That's when the whiskey enters the barrel, and barrels aren't just identical wooden containers. Distillers are quite specific about the wood in their barrels: where it's from, how long it's air-dried, and how deeply it's charred. As wood science advances, more changes are being made in how barrels are made; toasting the heads (the ends of the barrels) is becoming more common. Toasting doesn't char the wood, and

FOUR ROSES: FIVE YEASTS

Four Roses takes the concept of varying bourbon by using different yeasts and mashbills to extremes. Its distillers use a combination of 5 different yeast strains and two mashbills to make 10 quite different bourbons, which they then age in single-story, relatively small warehouses to minimize any differences from aging conditions. After all, why go to all that trouble making 10 different whiskeys only to introduce more variables?

Once the whiskeys are aged, master distiller Jim Rutledge will "mingle" them for the flagship yellow-label Four Roses bourbon, or select a smaller group to create the Small Batch, or pick a parcel of one type for a single-barrel bottling. The Four Roses single barrels can be unique, even idiosyncratic, and are a rare opportunity to discover just what yeast can do for a bourbon.

The different yeast strains, with their in-house letter code and the contributions they make to Four Roses, are:

V A slightly fruity, well-rounded classic bourbon character

K Spicy; needs longer aging to develop

F More floral, herbal, soft, and full

O Quite fruity and complex, with a long finish

Q Huge floral nose, quite fresh and delicate

The Maker's Mark distillery in Loretto, Kentucky, is a registered National Historic Landmark, being the site of a former mill and distillery erected in 1805.

"ALDEHYDE-Y"

The first time I went to the Kentucky Bourbon Festival was in 1998, and one of my favorite events was the Bourbon Heritage Panel, six eminent figures from the industry taking questions and discussing bourbon. One of the first things they did was taste a bottle of pre-Prohibition bourbon donated by the Oscar Getz Museum of Whiskey History in Bardstown (where the panel took place). The bottle was distilled in 1916 and bottled in 1933: 17 years in the barrel.

The panel swirled, sniffed, and speculated on how this bourbon might be different from today's whiskey. Heaven Hill president Max Shapira pointed out that there were no hybrid corn strains available then and that the ratios of the mash-bill would probably be different. Bill Friel, retired master distiller at Barton (now the Tom Moore

distillery), thought a big difference would be that the whiskey probably came off the still at a lower proof than is common today and went into the barrel at a lower proof as well.

The whiskey, unfortunately, was a disappointment. Wild Turkey's Jimmy Russell and Bill Friel put their heads together and discussed it, then announced that they found it to be resinous and "aldehyde-y" (aldehydes have a floral or fruity character, and too much is out of character for whiskey), probably from being too long in the wood, or something wrong with a stave in the barrel. "Maybe a sap pocket," said Jimmy.

That's one of the issues that drives the high price of super-aged bourbon: risk. Old doesn't always mean better. You have to know when to bottle it, before aging becomes destructive.

it creates a somewhat different set of chemical compounds in the oak, which in turn have a different effect on the whiskey.

THE WAREHOUSE

THEN THERE'S THE PART that's always held a special interest for me: the warehouse or, as it's sometimes called in Kentucky, the rickhouse (the wooden racks that hold the barrels are called "ricks"). Warehouses will age whiskey differently depending on how they're built. The ironclads, usually built to seven stories tall (some are four or five, some new ones are nine) with a metal skin on a solidly built wooden frame, are the most common. They have good air circulation, and the thin metal walls mean temperature shifts have a more rapid effect (although 20,000 or more 53-gallon barrels full of whiskey won't change thermal direction on a dime).

"It's just a shell to keep out the weather," said Jimmy Russell of the metal skin. "If it wasn't for the water damage, it might even be better to leave it off."

The height has an effect as well; rising heat concentrates in the top floors, and the whiskey is pushed harder into the wood there. The whiskey in these barrels will age more quickly, evaporate faster, have a woodier, drier, spicier flavor, and become astringent and smell sharply of acetone if left too long. "High and dry" has a whole different meaning in whiskey aging.

Stone and brick warehouses have less air movement in them because of their solid construction. They're also lower than the ironclads, generally topping out at three or four stories. Brown-Forman uses brick and stone warehouses for its "cycling" process in aging Old Forester, Early Times, and Woodford Reserve. The warehouses have steam heat, and during the winter the distillers use the steam to gently raise the warehouse temperature.

The historic Tom Moore Distillery in Bardstown, Kentucky, home of Very Old Barton

A RIVER OF FIRE

*T*hink about what an ironclad bourbon ware-house is: it's about a million gallons of fuel-strength alcohol, contained and supported by tons of either alcohol-soaked oak, or dry, seasoned timber supports. It's a bomb just waiting to go off.

That's what happened back in 1996, when Heaven Hill's Bardstown facility suffered a disas-trous fire. Seven warehouses full of bourbon were lost, and an 18-inch-deep river of burning whiskey flowed down the hill and destroyed their distillery.

The folks at Heaven Hill understandably don't even like talking about that day, but Fred Noe, spokesman for Jim Beam (and son of revered Jim Beam distiller Booker Noe) told me about the fire. "I couldn't get closer than about a quarter mile,"

he said. "It was just that hot, and loud. They could see the fire up in Louisville [about 30 miles away]."

The fire took place in pouring rain; the whis-key was burning too hot to even notice. "You ever seen a warehouse fire?" Noe asked. "It burns so hot when that whiskey gets going, and all that seasoned wood . . . when it burns out, all you've got left is just a pile of steel hoops. That's all that's left."

In the wake of the Heaven Hill fire, and smaller fires at Jim Beam and Wild Turkey, new regula-tions were put in place. Warehouses have to be surrounded by a berm to contain burning whiskey, and there are now sprinkler systems and multiple escape routes. Fire is still a distiller's nightmare, but it's a bit more under control.

As master distiller Chris Morris explained, there are temperature probes in some of the barrels, scattered through the warehouse. Say the temperature outside goes down to 20°F (–7°C); when the temperature in the barrels gets down to about 60° (16°C) (Chris carefully couched all of this in very general terms), the heat goes on. It stays on until the whiskey gets up to around 80° (27°C), which might take a week; then the heat goes off until the whiskey gets down to 60° again. Once winter's over they stop cycling and let nature do its thing.

Morris's explanation of how the cycling works applies to normal aging as well. "The absorption of spirit and water is pretty linear," he said. "Hot or cold, you have material from the wood being absorbed by the spirit. The 'breathing' of the barrel comes from the change of the seasons. It brings oxygen in

[through the wood], which creates oxidation and the creation of aldehydes, the fruit and spice."

"In an ironclad, that takes a long time," he continued. "Mother Nature does it slow. Back in the 1870s, it was thought that an aggressive cycling in the winter would lead to more fruit and spice flavors. The absorption still takes time, but you can use that time better. Old Forester uses both [cycling and non-cycling-aged whiskey], and you can really control your flavor profile by matching barrels with differ-ent flavors."

Why the different types of warehouses? "It's because every distiller has his own opin-ion," Heaven Hill master distiller Parker Beam told me. "Some people would say about [one type of] warehouse, 'Oh, I'd never build 'em that way.' Someone else may say, 'Oh, hell,

that don't matter.' These small quirks are what set them apart from another."

Where the warehouses are sited also makes a difference. I call it "Kentucky feng shui." Warehouses on hills catch more airflow from wind, though they can also be more vulnerable to thunderstorms and tornados there. Wind can blow the metal skin and roof right off a warehouse — you just replace it — and a tornado can destroy a warehouse, or in some cases twist it so badly that the barrels can no longer be rolled in and out. In those extremes there's not much to do other than laboriously take all the barrels out and put

A bronze statue of Booker Noe, master distiller for Jim Beam for 40 years, sits outside the distillery in Clermont, Kentucky.

them in another warehouse, tear the twisted warehouse down, and start over.

Some distillers insist on a north-south orientation for warehouses so they catch the day's sun evenly. Warehouses may be shaded by trees — or distillers may cut trees away from warehouses — or set near a river or stream. Former Buffalo Trace warehouse manager Ronnie Eddins told me that he was sure the regular fog off the Kentucky River beside the warehouses — and the way it would wetly come right in the windows — gave his whiskey a "sweeter, more mellow taste."

"You have to study everything," he explained, "and try to pinpoint what you could do to make it better. It's been a constant fascination. You find a piece and try to figure it out, and then, next thing you know, you've got a big project."

THE WHISKEY TEAM

HERE'S WHERE THE FINAL factor in what makes bourbon different comes in: people. Whiskey making tends to be a job with long tenures. Ronnie Eddins, for example, started at Buffalo Trace in 1961 and was the warehouse manager from 1984 till not long before his death in 2010.

The bourbon we're drinking today was shaped by an amazingly long-working group of men, all of whom worked at their respective distilleries for decades. Some have retired, and some, sadly, have died, but all of them have made decisions over at least 20 years that put their stamp on the whiskey. Here's who I'm talking about.

- Bill Friel (Barton/Tom Moore)
- Booker Noe (Jim Beam)
- Elmer T. Lee and Ronnie Eddins (Buffalo Trace)
- Jim Rutledge (Four Roses)
- Jimmy Russell (Wild Turkey)
- Lincoln Henderson (Brown-Forman)
- Parker Beam (Heaven Hill)

Even Jimmy and Parker's sons — Eddie and Craig, respectively — have already put in decades as distillers at Wild Turkey and Heaven Hill.

What decisions do distillers and warehouse managers make that the marketing and budgeting people don't? Often they have a lot of input on how much whiskey is made, where it's warehoused, what kind of warehouses get built, and the taste profiles of new whiskeys (and the slow evolutions of established ones). They also serve as the whiskey's memory, keeping the good traditions, letting the unimportant ones go, and making sure no changes affect the quality of the whiskey.

For instance, when cypress, the wood traditionally used for bourbon fermenters, was just no longer available in the quantities needed to build the big tanks, master distillers at the various plants were responsible for the tests that would determine whether steel tanks would still make the same whiskey (happily, they do). Some distillers still use cypress — but that's their tradition.

The real job of the distillers, and the warehouse managers, is to be aware. They need to be aware of the climate, the costs of their business, the quality of the grain and the wood they get from their suppliers, the conditions of their facilities, the quality of the work done by the staff. They also need to be aware of how the whiskey's doing, all the time, which is why regular sampling is a big part of the job.

That's the thought behind something Ronnie Eddins told me, barely 3 years before he died. "You know, in your life, you only get about two chances to learn from a 15-year-old bourbon," he said. "There's your first one, and you learn from it all along the time, and you put all that into the second one. By the time the second one's done . . . you're usually about done too." Poetic words from a man who had a largely unsung role in the development of some of the best bourbons Buffalo Trace ever produced.

Ricks of sugar maple billets are fired to create the charcoal used in Tennessee whiskey's Lincoln County process of "mellowing" or filtration.

TENNESSEE WHISKEY

YOU MAY BE WONDERING why I haven't yet mentioned Jack Daniel's (or maybe you're one of the smaller but just as loyal group of fans who are wondering why I haven't mentioned George Dickel). After all, Jack Daniel's is the biggest-selling American whiskey, in the United States and around the world.

Daniel's and Dickel aren't labeled as bourbon, though. They're Tennessee whiskeys (or "whisky," as Dickel labels say). There is no mention of Tennessee whiskey in the U.S. standards of identity, nor is there any mention of the "Lincoln County process," the filtering of the unaged spirit through 10 feet of hardwood charcoal (and a white wool blanket), a process that makes Tennessee whiskey . . . Tennessee whiskey.

That is, according to Brown-Forman, which makes Jack Daniel's, and presumably also according to Diageo, which owns George Dickel. But if you look at the standards of identity closely, you'll see that both of these brands do everything necessary to be labeled as "straight bourbon whiskey," and do nothing that would prevent them from being so labeled.

So what are they? Let's look at that. Jack Daniel was a real person, who really did distill whiskey at the current site of the distillery named for him, from the gushing pure waters of Cave Spring. The charcoal filtering — which the distillers usually call "mellowing" or "leaching" — was fairly common back in the early 1800s. Exactly how it came to be called the Lincoln County process is one of those tantalizingly unclear whiskey mysteries, but it's a cool name, so leave it be.

THE CORN CONTINUUM

Oaky | JACK DANIEL'S SINGLE | GEORGE DICKEL BARREL SELECT | GEORGE DICKEL NO. 12 | JACK DANIEL'S OLD NO. 7 | GEORGE DICKEL NO. 8 | GENTLEMAN JACK | Sweet

The Lincoln County process is something to see. At both Jack Daniel and George Dickel, the charcoal is made on-site from sugar maple wood. They get the wood already air-dried and sawed into 2-inch by 2-inch billets, about 5 feet long. These are then stacked into "ricks" by laying six billets side by side, with about a 6-inch gap between them. Another such layer is laid on crossways, and so on, until the ricks reach up to 6 to 8 feet high. The ricks are set in squares of four, with a centrally inclined lean so that they'll collapse inward as they burn, rather than fall apart.

When it's time to burn, the ricks are sprayed with alcohol and set on fire. They are burned in the open air to allow the release of any impurities in the wood that would contaminate the kilned charcoal. The wood will burn for 2 or 3 hours, being wet with hoses most of the time to control the burn. The fire burns hot, but the tenders never let it get roaring. Once the burning is over, the charcoal is allowed to cool before being broken up into pieces about the size of large peas.

The charcoal goes into the mellowing vats, which are about 10 feet deep and 5 feet across; a white wool blanket is stretched across the bottom to contain any charcoal dust that comes loose. At Jack Daniel the new make spirit trickles through the vats. At Dickel the vats are completely filled with spirit before any is tapped off the bottom, and they are refilled as they drain off; the charcoal is said to be "drowned." The vats at Dickel are also chilled; the story is that they noticed the whiskey tasted better when it had been mellowed in the winter, so that's how they filter all of it. (Astute readers may note that this is how you "chill filter" whiskey to remove compounds that can turn the whiskey cloudy if it gets cold, a practice used by many distillers, though not with so much charcoal.) Dickel also uses *two* wool blankets, one on the top and one on the bottom.

What's the process do? I tasted three samples of spirit at Dickel once. The first was right off the beer still: grainy, muddled in aroma and flavor. The next was off the doubler, the pot still–like step that

RYE FLAVOR RANGE

Older / Oaky

JEFFERSON'S PRESIDENTIAL
SELECT 21-YEAR-OLD

SAZERAC 18-YEAR-OLD

VAN WINKLE FAMILY RESERVE

KNOB CREEK

(RI)1

BULLEIT

WILD TURKEY 101

RITTENHOUSE BONDED

THOMAS H. HANDY

SAZERAC 6-YEAR-OLD

OLD POTRERO

OLD OVERHOLT

JIM BEAM

DAD'S HAT

FEW RYE

Younger / Herbal

follows the column-style beer still. It was remarkably cleaner, both to the eye and on the palate, and was unmistakably the taste of sweet, pure corn. The third sample was off the mellowing vat: it had pulled off the corn's oiliness and down-home cooked character, leaving a lighter, purer spirit: corn eau-de-vie. The process had not added flavor (which would be forbidden by the standards of identity anyway); it has been taken away, leaving only the gentle heart of the grain.

By the way, neither distillery is in Lincoln County. The only distillery making whiskey today in Lincoln County is Prichard's, a craft distillery, where the whiskey Phil Prichard makes is not mellowed through charcoal.

Jack Daniel is a huge distillery, and getting bigger; in mid-2013 it announced that it would begin a $100 million expansion of the distillery to meet growing demand. To put that in perspective, Diageo spent about $60 million building its new Roseisle distillery in Scotland, a distillery that has been described as "big," "large-scale," "enormous," and "the Death Star." Jack Daniel's whiskeys — the familiar Old No. 7, the lesser-known Green Label, Gentleman Jack, and the Single Barrel expression — sell well across a wide range of consumers.

George Dickel, although owned by Diageo, the world's largest drinks company, is a complete contrast. It doesn't have as much story as Jack Daniel: although George Dickel was also a real person, he was a whiskey broker, not a distiller, and his brother-in-law got into the distilling business, but production moved around quite a bit as temperance laws, national Prohibition, and World War II had their effects on the whiskey industry. The current distillery was built in 1959. It is small, is almost completely nonautomated, and has not received a lot of promotion or attention, although its whiskeys are well liked by critics.

But what are they? Are they bourbons that choose not to claim the title? Or is the charcoal leaching significant enough to make them something different?

I've given you the facts; now I'll advise you to make your own call on the issue. I'd also advise you not to get into an argument about it; one of the very few times I've ever been thrown out of a bar was after an argument over whether Jack Daniel's was bourbon or not . . . with the bartender. I've never made that mistake again. Jack and George have *very* loyal fans.

RESURGENT RYE

RYE AS WE NOW KNOW IT — *American* rye whiskey, as Canadian whisky writer Davin de Kergommeaux would insist on my saying it — is more like an exceptionally high-rye bourbon than what it used to be. Going back to the standards of identity, the only difference between rye and bourbon is that rye is the dominant grain in the mashbill instead of corn. Everything else is the same.

It's still a breathtaking difference. Rye whiskey won't give you that luxurious river of corn you get in some bourbons, or the cinnamon Red Hots you'll get in some others. Instead it will fly up your nose in a hot herbal rush and light up your mouth like a carnival midway with a flame of bitter, oily ryegrass; the only sweetness you'll get may be a shatteringly brittle sensation at first taste, and maybe some vanilla in older ryes. It's quite a ride.

Although rye whiskey used to be *the* American whiskey, the whiskey of my home state of Pennsylvania (and of Maryland) and what the state legislature ran on (because beer would get warm and flat during lengthy debate), rye had fallen on hard times. It never really came

Watching the white dog at the Jack Daniel's distillery in Lynchburg, Tennessee

back after Prohibition as strongly as bourbon did, and the popularity of Canadian whisky and the explosion of white spirits that started in the 1960s almost did it in.

By the time I started writing about whiskey in the mid-1990s, American rye was on the brink, down to well under a dozen brands: Wild Turkey Rye, Beam's Jim Beam and Old Overholt (one of the famous Pennsylvania brands), and Heaven Hill's Rittenhouse, Pikesville, and Stephen Foster brands were the only ones seen in any kind of regular distribution. Out of perhaps 200 days a year when Heaven Hill "mashed in" — cooked grain to make whiskey — I was told they were mashing for rye only 1 day a year.

How could this be? Rye was fascinating to all the staunch whiskeyphiles I knew. The earliest American whiskey, the stuff that launched the Whiskey Rebellion, the basis of many of the classic whiskey cocktails, a common bar call in classic movies — and it

was wonderfully different from bourbon. Rye was spicy, minty, explosive in the mouth, and it had a delicious evolution in character from when it was young (zesty, bright, and fresh as a sun-drenched meadow) to when it was mature (spicy, still explosive, and almost incapable of being drowned in a cocktail) and finally old (deep, capable of great synergy with the oak, and capable of going older, further, than bourbon).

One of the great moments of my whiskey experience came when I first tasted the Sazerac 18-year-old rye from Buffalo Trace. It was a prerelease sample at WhiskyFest (one of the great "under the table" things that happen when whiskey people get together), and it was smooth as sin at 110 proof, a gentle but explosive punch in the mouth that left me breathlessly grinning. Again, how could it be that a whiskey like this wasn't selling to more people?

Not long after, my question was answered, and we started to see movement in the rye niche. Cocktail writer David Wondrich deserves much of the credit for constantly championing it, convincing bartenders to try it in cocktails and demand that distillers make more. I remember him haranguing the Heaven Hill folks at an event one time, telling them what great stuff Rittenhouse Rye was and how they should be pushing it more (and charging more for it; Rittenhouse could be had for a ridiculously low $12 a bottle at the time).

Of course, we got our wish and should have been more careful about what we wished for. There are more ryes on the market now, including the great ryes that were being distilled at the old Seagram distillery in Lawrenceburg, Indiana, and are now coming out under a variety of labels (Bulleit Rye comes from there, bold and bright from a mashbill of 95 percent rye). Some companies are buying up stock of Canadian rye flavoring whisky and selling it on its own. But now we have the opposite of the problem we had before: plenty of people know about rye, and want it, and there's not quite enough to go around.

That's why Heaven Hill is mashing rye over 20 days a year now, and Buffalo Trace is in the rye game, and Beam has added new ryes to its portfolio, including a Knob Creek rye that just screams with the grain. Even Daniel and Dickel have rye now; Dickel's comes from the same Indiana source as Diageo stablemate Bulleit (the Dickel undergoes a post-aging version of the Lincoln County process), while Jack Daniel is mashing its own rye, which is only out in a clear, unaged version so far (and labeled as "spirits distilled from grain," since it is unaged).

American whiskey is growing. That's thanks to a combination of sticking to tradition where it works, innovating where possible, and making a fine product under all circumstances. At the Stitzel-Weller distillery in Shivley, Kentucky, there used to be a plaque, put there by Pappy Van Winkle himself, that sums up how the industry has survived, and why it is now thriving:

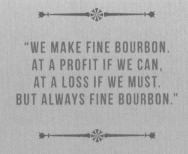

"WE MAKE FINE BOURBON.
AT A PROFIT IF WE CAN,
AT A LOSS IF WE MUST.
BUT ALWAYS FINE BOURBON."

The same plaque now hangs at Buffalo Trace, where Pappy's grandson Julian Van Winkle works with Buffalo Trace distiller Harlen Wheatley to make the next generations of his family's whiskey. They may be Pappy Van Winkle's words, but they're apt for this traditional industry as a whole, which has been through the wilderness and come out stronger than before.

CANADIAN:
BLENDED,
ALWAYS

Canadian whisky suffers from a reputation problem, which is amazing, because despite years of slow decline, it only recently slipped from first place as the largest whisky category in United States sales. Didn't know that? It's true: While bourbon and Tennessee whiskey — the home team! — *finally* edged past Canadian whisky sales in 2011, Canadian sales in the United States are still far bigger than Irish whiskey sales, and Canada sells more whisky here in America than single malts and blended Scotch *put together*. Top that with the latest export figures, showing the decline is over: the value of exports to the United States is up by 18 percent. And I say Canadian whisky has an image problem? We should all be so afflicted.

till, it's true, and you have to wonder if it could be doing a lot better if it weren't for some perception issues. It is blended whisky in an age that reveres the perceived purity of single malt Scotch and single-barrel bourbon. Canadian whisky drinkers are, at least in the large U.S. market, a graying category — not young trendsetters — looking for a low-priced mixing whisky rather than a superb sipping whisky. The category suffers from that very image: mixing whisky, a category that has derisively been called "brown vodka." It's not expensive and has been unable so far to create a high-end brand with large appeal.

And yet, all of that is beginning to change. Blended whisky is poised for a new respect as single malts continue to rise in price, and blends are created with more flavor rather than less. Canadian whisky can easily be part of that trend with a few nudges at the blender's bench, or simply some awareness (and export) of the more flavorful blends that are already available.

Canadian whisky drinkers in the United States are still older on average, but it is reaching a new, younger audience. My 22-year-old son and his college friends, for instance, prefer Canadian whisky over most other liquor, and I see it ordered by more younger drinkers than I've ever seen before. Canadian whisky cocktails are even featured on some bar menus.

Why the sudden popularity? It could be as simple as a desire for change, or it could be a smart substitute to meet the surging demand for rye whiskey that American distillers can't easily supply right now. But it's also the liquor of choice on two very popular television series, *Mad Men* and *Boardwalk Empire*, where bottles of Canadian Club wash up on shore in the opening credits every episode.

As for the questions of flavor, prestige, and price, those would also seem to be on the verge of changing. On a recent trip to some Canadian distilleries, I saw a category that was strong in its own country and ready to build on what is obviously a very strong base in the United States (U.S. sales are about five times the volume of home sales) with an array of new whiskies. Exciting times may well be just around the corner for Canadian whisky.

TWO STREAMS

CANADIAN WHISKY IS actually quite a varied creature. In 5 days I visited four different distilleries, and none of them did things the same way. There were different types of stills, very different approaches to mashing, and quite different grains used to make the whiskies. Canadian whisky makes an interesting comparison to the malt and pot-still monoculture of Scotch single malt distilling or the uniform stills and highly similar mashbills of bourbon. (I also have to mention that one distillery, Highwood, in High River, Alberta, was the first I've ever visited that did not have a mill or buy premilled grain. Instead, and rather astonishingly, the distillery staff put the whole grain — they use Alberta winter wheat as a base — into a large pressure cooker at 60 psi. After a fairly short time, about 15 minutes, the pressure and heat have exploded most of the starch cells in the grain. Whatever wasn't is blown open by the next step; the grain is blown into the mash cooker with a 120 psi burst of steam, where it hits a thick, curved steel plate and essentially disintegrates. It's astounding.)

The one common thread through most traditional, established Canadian distillers is that they produce two streams of whisky. They may not call them by the same names, but the idea is the same.

One stream is a "base whisky" (also called "blending whisky") that is distilled to a very high proof, up around 94 percent alcohol or even higher, and is much like the grain whisky in Scotch blended whisky. The second is a "flavoring whisky" (also called "high wines") that is distilled to a much lower proof (it varies, but it's between 110 and 140 proof). A single distillery may make one or more of each type, varying the grain or the distillation regimen, or doing a combination of both.

How they get those two streams can be confusing to someone who's used to the much more traditional whisky making you'll see in Scotland or America. Canadian distillers have left behind much of the romance and nostalgic parts of distilling. You won't see gleaming banks of copper pot stills here; instead you'll see a column still the size of an ICBM gushing spirit at 240 gallons a minute.

Malt as a source of enzymes for mash conversion has largely been replaced by purified enzymes, tailored to work with different grains and added directly to the mash, which mostly ferments in closed vats. I spoke to Bruce Rollag at Black Velvet, who'd been there pretty much since the plant opened in 1973, and he remembered when the switch was made to enzymes. "That was one of the better days," he said, "when we got rid of the malt. It was dusty, hard to handle, and unforgiving on temperature or pH. If either one was too high, or too low . . . you had a vat of porridge. The enzymes are very forgiving." That's part of the Canadian distiller's approach: don't be afraid to change to something that works better or is easier.

Each distillery I visited took pains to show me their "DDG" area, the "distiller's dark grains." This is what's called the "dryhouse" in Kentucky, or where they process the "pot ale" and "draff" (the stillage and the spent grains) in Scotland, but it's not usually on the tour. The Canadians seemed obsessed with it, proudly showing it off, but it wasn't till I toured Hiram Walker that I learned why.

We entered the huge warehouse-like space where the DDG was collected, and when my eyes adjusted to the dim light inside, I realized there was a huge pyramid of dry

9.09 PERCENT

If you know a little about Canadian whisky, you may know about the 9.09 percent rule for whisky exported to the United States. It allows up to that percentage of the blend to be of . . . stuff. This may be lesser aged spirits, American-made spirits, or "blending wine." Blending wine was described to me at Black Velvet as a very dry white wine, diluted and blended with grain neutral spirits (GNS). By using American ingredients the distiller gets a tax break on exports to the United States. The components are kept as carefully neutral as possible to make it easier for the blenders to match the flavor of the all-whisky version. It's weird, but that's tax law for you.

CANADIAN: FLAVOR PROFILE FOR ICONIC BOTTLINGS

This chart rates five core characteristics on a scale of 1 to 5, with 1 = faint to absent, and 5 = powerful and fully present.

Whiskey	RYE/SPICE	WOOD	CARAMEL/TOFFEE	MOUTHFEEL
ALBERTA PREMIUM	5	2	2	2
BLACK VELVET	1	2	3	2
CANADIAN CLUB RESERVE	3	1	3	3
COLLINGWOOD	1	3	2	3
CROWN ROYAL	3	2	4	3
FORTY CREEK BARREL SELECT	4	2	4	3
GIBSON'S FINEST 12-YEAR-OLD	2	3	5	3
LOT NO. 40	4	4	2	4
SEAGRAM'S VO	2	3	3	2
WISER'S 18-YEAR-OLD	2	4	3	4

bits of grain — and it didn't smell horrible. I'd always thought that the dryhouse of a bourbon distillery smelled something like a roasting chicken that the cook forgot to pluck, but this huge heap smelled like a pleasantly toasted cereal.

Dr. Don Livermore explained. "The dryhouse operations are much more important here," he said. "The DDG is not a by-product; it's a coproduct, a high-protein cattle feed. Three tons of corn makes one ton of DDG, and we sell it for a similar price per ton as we pay for the corn."

That's a tidy savings, but then he explained that it was also an indicator of plant conditions, specifically fermentation efficiency. "If fermentation isn't right, the whole plant won't work," he said. Too much residual, unfermented sugar will screw up the dryhouse. "I'll smell it as soon as I walk in the door, and someone's going to have a bad day."

Livermore has to be efficient. Hiram Walker is the largest beverage alcohol plant in North America. Not only do they make the very popular Wiser's brands, they also make Canadian Club under contract; it's a lot of volume. But the truth is, the other plants — Canadian Mist, Alberta Distillers, Black Velvet, Gimli, Valleyfield, even the smaller Highwood — are all running at a scale where efficiencies are important. They need to be trim, and it shows in most of their operations.

STEALING CANADIAN FLAVOR

*W*hen craft whiskey makers start their businesses, they always have a need for product, and they often buy bulk whiskey to bottle and sell. Some of it comes from places like MGP Ingredients, the old Seagram plant in Indiana, while some of it comes from distilleries that don't like to share their names. Recently, some of it has come from Canada, where craft whiskey makers are buying bulk flavoring whisky.

It's perfect for the craft bottlers. American whiskey drinkers aren't familiar with the character of straight Canadian flavoring whisky (few people are!); it's likely rye whisky, and that's hot right now. And the stocks are more plentiful than they are in the United States, where bulk whiskey stocks are drying up. You just have to know someone in Canada.

Some of the Canadian-stock whiskeys are quite good, command a good price, and garner critical acclaim: WhistlePig, for instance. The question that comes to mind is easy: Why don't the Canadians do this? They'd get a whole new market; a niche market, true, but one with a nice profit margin.

The answer, I've decided, after talking to people in the Canadian whisky business, is that they're just not interested. That's not how they make whisky. Rick Murphy, the production superintendent and master distiller at Alberta Distillers Ltd. in Calgary, told me that Canadian whisky makers develop a blender's mind-set. "It's a unique landscape," he said.

Who am I to say they're wrong?

There is also a dedication verging on fanaticism to the purity of the spirit for the base whisky. Some of the distillers use a process called extractive distillation, the "third still" I mentioned back in chapter 2. It's a counterintuitive way to purify the alcohol, since the first step is to dilute it. The spirit coming off the beer still at around 130 proof is diluted with water back down to between 20 and 30 proof, and then it is introduced to the extractive distillation column.

The aim is to force off the fusel oils and congeners, the chemical impurities in the spirit. These unwanted compounds are for the most part insoluble in water; raising the water content forces them out of the spirit. They're taken off the top and either sold as chemical feedstock or burned to heat the stills.

The alcohol now comes off neatly at about 94 percent ABV, squeaky clean.

The flavoring whisky is usually made much like bourbon: a single pass through a beer still, followed by batching through a pot still. The pot still will clean up the spirit a bit, but not too much, and leave it ready to go in the barrels.

When the whisky does go into the barrel, it's under a varied set of circumstances. At Black Velvet, for instance, the so-called high wines (flavoring whiskies) are aged in barrels for 2 years. The rye-based high wines go into first-fill bourbon barrels, while the corn-based high wines mostly go into first-fill bourbon barrels, but some are in refills. After 2 years of aging, they are dumped, blended with new

Toronto's Distillery District, formerly the Gooderham and Worts Distillery, is now home to a variety of shops and entertainment venues, including Balzac's Coffee Roasters, housed in the former pump house.

base whisky, and put back into barrels for at least 3 more years.

At Highwood all the whisky is aged in used bourbon barrels, and they reuse them; I was told that "a barrel is spent when it starts to leak." That's actually pretty common in Canadian whisky making. Wood management, which has become a huge quality issue in Scotland and Ireland, where each barrel is tracked through its life and sold off after two or three uses at most, is still a frontier in Canadian whisky making. I noticed the beginnings of a barcode tracking system on the barrels at Hiram Walker, but it's all new.

At the time of my Canadian tour, Dr. Don Livermore was experimenting with new barrels and new woods, such as red oak. It made a very forward, spicy, bright whisky,

and I asked him if people would want to drink that. "They're all tools in the box for the master blender," he said.

COMPREHEND THE BLEND

I HAVE TO BE HONEST with you. I really understood how Canadian whisky was made only in the last few years, when I began visiting Canadian distillers and talking to Davin de Kergommeaux, the author of *Canadian Whisky: The Portable Expert.* Coming to Canadian whisky from the outside is not easy. The way the distillers make this whisky is different from how other whiskies are made.

The fascinating thing for me is that tasting Canadian blended whiskies both *before* and *after* I fully understood how they were made and what they were intended to be has led me to reconsider some long-held prejudices about Canadian whisky, blended Scotch, and grain whisky. The frustrating thing now is encountering whisky drinkers who clearly still have those prejudices and not being able to get through to them with my newfound enlightenment.

The Canadians don't help this situation. Take the terminology, for instance. The people in production tend to be blunt and honest and call a thing what it is without looking over their shoulder to see what the marketers would rather they called it. The marketers, meanwhile, seem stuck in the 1980s, promoting Canadian whisky as a lifestyle product, when the growing interest in whisky worldwide has made focusing on the whisky itself a much more effective way to promote it.

For instance, when I toured the Black Velvet distillery in Lethbridge, Alberta, the technical staff flat-out called their base whiskey "GNS." That's industry-speak for "grain neutral spirits," the flavorless commodity alcohol that's distilled as pure as it can feasibly be done (you run into problems with water absorption above 96 percent purity). In America it's the stuff that's added, unaged, to bargain booze as a cheap enhancer; that's how Americans make "blended whiskey." Black Velvet's base whisky is as clean and pure as GNS when it comes off the still, but it's absolutely *not* used as a cheap booze enhancer; it's aged in wood and develops flavor and character of its own, a real contribution to the blend. For once, over years of visiting distilleries and talking to distillers, I thought the conversation maybe could have used a marketer's touch.

Similarly, I was interviewing Andrew MacKay, the revered master blender for Crown Royal, for the *Whisky Advocate* blog a couple of years ago, and he casually defined base whisky as the stuff that "comes off the still with the characteristics of a vodka." He then explained that the base whisky is aged in used barrels: "If you have a barrel that had just contained bourbon, and put that vodka in it, it pulls out the fruity aromas and flavors from the wood. That's part of our arsenal." He was explaining exactly how base whisky is used in Canadian whisky blending, but the blog readers seized on the word "vodka" and beat Canadian whisky to death with it.

Interestingly, when I toured Black Velvet and the Hiram Walker distillery (home to the Wiser's and Lot No. 40 brands; Canadian Club is also made there), they both offered their unaged base whisky for tasting (with plenty of water!). It was, in both cases, a briskly clean spirit, with the same bond-paper aroma I prize in a high-quality vodka, and just the slightest hint of dry grain. (Do you remember what good bond paper smells like? Dry, like well-washed linen, with a tiny tang of acid?) But the people at Walker also offered their Polar vodka as a comparison, and the difference was distinct; the vodka was not as zesty, though just as hot with alcohol. It was rounded and clean, as if the interesting bits had been sanded off, whereas the base whisky was lively, especially in comparison.

Is that enough of a difference to make one alcohol "vodka" and the other "whisky"? Likely not, but that misses the point, and it's an important one. Vodka is intended to be sold as is; base whisky is intended for aging and blending. Is it "really" whisky? It's made from grain, it's fermented and distilled, it's aged in oak. It is for all intents and purposes the same product that is called "grain whisky" in Scotland, and no one in the industry questions whether *that* is whisky.

EXCEPTIONS TO THE RULE

Canada is developing its own small craft brewers, and like craft brewers in America and Europe, they do things their own way. There are also two established Canadian distilleries that make whisky in a different way from the rest of the country. The first is Glenora, a malt whisky distillery that makes its spirit in copper pot stills; appropriately enough, it's located in Nova Scotia ("New Scotland"). Glenora took a good 10 years to find its feet, after a change in ownership and a long legal fight with the Scotch Whisky Association over its Glen Breton brand name. The SWA's hackles are raised whenever a non-Scottish whisky puts anything Scottish on its label, and "Glen" is near the top of the list. Glenora, with its Scottish heritage, located in the town of Glenville, eventually prevailed. It didn't hurt their case that their labels sport a large, red Canadian maple leaf.

Glenora suffered a bit from a lack of distilling experience in the early years, and its whisky was a bit murky in flavor, with the off-putting soapy/green vegetation character typical of poorly made spirit cuts. That's increasingly behind it, and it's developing a better reputation.

The other nontraditional distillery is Forty Creek, in Grimsby, Ontario, between the shores of Lake Ontario and the long, looming cliff of the Niagara Escarpment; it's part of the Kittling Ridge Winery. That's where John Hall uses the exacting care of a chemical engineer and the blending palate of a winemaker to craft his Forty Creek whiskies. He follows Canadian tradition to some extent: his whiskies are blended from different outputs. But he does it his way.

Hall makes whisky from three grains: corn, barley malt, and rye. He mashes, ferments, and distills each one separately and then ages them separately, in different types of barrels for each grain. Once the whiskies are mature, he blends them. He will then "marry" the blend in another barrel (some used, first-fill bourbon barrels, some in Kittling Ridge Winery sherry barrels). It makes an excellent whisky, and Hall is a great ambassador for it.

Glenora Distillery in Nova Scotia: It only looks like it's in Scotland.

EMBARGO!

So there I was, tasting whiskies at Black Velvet, making my way around the table, and Jan Westcott, who is the president of the Association of Canadian Distillers and was along on the trip (great guy; no sense of direction at all), is getting nervous. I can't figure out why, so I keep tasting, and I get to the Danfield's 10-year-old — the what? "What's this Danfield's?" I asked. Not exported, is the answer. Oh, okay. But it's got the wood shop/cedar-oak shavings aroma I've noticed in good Canadian, wrapped in sweet caramel, and a good flavor, but a bit of a drop-off at the end.

Okay, let's try this Danfield's 21. Hey, nice stuff! A big nose of fresh-sawn oak, vanilla, mint, rye zing, and a deliciously luxurious mouth of sweet cereal and more of that wood and rye popping on toward the finish. "Hey, why don't we get this?" I sang right out.

"There's not enough of it!" Jan quickly replied. "You can't have any of it!" He was grinning, but you know? The Canadians do that a lot! For the longest time we didn't get the good stuff. Gibson's Finest, nothing from Alberta Distillers, Wiser's, nothing from Highwood, the Canadian Club 20- and 30-year-old bottlings, and of course, the Danfield's: they kept it almost all to themselves.

Why? Well, they tend to underprice the stuff, so there's not enough money for marketing and promotion (especially after they've paid Canada's pretty stiff excise taxes), and that makes it hard to afford the education it's going to take to get us to understand Canadian. They've got a great market for it at home that drinks up all the good stuff they make, so where's the need? And they sell a lot of the regular stuff to us; the standard bottlings of Canadian whisky still do very well here.

But they could be doing better if they brought the good stuff and helped folks understand what's going on with this misunderstood whisky. Canada's an export economy, has been for a long time, and they should think about exporting some of their top whiskies.

If you're still not convinced, let me tell you what convinced me. Part of my job as managing editor at *Whisky Advocate* is to review whiskies for the magazine's buying guide, and part of that task is to pick a winner for the magazine's annual awards from the categories I review. I was reviewing Canadian whiskies for a time, and the winner I selected in 2011 was Wiser's 18-year-old. There were some whiskies that were more exciting that year, but the Wiser's was a better whole, a delightful whisky to sip, though I wouldn't hesitate to mix with it as well because of its well-rounded character. As I described it, it has "a nose of hot cereal with a dusting of dry cocoa and oaky vanilla, and hints of figs and sesame oil. The palate yields clean grains — a real crack of rye among them — and oak, dried apricot, unsweetened licorice, and a long finish of warming rich cereal." A delightful whisky, really, and Wiser's 18-year-old is still one of my favorite Canadians, even after a much broader tasting experience than I had at the time.

When I was at the Hiram Walker distillery and tasted the base whisky, as I related above, master blender Dr. Don Livermore had laid out a tasting of a huge range of whiskies and aging spirits from all the distillery's different "streams," at varied ages. One of them was the Wiser's 18-year-old, and I enjoyed it again, and asked him what ages and streams went into the whisky.

I was stunned — yes, "stunned" is not an exaggeration — to learn that the Wiser's 18-year-old is made entirely from base whiskies, aged in barrels that had been already used once to age Canadian whisky. There's none of the more complex, lower-ABV, "better" flavoring whisky in there.

After I recovered my composure by having another sip, I continued tasting the other whiskies, but my mind was turning. This was it, the key to Canadian whisky. Things I'd heard, things I'd tasted, things I'd read — it all fit together now. It made me think of something Andrew MacKay had said about Crown Royal's creamy, smooth, sweet character.

"It's *designed* to feel and taste this way," he said. "It's quite distinct from bourbon; it's quite distinct from Scotch. We try to be very distinctive, and we know we have to make our distillate the best it can be; we can't just depend on the wood. All the whiskies are aged separately, in individual barrels, different [batches]."

"The calendar is really a guide," he said. "You're moving backward and forward in time. What I'm making today is for 10 years from now: these are the whiskies I need to make, these are the barrels to put them into. But I'm also looking back, seeing what I actually have from 10 years ago, and how it's matured. You have to consider the evaporative loss, where it's produced, the barrels you have, how much they cost."

I had told him at the time that this was exactly the kind of thing Canadian distillers should be explaining to consumers, why Canadian whisky is the way it is, and what a painstaking process blending really is. He laughed, and agreed, and confirmed what he'd said. "We make it this way on purpose," he said again.

Any marketers listening?

JAPANESE:
THE STUDENT
BECOMES
THE MASTER

"The reason we started making whisky at Yamazaki was the very, very good water there. To make a good tea, you need good water. Tea master Sen Rikyu built his first teahouse there. Very humid air, which is important to whisky maturation; if it's too dry, you lose too much whisky through evaporation. Even in the winter, it is not dry. Three rivers meet there, and the difference in temperature creates fog. The air is always filled with moisture."

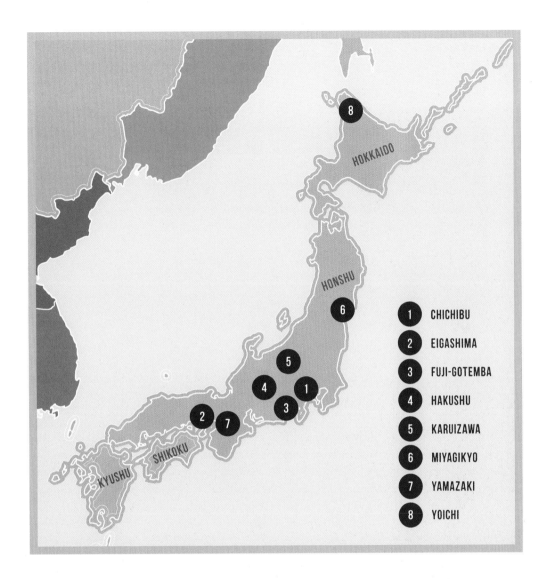

1	CHICHIBU
2	EIGASHIMA
3	FUJI-GOTEMBA
4	HAKUSHU
5	KARUIZAWA
6	MIYAGIKYO
7	YAMAZAKI
8	YOICHI

Mike Miyamoto, the former master distiller for Suntory and now its global brand ambassador, was explaining to me why Shinjiro Torii built the first whisky distillery in Japan at Yamazaki, on the island of Honshu, back in 1923. Yamazaki is also situated between Kyoto and Osaka, two major markets. Although the distillery sits on the edge of town, with thickly wooded hills rising steeply behind it, it was built within shouting distance of the railway and near the old main road between Kyoto and Osaka; today the multilane Meishin Expressway tunnels under those background hills. Commercial convenience is not to be overlooked, but you can always find a way to ship good whisky — just ask the distillers on Islay — while good water is not always easy to find.

As we've already learned, Torii's first distiller, Masataka Taketsuru, left Suntory and Yamazaki in 1934, not too long after the release of the first whisky, which was not a

JAPANESE: FLAVOR PROFILE FOR ICONIC BOTTLINGS

This chart rates five core characteristics on a scale of 1 to 5, with 1 being faint to absent, and 5 being powerful and fully present.

Whiskey	PEAT	FRUIT	OAK/SPICE	MOUTHFEEL
HAKUSHU 12-YEAR-OLD	2	2	2	3
HAKUSHU HEAVILY PEATED	5	3	1	4
HIBIKI 12-YEAR-OLD	1	3	3	3
YAMAZAKI 12-YEAR-OLD	1	3	3	3
YAMAZAKI 18-YEAR-OLD	1	4	3	4
YOICHI 15-YEAR-OLD	3	1	3	4

commercial success. After some ventures in nonwhisky companies, he would, with the help of interested investors in the Nikka distilling company, build a competing distillery, Yoichi, on the northern island of Hokkaido. Yoichi sits on the west coast, a fishing town of some 20,000 people, noted for the quality of the local apples. It is almost as if Taketsuru wanted isolation to create the whisky he wanted to make.

These are the Big Two whisky makers of Japan. Suntory and Nikka would each build an additional distillery. Suntory built the giant Hakushu plant in the 1970s, at the foot of the Japanese Alps, near Hokuto, west of Tokyo. Taketsuru would build Miyagikyo on the northern end of Honshu in the late 1960s, tucked into a valley west of Sendai, personally selecting the spot — reportedly for the water — and planning the distillery while in his 70s.

And that is about it. There are four other whisky distilleries in Japan, all small and all on Honshu: tiny and independent Chichibu; Eigashima, where whisky is made only 2 months a year when the plant is not making sake and shochu; and Fuji-Gotemba and Karuizawa (which is currently mothballed, as is half of Suntory's Hakushu plant, victim of the early 1990s crash of the Japanese economy), both owned by Kirin Brewery. Their whisky is hard to find even in Japan.

Happily, the whiskies from Suntory and Nikka not only are easy to find in Japan but also are becoming easier to find in world markets. That's leading to a reassessment of Japanese whisky, as the rest of the world discovers that it's not only good but also distinct, despite its obvious Scottish roots and connections and similar label terminology.

AN IRISH TWIST

JAPANESE WHISKY MAKING had its origins in Scotland, with the direct experience of Taketsuru-san in Campbeltown. But Torii-san quickly moved to put a Japanese sensibility on Suntory's whisky, moving away from the bold character of Taketsuru's first effort toward a more subtle and balanced whisky.

Again, Mike Miyamoto explains. "Shinjiro Torii wanted to create whisky to appeal to the Japanese palate, a delicate palate. We like well-balanced, mild, and sophisticated whisky. Once you sip it and taste it on the palate, you taste many different characters, different tastes coming out."

To get a Japanese palate from a Scottish type of whisky, Suntory (and Nikka) used a very Irish kind of process. Japanese distillers needed a range of whiskies, and unlike Scotland, they couldn't just go out to other distilleries that made different whiskies and start trading to get what they needed. (Given the history between Torii and Taketsuru — which was never openly hostile, but distant — it's not surprising that they don't even trade between each other.) The only way to get different whiskies was the Irish way: make them yourself.

Suntory and Nikka both vary every angle of the fermentation and distilling process to get that variety. They use different yeasts, vary

Japanese whisky makers use wild variety in their fermentation and distillation processes to produce a wide range of whiskies from what is, for now, a small number of distilleries.

Copper gleams everywhere at Suntory's Yamazaki distillery.

fermentation times for different aromatics from the yeast, employ both wooden and steel washbacks (the wooden ones will harbor microflora that will add flavors to the wash), and use varying degrees of peated malt.

Suntory's stillhouses are not the uniform ranks of identical pot stills you'll see at big Scottish distilleries like Glenfiddich and Glenlivet, but a somewhat jarring assembly of different designs, paired off with each other for different amounts of reflux; they can even be reconfigured to a degree as needed, all of which will affect the weight and mouthfeel of the spirit. The cuts of foreshots, hearts, and feints are varied. There are steam-heated stills and ones heated by direct contact with flame; Nikka uses coal at Yoichi, a delightful throwback to the old days in Scotland. The grain whiskies are changed up in similar fashion, though not as varied.

Aging in wood simply runs riot in these distilleries. There are the familiar varieties — sherry barrels made of American or European oak, along with bourbon barrels — in first-fill

Whisky is very much a part of metropolitan Japan.

Canned highballs — whisky and sparkling water, canned like a soda — are a uniquely Japanese invention. Both Suntory and Nikka produce them.

and refill condition. But also, as Miyamoto noted, Suntory makes its own oversize casks, at its own cooperage. "Puncheons," he called them. "We import the timber from the U.S., and bend it to make our own barrels. [They're] 480-liter casks, compared to 180 or 230 for the bourbon barrel or hogshead [the size common in Scotland]."

It doesn't end there. "We also make *mizunara* casks, made from Japanese oak," he said. "The timber is slow growing and requires a long maturation. When we had the war, it was sad, and tragic. The importation stopped, so we had no bourbon barrels or sherry butts. We had to source our own supply. We used the *mizunara* timber. Bourbon and sherry casks give flavor after 5 years. *Mizunara* didn't, so we thought, 'That's bad wood,' and left the casks in a corner. Twenty years later we tried it. 'Wow, amazing taste!' We don't char it, just

toast. We specify the color of the fox (light toasting) or the raccoon (deep toasting)."

He told me about one more type of cask that they use to make whisky that goes in their delicious Hibiki blend, along with about 20 others. "It is finished in plum liqueur casks," he said. "They're old casks that would be taken away from the system, but we give them a treatment with infrared rays and then put plum liqueur in the casks. It picks up a very nice oakiness and sells very well. Then we finish whisky in that cask."

Hibiki is a top-end blend, delicately complex and floral, and a beautiful presentation in a heavy bottle. "There are 24 facets on the bottle, represents 24 seasons in Japan, and 24 hours in a day," said Miyamoto, who then noted, "We care about the small details. Sometimes too much!"

Suntory's Scottish roots are evident here.

HIGHBALLING IT

Blends are the lion's share of the Japanese whisky business, just as with Scotch whisky, and always have been. They were hugely successful in the boom years of the Japanese economy, consumed as *mizuwari*, "mixed with water." Reminiscent of the "Kentucky tea" that bourbon drinkers will make on a hot day, a *mizuwari* is perhaps one measure of blended whisky, ice, and two (or two and a half) measures of water.

Whisky sales, driven by the ease and refreshment of *mizuwari*, were immense in the 1970s and 1980s. Dave Broom notes in *The World Atlas of Whisky* that in the 1980s, sales of the Suntory Old brand alone hit 12.4 *million*

cases, almost as much as the global sales of the entire Johnnie Walker brand line today. That's simply immense.

It didn't last. When the economy crashed, whisky crashed with it, and the Japanese turned to a cheap, low-malt type of beer known as *happoshu*. What brought whisky back was an old twist on the once popular *mizuwari*: soda water, the highball, or as it's sometimes called, "soda-wari." It's growing quickly, and Suntory is packaging a canned premixed version.

"When we enjoy whisky in Japan, we add water, or soda, the highball style," Miyamoto said. "Canned highball, that is very, very good, and handy on a train! We have the bullet train between Tokyo and Osaka, it takes two and a half hours. Most businessmen [going on the train] will buy a can or two of highball and have that instead of beer." Japanese brewers are feeling the pinch; beer sales are dropping rapidly.

Still, drinking whisky in Japan has changed, and not just switching water for soda. Previously there was a hierarchy, an almost rigid progression of the whiskies you drank as you progressed in your career, starting with a basic blend. Now young Japanese men or women may have a Suntory Highball (basic) or a glass of Yamazaki single malt (highbrow). The hierarchy has faded. If they can afford it, they will try it.

Even single malts have changed with the Japanese bent for innovation, though. Where a Scottish distillery may bottle several expressions of its malt, mainly differentiated by the age of the whisky, the Japanese take those different whiskies they've been making and create single malts that can vary much more among bottlings.

"We introduced the blending concept of single malts," Miyamoto said. "All the different whiskies that go into Yamazaki are made at Yamazaki, so it is still a single malt. It makes a very balanced single malt. That makes the Suntory whisky different from the other [single malts]. Different from Nikka, also."

Sample some of the whiskies, and you can taste the differences:

- The Hakushu 12-year-old: fresh, green, and possessed of a nectar-light sweetness; the mouth is grassy-sweet with a lime-pith edge around it and just a touch of soft smoke in the finish.
- The Yamazaki 18-year-old: full, rich, with ripe harvest fruit notes in the nose; the same in the mouth with a solid weight of wood that lasts into the finish, a whisky with gravity.
- The blended Hibiki 12-year-old: softly floral, fruit pastilles — I can smell that slightly dusty note — and lemon sand tarts; the palate is more settled, with

touches of light pit fruits and a juicy sweetness that tapers to a dryly spicy finish; elegant blend.

Is Japanese whisky more or less the same as Scotch whisky, or is it very different? There are similar elements, to be sure, and I'm not at all certain that I could pick a lone Japanese malt out of a lineup of 10 single malts. But *mizunara* oak, the uninhibited experimentation with process that comes from necessity, and the fascinating sensibilities of Japanese blended whiskies make for an excellent addition to the world of whisky.

"The Japanese climate makes the Japanese style," Mike Miyamoto says. Given the wide range of climate from the subtropical southern islands to the snowy winters of Hokkaido, I think he may have put his finger on it.

The Mash Tun whisky bar in Tokyo dislays a decidedly Scottish flair — and an impressive range of whiskies from around the world.

CRAFT WHISKEY

One aspect of whiskey making that's getting a lot of attention these days is the new wave of distillers setting up shop all over the world. No one is quite set on what to call them yet: artisanal distillers, microdistillers, craft distillers. I'm calling them "craft distillers" now, because I can see that coming, after 30 years of watching the craft beer business. "Artisanal" is too long, and a bit pretentious; "micro" becomes a problem when you get successful. "Craft" is likely where it's going to wind up.

ut for now they're small distillers, although small distillers are nothing new or even particularly different. After all, that's how things started, over 600 years ago, and how things were till the Industrial Revolution. There have always been a few small distillers around. Some folks are just hardheaded enough that they want to do things their own way.

I visited a small distiller back in the 1980s, before we got all excited about them. That was Michter's, up in the Pennsylvania hills outside Schaefferstown. There had been distilling going on at the spot since the mid-1700s, and you could see why. The surrounding area was rich farmland, but the ridges around the spot would make travel hard. The distillery sat in a fold of hills, protected from wind and blessed with a clean-flowing creek of limestone water.

Michter's is proof that small distilleries can do great things. That's where one of the best bourbons I've ever tasted was made: A. H. Hirsch 16-year-old, a legendary bottling of well-aged whiskey that is still talked about reverently for its deep, complex aromas and rich but not over-oaked mouth. Knowing that a great American whiskey came from a small distillery in eastern Pennsylvania makes it easier for me to believe something like that can happen again.

I am going to speak almost entirely about American craft distillers, because I know more about them, have visited some of them, and have sampled more of their whiskeys. I have also tasted some very good whiskey from craft distillers like Penderyn (Wales), Armorik (France), Mackmyra (Sweden), Zuidam (Holland), and Limeburners and Lark (Australia).

Balcones: a fiercely independent — and idiosyncratic — Texas distillery

I've also very much enjoyed the whiskeys of Kavalan (Taiwan) and Amrut (India), but they are definitely not small craft distillers; they are large and rapidly growing. The craft movement itself is also a growing one that is going to change the face of whiskey making; in fact, to some extent it already has.

A SMALL START

MODERN CRAFT WHISKEY got its start in America in 1993. That's when two guys started making whiskey on small stills in idiosyncratic ways; coincidentally, both were on the West Coast. Steve McCarthy of Clear Creek Distillery in Portland, Oregon, was probably a couple of months ahead of Fritz Maytag's Anchor Distilling in San Francisco, but they were almost synchronous.

The year 1993 was a time full of expectations for a small but growing number of drinks fans. Over the preceding few years we'd seen small breweries pop up and start making beer that was completely different from what the big national breweries made; Fritz Maytag's Anchor Brewing was one of them, in fact. By 1993 around 450 small breweries were in operation in America, more than at any time since World War II. More amazing yet, that number would double in the next 5 years.

Across the country I and other craft brew fans — mostly young, professional, mobile — saw this happening and thought it presaged a whole new era of small, cool, interesting producers. When we saw Fritz Maytag, who was revered as one of the fathers of craft brewing, starting a *microdistillery*, we were sure that craft distilling would be the next big thing.

It wasn't. The output was tiny (I think the first bottling of Anchor's Old Potrero totaled

CRAFT DISTILLERIES IN PRODUCTION

Craft distilling has seen explosive growth in recent years, more than quadrupling from 2008 to 2012.

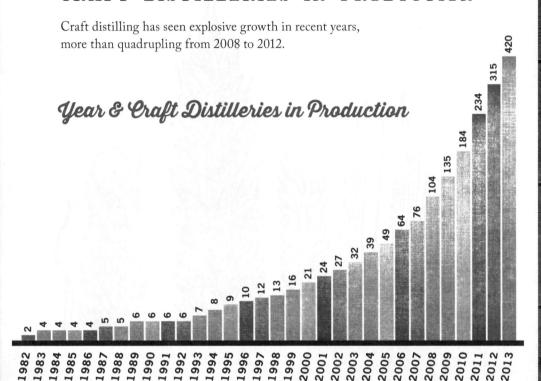

Year & Craft Distilleries in Production

about 1,400 bottles, and most was sold to restaurants) and expensive, and not at all what people were used to.

But it was full of promise. I got a sip of that first bottling, and I still recall the way everyone in the small room went silent as we passed around the glass and just smelled it (it was around 120 proof, so we weren't in a rush to taste it). It was only about a year old, and made with rye malt, and it was stunningly aromatic: zesty-fresh grass, rolling waves of mint, and just a bare wreathing of wood. It

was young, powerful, and invigorating. It was very different from what we usually saw from American distillers, and rye whiskey was still under the radar at that point.

Steve McCarthy's malt whisky was also different. He'd been inspired by a visit to Scotland, where he discovered the Lagavulin 16-year-old and wanted to make something similar at the eau-de-vie distillery he'd opened in 1985. "I wondered if we could make whisky on an eau-de-vie still, and we could!" he told me recently, still excited about that moment

WHOSE WHISKEY IS IT, REALLY?

*C*raft whiskey makers are at a distinct disadvantage compared to other craft distillers and brewers: Whiskey takes a lot longer to be ready for sale. Unless distillers want to get into the white whiskey game (see page 187), they'd better have a solid capital reserve so they can keep making whiskey till the first barrels are ready to bottle and sell. Even the quickest small-barrel stuff usually takes 6 months.

Craft brewers had their own problems with capital. It takes a lot of stainless steel to brew the large volumes of beer they need to succeed: kettles, tanks, pipes, whirlpools, more tanks, and hundreds of kegs, some of which never find their way back to the brewery. Then there's the bottling line, glass, and labels and packaging.

Some brewers found a way around those capital requirements through a practice called contract brewing. They would pay established brewers that had extra capacity — usually the old regionals, such as Genesee, F. X. Matt, or August Schell — to brew beer for them and then spend the money they saved on not building a brewery for marketing and promotion. The beer might be the brewery's regular line relabeled, it might be brewed to different specifications, or it might actually be brewed by the contractor, who would lease the facilities for a day or so every month. It caused bad feelings in the industry for a long time; brick-and-mortar brewers felt that contract brewers were cheating, that they didn't have enough skin in the game.

In craft whiskey a similar procedure is to find distillers or brokers with an excess stock of aged whiskey and buy it to sell under your own label. *Whisky Advocate* calls that "sourced whiskey," while whiskey blogger Chuck Cowdery calls such operations "Potemkin distilleries" and craft distillers call them things I won't repeat (the gentlest is "fakers").

It's not just craft distillers, either: Bulleit, a large brand owned by Diageo, currently has no distillery. Bulleit buys bourbon from Four Roses and rye from the former Seagram distillery in Lawrenceburg, Indiana, which is now operated by MGP Ingredients.

As in brewing, there are varying degrees of how much the sellers add to the process. They

may just show up, pick out a taste profile, and leave it to the warehouse manager to pull a parcel of barrels and bottle them. They may go warehouse crawling and pick their own. They may do what folks like David Perkins at High West distillery did, not just picking out their own but blending them in their own interesting ways: a young rye and a much older one, a bourbon and a rye, and a blend Perkins calls Campfire, with bourbon, rye, and a smoky Scotch. Or they may buy some good older whiskey and either blend it with their own younger whiskey or "finish" the whiskey in barrels that once held other spirits or wine.

Is bottling other people's whiskey bad practice? I'd say it comes down to intent: whether the bottler's intent is to deceive the consumer into believing that the whiskey in the bottle is its own. Perkins, for instance, has always been ready to let you know that he's bottling sourced whiskey. Other distillers say not a word about where their aged whiskey comes from, and unless you read their label very closely, you won't know it's not their own. Look to see if it only says where it was "bottled." See if the town name is different from the distillery's. And do a quick check on age; if it's a 4-year-old whiskey and the distillery just opened, it's sourced! Remember, you can't really guess the age by color in these days of small barrels.

If a craft distiller is selling whiskey that isn't its own make under a label that doesn't identify it as such (or at least have information on their website or Facebook page that shows it), exactly where does the "craft" come in? They may well be making whiskey and aging it with all kinds of good intentions, but there are other ways to make money while they're waiting; gin or vodka, for instance, both grain spirits, or unaged whiskey, which can be done a lot better than many are doing it now. If they're buying whiskey, and reselling it under their own label without telling you or making the information easy to find, I'd buy another whiskey.

The fact is, you have to be careful. If you want to support your local distiller, that's great, but it might be a bit different if you're supporting your local distiller by paying a $20 premium for whiskey you could be buying under a different label!

St. George Spirits, Alameda, CA

Spring rye crop in Tennessee

from 20 years ago. "We brought in peated malt from Scotland. And now we're using all Oregon oak. I don't think it's any good at all for wine, but it's fantastic for whiskey. This is Oregon single malt, and I've stayed with that."

Like I said, craft whiskey looked ready to follow immediately on the heels of craft brewing. We were terribly disappointed when it didn't explode into popularity as microbrewing had. But we'd seen and tasted the future, even though we didn't realize it at the time. The whiskeys Anchor and Clear Creek made would point the way for American craft distillers: different, small, the product of individual passion.

Look around today, and you'll see a whiskey landscape that looks a lot like the craft brewing landscape of 1993. There are the established big distillers (American and imported), a few established small distillers who've been around for over 15 years, and a burgeoning broth of tiny upstarts — over 300 of them. The media loves them (they're great stories!), they have enthusiastic local support (and local opposition to the devil's juice in some areas), and they have a lot of innovative ideas and are resurrecting old, forgotten ones.

An important difference in the comparison to craft brewers is that the craft whiskey makers actually have it easier in one very important respect. The people they're selling to — wholesalers, retail stores, and bars and restaurants — have already seen this work with craft brewers, and work well.

Craft brewers were still a long shot in 1993. People didn't know what they were, or why they were around. Wholesalers and retailers had no idea how to sell them, and most bars had six taps or less. All they could see was that more beers would cost them more money — and who was going to buy them?

The answers to those questions seem obvious 20 years later. Thanks to the success of craft beer, for the wholesalers and retailers of whiskey that's exactly what it is: obvious. They're much more willing to take a chance on a new, unknown product if the packaging and marketing are good and the whiskey in the bottle delivers. That's been an immense help to craft whiskey makers.

Where craft distillers have it harder than craft brewers is in selling their wares to the consumer. Craft brewers had it easy there: the beers being made by the major American brewers were all the same, and they were all bland, light lagers. Big was bad.

That's definitely not true with whiskey. Bourbon and Scotch and Irish are anything but bland. (I'd argue that what most Americans expected when they asked for Canadian whisky 20 years ago was bland, but that was influenced by a marketing decision on what was exported; there's great Canadian to be had!) But the craft brewing story is so temptingly parallel to the craft distilling story in so many other ways that it may seem irresistible to disparage "the bland whiskey of the big distillers." That's a mistake, as anyone who's had a dram of Lagavulin or a snort of Booker's can tell you.

The story of craft whiskey — the details that pull in aficionados and newcomers alike — has to be about something else. And here's where craft distillers are making headway.

CRAFT WHISKEY: THE REAL STORY

LET'S TALK ABOUT THE real story that craft distillers have to tell: the things about craft distilling that set them apart from the big distillers, and the reasons that people should consider spending the extra money that a bottle of craft costs. (I'll tell you about why the cost is higher a little later.)

LOCALLY MADE: LOCAL PEOPLE, LOCAL INGREDIENTS

JUST AS CRAFT BREWING STARTED with "local" as a strong draw (and is moving back to that concept now), just as community-supported agriculture farms are enrolling more and more participants who want to know where their food comes from, and just as the "farm to table" movement in restaurants is bringing food suppliers and chefs closer together, so is local production making craft distillers more interesting and more authentic.

Take my local distillery as an example. Mountain Laurel Spirits makes its Dad's Hat Rye whiskeys in Bristol, Pennsylvania, a town on the Delaware River just north of Phila-delphia. Business partners Herman Mihalich and John Cooper use Pennsylvania-grown grain. They know that their distillery is sited only 5 miles from where the once-famous Philadelphia Pure Rye distillery made whiskey until Prohibition, and they make rye

Pennsylvania style (with rye, rye malt, and barley malt and no corn), like the old Monongahela Valley distillers in western Pennsylvania, where Mihalich grew up. They stress their regional focus in their marketing, and it works even outside the area; local roots are authentic, even when it's not your locale.

Hillrock Estate Distillery in Ancram, New York,

takes it even further. Here in the old grain-growing region of the Hudson Valley, south of Albany, owner Jeffrey Baker is growing rye and barley on his land, including two fields right beside the distillery. He buys his corn from local farmers. The grains are malted and milled on-site, and some of them are smoked with peat here (Baker is looking at old maps to find local sources for the peat as well).

Hillrock's maltings (another name for a malt house) was built for them by Christian Stanley, who, with his wife Andrea, runs Valley Malt, a small custom malting operation in Hadley, Massachusetts. The Stanleys know by name every farmer who supplies grain to them, and they can prepare specialty batches of almost anything a distiller can think of; I saw Andrea packaging a batch of cherry wood–smoked triticale malt once when I was there. They supply distillers in places ranging from Gloucester, Massachusetts (Ryan & Wood), to central New York (Finger Lakes Distilling, which sends barley from a local farm to Valley Malt to be malted).

You'll see a local bent in some big distillers, too, of course. Quite a few have a protected source of water from a spring or well. Some Scotch distillers, such as Bowmore and Highland Park, make some of their own malt, and Highland Park cuts the distinctive peat found there on Orkney to smoke its malt. Heaven Hill gets part of its corn from farmers' fields around its warehouses. But the craft distiller who can take you to the spring, show you the field, and let you hold the green malt and lay your hand on a barrel filled with aging whiskey — that's a story, and a link.

Ryan & Wood, the Gloucester distillery that uses Valley Malt, has built up a solid trade with area restaurants and retailers, like the Blue Ox Inn, in Lynn, Massachusetts. The bar manager at the Blue Ox told me that Ryan & Wood owner Bob Ryan had dropped

Finger Lakes Distilling in New York State proudly uses a 12-inch column still.

off sawn chunks of used barrel wood and the chef had cold-smoked steaks with it. "He loved it, the best flavor; [now] we have it on special every day. Can you imagine, having a rye Manhattan with a steak smoked with the barrels the whiskey was made in?" Only from a craft distiller. People like the idea of a whiskey with that kind of personal touch.

THE MOONSHINE MYSTIQUE

WE TEND TO LIKE THE IDEA of the honorable outlaw, that person who's working outside the boundaries, not to cheat anyone but to serve the people, Robin Hood style. When we hear stories of illicit distilling, do any of us cheer for the revenuer or the exciseman? No, we cheer for the moonshiner, for the crofter with his sma' still, for the wily *poitín* maker. Craft distillers tap into that mystique almost automatically, because there's something in us that just can't believe a small distillery can be legal; these people sure look like they're getting away with something!

That mystique is clearly boosted when the distiller's selling unaged whiskey, a.k.a. white dog or new make. You and I, we know that upstart distillers sometimes sell white dog because they have to; it's quick cash flow, but at the same time this is something the big distillers could have done all along. The big distillers are doing it now, and the craft distillers led them to it!

They should have been doing it before, because people are bubbling with curiosity about whiskey. They want to know what it's like, and tasting the stuff before it goes in the barrel is a hugely interesting part of the whiskey experience. It's educational, it's fun, it's interesting, it's revealing. These days you can even buy small barrels so you can age your own.

White dog shows the skill of the distiller, and it can show the intent of the distiller.

What's more interesting, some distillers change the run for what they'll be selling as white dog, and what they'll be barreling. They want the stuff for the white dog coming off cleaner. The barrel, I've been told, needs more to work with. As I said, it's educational.

There are craft brands that claim moonshining heritage, or at least a link to illicit distilling, like Templeton Rye, Popcorn Sutton Tennessee White Whiskey, or Junior Johnson's Midnight Moon. At least one distiller has employed three ex-moonshiners, or "wildcatters" as they refer to themselves. Short Mountain Distillery, about 50 miles southeast of Nashville, works with Jimmy Simpson, Ricky Estes, and Ronald Lawson, who legally make Short Mountain Shine according to the recipe they all used independently.

"That's how it's made in Cannon County," said cofounder David Kaufman. The recipe is fairly simple: 70 percent cane sugar and 30 percent corn and wheat "shorts" (roughly milled bits of wheat bran, germ, and flour). That mixture is fermented, and the wash is drained out from under the fairly solid "cap" of grains that forms and is sent to the still; the cap and slurry are used as sour mash in the next batch. The three wildcatters make it their way on a hand-hammered still outside, a live working display. The main work goes on inside, on a bigger still, with a full-time distiller, but the output of both stills goes into the bottles. It's a real link to how things used to be done.

Not all white whiskey is good, not by a long shot. I've received samples that showed a bit of green — actual green color! — and tasted like that would imply. But I have also had samples of unaged whiskey that were quite good — the R5 from Charbay and Low Gap from Craft Distillers — that I would choose to have again. White dog also shows well in some cocktails. We drink white rum

IT REALLY IS ILLEGAL

*W*hile we're discussing moonshine, remember: real moonshine *is* illegal. Make no mistake about it: Making whiskey — or vodka, grappa, brandy, or eau-de-vie — at home without a distiller's license is very much illegal. Period. No wiggle room, no "if I'm just making it for myself, it's okay" escape hatch.

There are hobby stills being made and sold, there are books out on the subject (I'd recommend *Moonshine!* by Matt Rowley), and there is a lot of Internet discussion about technique, but unless you live in New Zealand, the only country in the world where home distilling is currently legal, you should know what the risks are.

For instance, not only does U.S. law completely forbid home distillation of alcohol, but you are not even allowed to own a still larger than one gallon (smaller ones can legally be used for making distilled water or plant essences but are subject to inspection). If you buy one of those hobby stills, beware: if asked, the companies that sell them have to supply the Alcohol and Tobacco Tax and Trade Bureau (TTB) with the names and addresses of anyone who's ordered a still, and the feds don't even need a warrant. If you are caught and prosecuted, it's a $10,000 fine and *5 years* in federal prison.

Herein lies one of the other disadvantages craft distillers have in comparison to craft brewers, as Corsair Distillery's Darek Bell explained it to me. There's no "farm system" like there is in homebrewing to develop the next generation of distillers.

"Craft brewers have tremendous bench strength in homebrewers," Bell pointed out. "There are tens of thousands of people with at least some hands-on understanding of brewing. But home distillation is 5 years [in prison] and 10 grand; it's life destroying. We'll see legal pot before home distilling is legalized." (Bell had homebrewing experience but also had an odd kind of legal distillation experience: he and friends were making biodiesel when one of them had the brainstorm that making liquor would be a lot more fun, and smell better, too.)

There is home distilling going on in the United States; I've tasted the results. But I stay away from it, and most craft distillers are even more careful. They want to have nothing to do with something that could potentially cost them their license just for being associated with it. So don't take your homemade samples to the local distiller, the way homebrewers will take beers to the craft brewery. You won't find a warm welcome. Better yet, don't make any samples at home. *It's very much illegal.*

and blanco tequila, after all; we drink grappa and marc. Why should whiskey be different? We need a name for it, though, or a rule change. The name "white whiskey" isn't accurate if it's unaged, and the idea that "aging" the spirit in a barrel for a day, an hour, or a minute legally makes the spirit whiskey is silly. Beam's new Jacob's Ghost is white whiskey; they age

spirit for about a year, then filter the color out, leaving an interestingly flavored spirit that's definitely not white dog. Highwood in Canada does the same kind of thing with its White Owl whisky, and it's been a huge hit. This is closer to what white rum is: "lightly" aged, enough to take the edges off and to filter some of the nasty bits out.

Checking lab samples at St. George Spirits

There has been talk of making changes to the U.S. standards of identity, to create a category for these unaged or lightly aged grain spirits that are not vodka, straight whiskey, or blended whiskey. It might also be helpful for the standards to allow more flexibility about aging in used wood, an option that would make it possible to make malt whisky in the traditional Scottish manner, before fiddling with it in some innovative way, which brings us to the final twist in the story.

VARIETY AND INNOVATION

VARIETY AND INNOVATION ARE the craft distiller's bread and butter, or should be. They're similar to what made craft brewing successful: being a genuine alternative to the major brewers' beers. Even the first brewpub I visited, way back in the early 1980s, at the onset of the microbrew movement, had three different beers, unlike each other and so very different from the light lagers that occupied the vast majority of the market at that time.

Some craft whiskey makers have taken to innovation tentatively. Stranahan's (out of Denver), for instance, makes essentially one whiskey, an all-malt whiskey (using exclusively regionally grown barley; there's that local factor again) that's aged in new, charred, white oak barrels, as required by the standards of identity. That's different, in that there are no big American distillers making all malt whiskey, but it's the regulated model for an American malt whiskey. Stranahan's varies things a bit by distilling in a hybrid pot still — pretty common for a small distiller — and with occasional cask-finished Snowflake bottlings, but its real selling point is that it's "Colorado whiskey": malt whiskey from a new charred barrel aged at high altitude.

With its peated malt whiskey, Lost Spirits Distillery in Monterey, California, is doing it more like Steve McCarthy at Clear Creek (see page 180) but throws in a handcrafted aspect or two. Lost Spirits uses California-grown malt, which is then wetted at the distillery and smoked in a self-built smoker with Canadian peat, from Manitoba, to pretty stiff levels. After fermentation, distiller Bryan Davis puts the wash through a wooden, steam-heated still. It's not the primitive "box of rocks" wooden column still full of smooth stones; it's a wooden pot still that looks like a very large barrel with a copper dunce cap on the top. This intensely smoky whiskey, aged in California cabernet casks, is *very* craft distilled.

Take it up a step, and you've got what Chip Tate is doing at Balcones in Waco, Texas. Tate wanted to create a Texas whiskey, something imbued with Texan grain, wood, and climate. So he and his crew fabricated their own stills to their own design (they used the more conventional copper). They make whiskey from roasted blue corn, and they also make whiskey from blue corn smoked over Texas scrub oak — which is jaw-twistingly smoky — and they age both in the Texas heat, which speeds up the evaporation rate tremendously.

For mad variety, though, it's hard to beat Corsair Distillery in Nashville. The distillery team uses many different grains: corn, blue corn, millet, buckwheat, triticale, spelt, oats, sorghum, quinoa, malt, barley rye . . . and that was all in one whiskey, the Insane in the Grain bourbon. "Some of the grains are a pain in the [butt] to process," said cofounder Darek Bell. "They all have different personalities." They have also made whiskey from imperial stout, oatmeal stout, and pilsner, and they've flavored the whiskey by running the alcohol vapors through a stack filled with hops or elderflowers.

Corsair has made something of a side project out of smoke. They smoke grains with different peats and woods; the Triple Smoke

Corsair experiments with hopped whiskeys.

uses peat, cherry, and beech and manages to taste like Scotch, German *rauchbier*, and pipe tobacco. Bell told me he was experimenting with forcing smoke directly into the rectification column. "There are a lot of different ways to get smoke flavor in."

He then delivered the distillery motto. "Imitation is suicide," he quoted with obvious pleasure, then added the second dose: "If it has been done before, we do not want to do it. Look, I live in the shadow of Jack Daniel's. I can't match them on marketing, on equipment. But creativity is free. Craft brewers know that; they're trying everything. The diversity of beers is incredible, and I keep waiting for that to happen with distilling!"

It's going to take a while for excitement like that to spread, although Bell has written a book about it (*Alt Whiskeys*) that is stuffed with inspiration, ideas he's simply giving away. It took a while for craft beer brewers to really start experimenting as well, if only because they were getting their practices down and looking back to the classics that had been overlooked or marginalized. That's something we're soon going to see more of in craft distilling. For all our talk about traditions in whiskey making, there are a lot of changes that have happened over the years. A quick list would include the dominant use of the column still and the all-but-exclusive use of new charred oak barrels by American distillers, the subsequent wide use of those bourbon barrels by Scottish and Irish distillers, much less use of direct fire on still coppers, the blending/flavoring whisky model of Canadian distillers, and the use of newer hybrid grains.

These are all areas in which a craft distiller could "go retro," making pot-stilled American rye, or aging in a much wider array of barrels, or using heritage grains. Some distillers are already headed in this direction,

but I see much more potential. One that is likely unique is Indian Creek Distillery in New Carlisle, Ohio. Joe and Missy Duer are using a set of small stills that were used at a family farm distillery to make rye whiskey from 1820 to 1920 — at the same site where they're distilling today. The family disassembled the stills at the start of Prohibition, and they were in storage until 1997. In 2011 they were finally put back into service, with the same recipe and water source.

CRAFTING A CATEGORY

WHEN YOU HAVE A GROUP of distillers relying on their innovations and differences to set themselves apart, it begs the question: what makes them similar? It can't just be size. The craft brewers thought that was their difference at first, but they quickly grew larger. Boston Beer Company, one of the original craft brewers, is now one of the five largest brewers in America.

I don't think there's anything wrong with being united in *not* being like the established distillers. They have a lot invested in being large, and in making whiskey pretty much just like they've always made it. Warehouses stuffed full of tens or hundreds of thousands of aging barrels of whiskey make whiskey makers like supertankers; it takes a long, long time to significantly change course. They can change older whiskey to an extent by careful blending, they can work with younger whiskey pretty easily, and clearly they can do flavored whiskey at the drop of a hat. But to start in a whole new direction, with new stills or a whole new grain? That's small and nimble craft distilling territory and will be for quite a while.

Craft whiskeys are still young. But to some extent, they're caught in the same kind of difficulty as the big distillers. As they make better whiskey, they'll sell more whiskey. But to have enough whiskey to sell as much as your growth projections say you'll need in 5 years, you have to make a lot more whiskey today than you're selling today. You have to pay for the grain and barrels you need today with the proceeds from the sales of the much smaller amount of whiskey you made 3 years ago. Where do you find time for change? How do you put aside whiskey to age for longer periods?

One way to attack that problem is something you're already seeing: price. Craft whiskeys are almost always more expensive than comparable whiskeys from traditional distillers. A price tag of $50 for a 3-year-old craft whiskey is common, when a 4-year-old bottle of Jim Beam can be had for under $20, and a 12-year-old single malt can be bought for around $40. What's going on?

It's simple scale. Buying in tiny quantities costs more per unit. Anyone who buys ground beef at the market knows that. Simple grocery shopping also teaches you that buying better-quality food costs more, buying organic costs a lot more, and buying out-of-the-ordinary food — ostrich, papayas, farmhouse cheeses — costs even more. And that's also the case for some craft whiskeys. Their distillers are paying for a new distillery (even a small one isn't cheap), equipment, labor-intensive processes, all the legal and regulatory costs, and energy, and none of it is at a volume discount.

But higher prices also keep demand in check and give distillers some breathing room so they can get their warehouse full. If they can balance demand and supply and price, they can start aging whiskey in larger barrels for longer times.

But do they want to? Craft whiskey is finding ways to make better young whiskey, using different distilling methods, different warehousing, and different grains. More importantly, tastes may be changing. After our long love affair with ever-older whiskeys over the past 15 years, the supply is running out. Craft distillers are going to be there with different stuff to tempt us. That stuff will challenge you. It will expand our definition of whiskey. Not everyone will like it; there will be different ways to enjoy it, new cocktails, and new rituals. But in the end it comes down to whether or not you like the way it tastes. That's what it's always about. And that could be part of the future of whiskey.

ST. GEORGE

Handcrafted in California

SINGLE MALT
WHISKEY

An American original

DISTILLED FROM
BARLEY
MALT MASH

43
PERCENT
ALC. BY
VOL.

43% ALC. BY VOL

Lot No. SM013

DILUTION:

WATER, ICE, AND COCKTAILS

Let's put that old canard about drinking whiskey neat to rest. You'll be urged by whiskey aficionados to only drink your whiskey neat: no water, and *certainly* no ice. You'll read it in books — there's no end of bad whiskey advice in detective novels — and you'll see it in movies and television shows, where there's always some self-righteous old man or know-it-all young dandy telling you that the *only* way to drink a good whiskey is neat, straight, up!

"When I drink whiskey, I drink whiskey," says Barry Fitzgerald in *The Quiet Man*, "and when I drink water, I drink water." He then proceeds to toss the whiskey bottle's cork away.

But as we discussed in chapter 5, adding water to whiskey is exactly what tasting pros do! So can't you add a few drops of water to open up the nose, a splash to quell the heat, or even a glass on the side to sip: "Whiskey, water back," as the traditional bar call goes? Of course you can. If you're tasting for education or enlightenment, you'll want to go easy and incrementally, but if you're simply drinking for enjoyment, add it as you see fit. Just remember: You can only put water *into* whiskey. Taking it out makes putting the toothpaste back in the tube look easy.

Don't let yourself be bound by the personal conventions of whiskey snobs . . . unless it's their whiskey. In that case, you might want to go easy on the water and keep it down to a few drops, just to be polite. There are still some specialty whiskey bars where a heavy hand with the water in the wrong whiskey could get you ejected, or at least refused service.

But there are some cultural conventions that welcome water. Japan is in love with the highball, a joyfully refreshing dilution of blended Scotch whisky with cold soda water, knocked down to 20 percent ABV or less. I've picked up the soothing habit of Kentucky tea, a blend of two parts water to one part bourbon in a tall glass that gives the water flavor (while killing anything lurking in it) and gives the bourbon quaffing power; it's a great drink with a meal, or when you just feel like drinking bourbon as if it were beer. In the hot countries of South America, whiskey patrons — notably in Venezuela and Brazil — cheerfully quench their thirst with a tall glass of Scotch and soda, clanking with ice.

Adding ice is perhaps even more controversial; you're not just adding water, you're chilling the whiskey as well, which fills some people with unspeakable horror. "You'll chill your inner organs," as a friend of mine swears he heard a Scotsman once say with horror at the very thought. Well, it's not usually that hot in Scotland (Scotland's on the same latitude as Juneau, Alaska; no wonder they don't want ice!), but here in America, it can be sweltering.

There are just times in life when an American is going to need ice. Chilling the whiskey is what you want when it's sweltering hot and you're out on your back porch watching the kids in the pool, or tending the grill. Take a low tumbler, what's rightly called an old-fashioned glass for reasons we're going to get to shortly, put some chunks of ice in there, and douse them with whiskey.

Ah. It's like Colonel Davy Crockett said: "It makes a man warm in the winter, and cool in the summer." And a little bit of ice sure helps the cooling.

If you're going to drink good whiskey when you're in the summer heat — and I do; why drink something that's substandard just because it's hot? — you'll want to use big, hard, *cold* chunks of ice, stuff that will chill more than it dilutes, not some crushed slurry that will quickly melt. You can either buy block ice and get handy with a pick or mallet — an impressive skill, but keeping block ice around can be wearying — or get some of the extra-large sphere or cube ice molds (the Tovolo ones work well at a very affordable price). I don't hold with the whiskey stones or metal balls; you can chip your teeth on the things, and the set of stones I had picked up food odors in the freezer. Stick to ice, that's my advice.

As for drinking your whiskey neat, well, I do, a lot of times. To keep warm in the winter, for instance, or when I'm first tasting a new whiskey, or simply because the whiskey

Neat

with Water

with Ice

is one that I've found I enjoy drinking neat. You should feel as free to drink your whiskey neat as you do to add water or ice. After all, what does "neat" mean? It's defined as free from admixture or dilution. See, if you want to avoid dilution, by the time the whiskey is in the bottle you're too late. Unless you're drinking cask-strength, single-barrel whiskey, it's already been mixed and diluted. So stop shilly-shallying, and have a drink. Any way you like it. It's your whiskey, after all.

WHISKEY
IN COCKTAILS

FOR OVER 200 YEARS we've been putting whiskey in cocktails, and there's good reason: they taste good. An Irishman loves his hot whiskey, Manhattans are the standard of many a bourbon drinker (though in my opinion they work better with rye), Canadian is a shamelessly good mixer, and a stiff Scotch and soda can make a big difference in your day.

Here again, you'll want to let your own taste be your guide. As you're learning, although all whiskey is made from grain and aged in oak, there are different grains, different oaks, and different makers. There are great differences among whiskeys, and they will go together with cocktail ingredients in very different ways.

I've lined up a baker's dozen of cocktails, most of them classics and a couple that are new, or perhaps not something you'd thought of as a cocktail. We'll go through them and talk about what's in them, and why those ingredients work with the particular whiskey bartenders have chosen. I'll be telling some stories as we go, and that's all part of the cocktail experience. Take your seat at the bar, and have your tip money ready.

NOT *THAT* WHISKEY!

*Y*ou may be told by your friends not to put "good" whiskey in cocktails; bartenders may say or strongly imply the same thing. Those annoying whiskey snobs, always ruining your fun. Well, this time, I agree, mostly. I've done it a few times to see what happens, and you should feel free to as well. It's your whiskey, after all. But you should think a bit before ordering a Rob Roy made with Macallan 18-year-old, or a Van Winkle Manhattan, or — good God — Irish coffee with Jameson Gold Reserve.

Why? Think of it like cooking with wine. There's the old "don't cook with wine you wouldn't drink" advice, but that's more about flawed or corked wine, or the so-called cooking wine that's been heavily salted to make it undrinkable. When you're drinking whiskey, there's a certain level of quality you don't want to go below, and really, it's a fairly low level; as I've mentioned elsewhere, most of the truly bad whiskeys are no longer with us. But using a really fine whiskey doesn't affect the cocktail enough to make it worth the loss of savoring the whiskey by itself, or the stiff bump in price it will mean.

That goes back to my praise of "table whiskey," or the "house bottle." I keep in stock a bottle of each of the major types: a blended Scotch, a standard bourbon, a rye, an Irish, and a Canadian. Those are the bottles I reach for when it's highball time, or poker night, or when I want a casual cocktail.

In general, there's certainly something to be said for not casually tossing a rare, ancient, and wonderful bottling into anything more involved than your favorite whiskey glass. But when it comes to everyday drinking of regularly available whiskeys, no matter how "fine" or "hand-crafted," I maintain the philosophy that Wild Turkey master distiller Jimmy Russell explained to me shortly after I met him. "We don't really care how you drink our whiskey," he told me, smiling broadly, "just so long as you drink it." Cheers to that!

HOT WHISKEY

Simplicity Itself

A HOT WHISKEY IS as simple and easy as it sounds. If it weren't for the boiling water, a six-year-old could make one. Put the kettle on, and while you're waiting for it to sing, take a slice of lemon and poke a few whole cloves through the skin; you don't *have* to use the cloves, but it makes a better drink. Get out a glass — it should be a tempered one or a mug; a handle helps, because it's going to get warm. Have your Irish whiskey and sugar

ready. White sugar will do, honey is better, and demerara is more authentic, if you have it. When the water is boiling, rinse the glass with it, to take the chill off the glass. Then add a teaspoon of sugar and an ounce of boiling water, and stir until the sugar is dissolved. Add 2 ounces of whiskey — Powers, Jameson, Black Bush, Kilbeggan — and your cloved-up lemon, then pour in another ounce of boiling water. Stir once. Enjoy. Easy-peasy.

Sugar. Hot water. Whiskey. A bit of lemon. It doesn't get much simpler than that, boyo, but truth be told, it's quite a different drink from just a tot of whiskey. You're re-creating how people used to drink whiskey back before it was good enough to drink on its own, to be blunt. This was the original idea of "punch," a word that is said to come from the Hindi word "panch," meaning "five," for the number of ingredients (water, whiskey, sugar, lemon, and spice). It seems more likely to me that it derives from "puncheon," a type of cask.

The sugar and lemon accentuate the sweet malt and fruity notes of the whiskey, while the cloves' bright but intriguingly musky notes perk up the senses and blend so well with citrus. The hot water brings it all together, facilitating the melding of the flavors and aromas, and then pushes them into your senses, opening up your sinuses and the nasopharynx, the part of your throat that connects the back of the nose and the back of the mouth. If you think of how a cup of hot tea opens you up and lets you breathe for a bit when you have a cold, you'll understand how a hot whiskey gets the flavors into your senses.

It's not just for the winter, either. A hot whiskey works well as the day winds down in the summer, too. Why? It's just that good. And did I mention that it's easy?

If you want to try the hot whiskey with Scotch, it's done pretty much the same way, but it's called a Whisky Skin. Just use a piece of peel off the lemon — no cloves — and suit yourself on the whisky: try a good blend, a solid Speysider like Glenfiddich or Glenfarclas, or loft the smell of peat into the air with a tot of Talisker.

OLD-FASHIONED

From the Dawn of Cocktail Hour

THE OLD-FASHIONED IS well named. Look at the ingredients: whiskey, sugar, bitters, and a bit of water. This is a "cocktail" from the dawn of drinks history, what people were drinking in New Orleans at the turn of the nineteenth century. That's the original idea of a cocktail: liquor, some sugar to take the edge off and make it pleasant to the taste, some bitters for rounding out the bumps, and a splash of water to bring it down to comfortable drinking strength.

The old-fashioned is a familiar cocktail, and a real go-to for me. Just as Negronis are popular with some cocktail enthusiasts because of their dead-simple 1:1:1 ratio of gin/Campari/sweet vermouth, the old-fashioned is something even the most inexperienced of bartenders can be easily coached through. It's a simple recipe, but let's consider some questions first, before determining just which simple recipe we'll use.

WAS THE DRINK REALLY INVENTED AT THE PEN-DENNIS CLUB IN LOUISVILLE? They certainly serve a lot of old-fashioneds — or so I'm told; it's a private club — and they claim to be the site of its invention, but there are references to the cocktail that predate the club's founding. Given that early cocktails were exactly this sort of mixture, and bourbon and rye whiskey were around for about 100 years prior to the club's founding in 1881, it seems unlikely no one would have mixed up an old-fashioned before that.

IS IT MADE WITH RYE OR BOURBON? In Kentucky, it's almost certainly bourbon; in hip cocktail bars in New York and San Francisco, probably rye. As Canadian starts to catch on again, maybe a high-rye Canadian. Rye will spice things up, while bourbon may be too sweet for some. The important question is, how do *you* like it? I look on questions like this as an opportunity for drinking different cocktails, an activity I'm pleased to call "research," as in, "More research is needed."

IS IT MADE WITH FRUIT, OR NOT? Ah, well, there's the sticker. Of the questions that divide mixologists, this is one of the big ones. I was taught basic cocktail making back in the dark days of the early 1980s, the days of jugged sour mix. The way my boss made old-fashioneds was to put the sugar in the glass and then gun a quick squirt of club soda in there, followed by two dashes of bitters, a slice of orange, and a maraschino cherry, which he would then muddle with great abandon; the cherry would be neon-red mush, the orange would be the peel, usually in two or three pieces. Then ice, whiskey (Windsor Canadian), a quick stir, a cocktail straw, and another cherry, with stem. I don't make old-fashioneds that way anymore. I don't think anyone does, actually; the orange (or pineapple, peach, or lemon; I've seen all

called for), if it's in there, gets lightly muddled in the sugar to bring out some juice, or sometimes it's merely hung on the side as a garnish.

Here's how I make an old-fashioned, and you're welcome to fiddle with it. I put a teaspoon of sugar (plain table sugar; we keep things simple around here) in the glass, pour in a bit of water (just a splash), and add 2 dashes of Angostura bitters. I stir a bit to dissolve the sugar, then fill the glass with chunked ice, pour 2 ounces of bourbon over it, and stir once or twice. It's satisfyingly simple, solid, and tasty, and it's a cocktail even a guy like me can make.

WHISKEY SOUR

Not Like Aunt Tillie Made It

I TENDED BAR DURING grad school, and what a waste of time that was. Grad school, I mean. I can't remember the last time I ever used what I learned there, whereas tending bar led me into this career. I should've been paying more attention behind the stick!

That was back in the early 1980s, and the three most popular drinks at the bar where I worked were draft beer (Miller High Life; it was the only draft we served), highballs made with Windsor Canadian and grapefruit soda (a local anomaly), and whiskey sours. Any kind of sour, really; I also regularly made them with apricot "brandy" and rum, and one guy got Kahlua sours.

I was okay with that, because sours were easy. Grab a shaker glass and dump in a three-count of booze (I had to measure the Kahlua because it poured slow), 1 barspoon of superfine sugar, and 2 glugs of sour mix, and fill it with ice. Cap it, shake it, strain it, and drop a cherry in it: instant tip if you got it to them while the fizz was still popping off the top. The older women loved them.

Only thing was, I thought they tasted like crap. "Whiskey sour" became my codeword for cheap cocktails and the people who drank them. I'd rather have had an honest 7 & 7 than the slumming whiskey sour.

Then I dropped by to see a friend at a new restaurant he'd opened. It was the first real cocktail bar I'd ever been in: bartenders in white jackets and black bowties, slick and smooth wood bar, eye-popping selection of booze on the backbar, and some strange mechanical contraption bolted to the bar surface. I got a beer and talked to my buddy, but I was entranced by the whole scene, and kept an eye on that . . . thing.

Then someone ordered a whiskey sour, and the bartender grabbed a fresh lemon, sliced it in two, placed half on the bottom jaw of the device, and rotated the handle. It was a juice press! Lemon juice poured into the glass, and then he added the whiskey, sugar, and ice, shook it, strained it, and . . . damn, I had to have one. *He used fresh juice!*

It was a revelation. For all the terrible things mixologists have said about sour mix, I have to judge: they haven't said enough. Thick, sweet, mystery-citrus sour mix emasculates this drink. With the fresh lemon juice slamming against the whiskey's sweetness (and the sugar direct-dialing down the acidic bite just enough), it was a drink that made my mouth jump and brought that tingling tightness back at the joints of my jaw. As a Tennessean acquaintance of mine would say, "It made my glands squeeze!"

Two things: obviously, use fresh juice. And use the whiskey that works for you: bourbon's plenty authoritative, rye will amp the explosion, Canadian plays well. I probably wouldn't go for Irish, as it might get overwhelmed, or Scotch, though the right one might work for you.

Here's how I make a whiskey sour now: fill a shaker with ice. Add 2 ounces of bourbon or Canadian, the juice of half a lemon, and a teaspoon of sugar (if you use superfine sugar, you'll get that nice fizz and pop; it means a better tip, I'm telling you). Shake it for a while, and not halfheartedly, either. Strain into a chilled cocktail glass, and garnish with a maraschino cherry with a stem. If you use sour mix, I don't know you.

(Oh, and the Kahlua sours? They were horrible, iridescent, like used motor oil. But since I mentioned them, here's a bonus cocktail recipe for you: Kahlua sours, made the right way, as I learned it in Mexico and have practiced many times since. Fill a rocks glass with ice, add 2 ounces of Kahlua, and squeeze half a lime over it, *hard*. Drop in the lime shell, and stir twice. The fresh lime juice lightens and lifts the heavy sweetness of the coffee liqueur and brings out the vanilla and caramel. *Delicioso!*)

BITTERS

itters are called for in many cocktail recipes. You've probably seen the paper-wrapped bottles of Angostura bitters, and you may well frequent bars where the mixologists make their own.

What are they? Tinctures, essentially, and not difficult to make. Choose your aromatic elements — herbs, seeds, spices, bark, flowers, roots, grasses, fruit or fruit peels — clean them as necessary, and put them in a bottle with unflavored alcohol. A clean 80-proof vodka will do, though 100 proof is better — more extraction, better concentration. If you can get it, use grain alcohol (a bottle of Everclear will make a *lot* of bitters). Cap the bottle, put it in a dark cupboard, and leave it alone for a month.

Did I say bitters weren't difficult to make? Sorry, they *are* difficult to make *well*. Balancing the aromatics isn't easy, nor is choosing the right ones, but it is fun to try. I just buy them. I usually have a bottle of Angostura (clove, cinnamon, a Moxie-like scent of gentian) and a bottle of Peychaud's (anise-tilted, red fruit), and sometimes a bottle of Regan's Orange Bitters (orange zest, freshly twisted).

I'm not really good at making cocktails, which is why I love and respect good bartenders. But a couple of dashes of good bitters makes an old-fashioned a drink I can always pull off with panache. Bitters don't really flavor a drink so much as they meld it, bringing together the opposites, and putting just a nip of aromas across the top. A subtle but important component.

Bitters are also useful in other ways that may appeal to the whiskey drinker. When I was growing up in rural Pennsylvania, my Amish neighbors always kept a bottle of Angostura bitters for stomach upsets, dosing themselves with a tablespoon of a 50:50 mix of bitters and water. (The popular German *digestif* Underberg performs the same service in a handy single-serving bottle.) If I'm the designated driver, I'll ask the bartender for ginger ale or club soda with a dash of bitters. It's a tasty addition. It still feels like I have a cocktail, and a manly one at that.

Finally, if you have an intractable attack of hiccups, I swear by the old bartender's cure of a slice of lemon, sprinkled with bitters. Bite down and hold it, sucking the bitters and lemon juice out of the slice. It's worked every time for me.

SAZERAC

A Reason for Rye

ONE OF THE MOST disappointing cocktail experiences I've ever had was with a Sazerac cocktail. I ordered it in a hotel bar in Montreal, where the bartender was dressed right, had the right booze, and had a great manner. And yet as I watched, brow furrowing in perturbation, he put together sugar, Canadian whisky (an acceptable substitute for American rye, given the location), bitters, and *lemon juice*; shook it; and strained it into a cocktail glass, serving it with a twist of lemon peel. It was a whiskey sour, a fairly good one, but it wasn't a Sazerac.

After some years of asking for Sazeracs and getting a variety of bad responses — some like the aforementioned sour, some of stunned ignorance, some of "Yes, we have Sazerac rye, do you want it neat or on the rocks?" — I think we've finally gotten to the point where most cocktail bars and good restaurants will make you a good Sazerac cocktail with little urging. My little heart skipped a beat at San Francisco's House of Prime Rib last year when the response was, "Yes, sir, which rye would you like it made with?"

Because, you know . . . it's not that hard! It's pretty much a rye old-fashioned with an absinthe rinse. Here's what you do. Muddle a teaspoon of sugar with just enough water to wet it in an old-fashioned glass, give it 2 dashes of bitters (Peychaud's to be authentic and right, but you can use Angostura, or some of each) and a good 2 ounces of a better rye whiskey (Sazerac 18-year-old or the younger "Baby Saz" bottlings are great, as is Rittenhouse if you've got it), add ice, and stir.

Once you've got that built, splash about half a teaspoon of absinthe (or Herbsaint) in a second, chilled glass, swirl it around to coat the glass, and pour the excess out. Strain the built cocktail into the rinsed glass. Twist a swatch of lemon peel over the drink, and enjoy. The hardest part is the rinse, and that's just because I'm fussy about catching every bit of the glass.

Rejoice that it's easier, because it's delicious. The old-fashioned part is already good — the Peychaud's adds a zesty extra snap of anise to things — and the absinthe rinse will bring the enhancing aromas of this herbal spirit to the rye. The anise/fennel/wormwood blend goes so well with the grassy, minty, herbal aromas of rye that everything gets intensified, the kind of synergy you're looking for in a good cocktail.

It's hard to lose with the Sazerac. It's a great way to start your night, to aromatically get the juices flowing, and the ritual of the rinse helps set the mood that you're just not at home anymore. But it's simple enough that you can have one before your commute home (via train or taxi; the Sazerac packs a solid slug of liquor) and not feel underdressed.

Best of all, like an old-fashioned ordered *sans* fruit, there's nothing froufrou about it. This is a solid cocktail, a drink the pros drink, and one that will get the bartender's tacit approval. You're not messing around when you get a Sazerac.

MANHATTAN

The Chameleon

WE'RE INTO SERIOUS slugging territory here. The Manhattan is a no-nonsense, big-boy drink that demands respect. It's all booze, made with a martini-strength slug of whiskey and a good dollop of vermouth, with enough bitters splashed in to encourage the whiskey and wine to shake hands. Stirred, strained (or not; this is one you can do on the rocks if that's your pleasure), and garnished with either the traditional cherry or a more sophisticated orange twist, it sits there, eyeing you as you eye it, simmering, quivering, powerful.

And the dangerous part is that it tastes so damned good.

Whatever origin story you like, the real story with the Manhattan is how it has changed, and keeps changing, a veritable Lon Chaney of cocktails. The basic, "real" Manhattan is, as is often the case with the classics, quite simple: 2 ounces of rye, an ounce of sweet/Italian vermouth, and a couple of dashes of Angostura bitters in a mixing glass full of chunk ice; stir, strain, and garnish. The spices and sweetness of the vermouth (and

don't give in to martini thinking and skimp on it; you need the full ounce) complement the spicy, dry rye, and the bitters perk it, round it, meld it. What more would you need?

But mixologists like to fiddle with every ingredient and come up with something new — really new, not just a new name. Exchange half the vermouth for dry white vermouth, and it's a Perfect Manhattan. Replace the bitters with Amer Picon, and it's a Monahan. Switch the rye for Scotch, and it's a Rob Roy. It goes on and on; it's like a bartender isn't a mixologist till he or she has cut a notch on the Manhattan.

Some of it was evolution. There's a bar I go to just outside Boston, called Deep Ellum. I usually go for the beer (they have a great selection of lower-alcohol craft beers, my faves), but they also have a cocktail menu with almost a dozen variations on the Manhattan variants. One of the owners, Max Toste, told me the story of the Manhattan menu.

"A guy named Billy Rose taught me how to make Manhattans in 1994," he said. "His Manhattan was of its day: Maker's Mark, sweet vermouth, a big cherry, Angostura, and a barspoon of cherry juice. That's what got me into it." (I remember those Manhattans. I drank them in the mid-'90s, sweet and juicy, 180 degrees from the spicy rye Manhattans I drink today.)

"Then I found this book, *Famous New Orleans Drinks and How to Mix 'Em* [Stanley Clisby Arthur, 1937]," he said, "and it was a moment. His Manhattan is a rye Manhattan, uses Peychaud's bitters, and vermouth at 2:1. It opened my head up to the drink and made me think about how different eras looked at cocktails."

It was that era idea that caught my eye. Deep Ellum does a 1950s Manhattan: "Classic Dean Martin," Toste describes it. "Bourbon, big old dash of bitters, and a Luxardo cherry."

I had the '70s Manhattan the last time I was in. "That's my granddad's Manhattan," Toste said. "Canadian Club, 2:1 with vermouth, a dash of housemade bitters, served over ice with a twist."

The Manhattan morphed to meet changing tastes and changing availability, when rye whiskey started to go missing from American bars. It changed to meet different demands, when people wanted flavors they couldn't get in other drinks, or just a change. It changed at the whim of the mixologists, which is how we've been blessed with some great cocktail discoveries.

But it's still around, in all its forms, including the original, thanks to cocktail revivalists and the rye comeback. Celebrate that, with the Manhattan that meets your particular tastes.

THE HIGHBALL

Whiskey and . . .

THE FIRST TIME I HEARD the word "highball" was in a children's book (appropriately enough, since I was a child at the time), *Mr. Twigg's Mistake*, by the noted illustrator and author Robert Lawson. Lawson had a gift for writing books that appealed to children without talking down to them (and an absolute genius for illustration), so his books often included adults, having adult conversations.

In this case the main character's father made highballs for visiting town officials, who had come to complain about the boy's giant mole. The highballs made everyone friendly and I wondered what kind of drink they were to be so good, and so effective!

I would keep wondering for a while. *Mr. Twigg's Mistake* was written in 1947, in the American golden days of this tall, refreshing style of drink, and by the time I started drinking, 30 years later, no one near my age had any idea what I was talking about. It would take another 10 years before I got hold of a cocktail book and figured it out: a highball is simply liquor, a mixer (juice, water, club soda, or a soft drink), and ice in a tall drink. It was a leisurely drink, something you could sip or gulp, a way to stretch the enjoyment of your drink by making more of it.

There are plenty of nonwhiskey highballs — the Cuba Libre, the Moscow Mule, the humble yet perfect gin and tonic. Even the Wisconsinite's beloved Brandy Old-Fashioned Sweet is a highball with cherry juice and bitters. But let's stay on topic. The best thing about this cocktail category is that everyone gets to play. It's time for the Whiskey Roll Call!

SCOTCH! Let's have a big glass of Scotch and soda, the classic champion of hot-weather Scotch drinks. Pour a couple of ounces of blended Scotch into a tall glass, fill it with ice, and top off with club soda. (I've been drinking the Compass Box Great King Street Scotch recently, a project by this whisky blending company to bring back respect for the blends, and it's tasting great in Scotch and soda.)

This so-called cocktail is actually pretty interesting: what you get is more than what you put in, which is essentially whisky and water. You'd think you'd just get diluted whisky, not all bad when you're pacing or refreshing yourself. There's more to it, though. Of course there's the physical snap of the bubbles from the club soda, which your tongue feels as effervescent tweaks, but it also turns out that some of the carbon dioxide is converted in the mouth to tiny bursts of carbonic acid, which tweak those same nerves in your tongue as your old friend ethanol. It gives Scotch and soda a bite that Scotch and water just doesn't have. Add the extra aroma carried up from the bubbles, and you can see why this drink is so popular. Try one soon.

IRISH! Irish whiskey had been quite resistant to the idea of highballs, because an amazing amount of the stuff is polished off neat, often with a glass of beer nearby. I've only recently been able to train myself to stop saying "and a shot of Powers" whenever I order a Guinness; it had become a reflex because the combination was so good.

But the crafty sons of fun at Jameson have hit on a highball that people love: Irish and ginger ale. It actually started at a bar in Minneapolis, called The Local, where they were serving a highball made with ginger ale and Jameson that they called Big Ginger. It went over *so* big that they became the biggest Jameson account in North America . . . so big they decided to cut out the Jameson middleman and went direct to Ireland, developing their own Irish whiskey brand, 2 Gingers. After reaching a legal settlement about the drink last year — a legal settlement over a *highball*? — Jameson is pushing the drink all over the world. And you know, it is quite tasty. Ginger ale works pretty well with a lot of different whiskeys!

BOURBON! If you've ever heard of "bourbon and branch" and wondered just what "branch" was, it's water. "Branch" is a Kentucky term for a small creek flowing into a larger one. Branch water is cool and pure — if you're lucky! — and thus a good addition to whiskey. I do like adding cold water to bourbon (I might even chill the bourbon) for Kentucky tea, a 2:1 ratio that is quaffable and still tastes clearly of the whiskey. It's great with a meal, and you can pace yourself on a hot day. If you've never had it, do yourself a favor.

Today, though, the big highball with bourbon is made with cola, but it's most famously connected to another whiskey, so it's time for . . .

TENNESSEE! Jack and Coke is the call. I've been told that as much as 70 percent of Jack Daniel's is consumed with Coca-Cola or ginger ale, and I'm willing to believe it. Drop in any bar in the country, and it's almost even money that someone will be drinking a Jack and Coke.

Except, of course, that I should say Jack and cola, because my first experience with Old No. 7 was a Jack and Pepsi. It was fizzy, it was sweet — it's Pepsi! — and the vanilla-corn sweetness of the whiskey tasted a lot better to me than the syrupy Cherry Cokes the girls at work were always drinking.

It's a combination that goes way back, and it even found its way into Prohibition. H. L. Mencken's account of visiting the Scopes trial (in 1925) gives a moonshine account: "Exactly twelve minutes after reaching the village I was taken in tow by a Christian man and introduced to the favorite tipple of the Cumberland Range: half corn liquor and half Coca-Cola. It seemed a dreadful dose to me, but I found that the Dayton illuminati got it down with gusto, rubbing their tummies and rolling their eyes." They still do; they just age the liquor a while now.

RYE! When it's hot and sticky in my far southeastern corner of Pennsylvania — and Lord, does it get humid here in the summer — and I have to tend the grill (or laze about in the hammock), I don't turn to beer. Beer's good up to a point, but when the dewpoint hits 80, I look at a cold beer and start to think about death, and where its sting might be.

That's when I turn to a big tumbler, plenty of ice, a good ginger ale, and cheap rye whiskey. Whenever I cross the border into Maryland, I'll pick up a handle of Pikesville Rye, and that's my hot weather buddy. I've heard the drink called a Rye Presbyterian (the original's made with Scotch), but I just call it a Rye and Ginger. The spice of the rye, the zing of the ginger: rye is just amazing, baby. How did you old guys do without it for so long?

There's another rye drink I wanted to tell you about, if only because of its nickname. The Black Water Cocktail is another one from the fertile minds at Deep Ellum, the place I mentioned in our discussion of Manhattans. It's equal parts Old Overholt and Moxie over ice, with a generous squeeze of lemon on top. "It's *gentian soda*," Max Toste says gleefully. "It doesn't even need bitters!" Max's bartender, Dave Cagle, calls it — and this is the nickname that grabbed me — "the thinking man's Jack and Coke."

I had to try it, and you know, it's quite savory. In fact, I was moved to add more Moxie to bring it up to a more highball-like ratio. It may be the best whiskey aperitif I've ever had, come to think of it. Moxie's weird gentian assault grabs the rye by the scruff of the neck — rye whiskey, pushed around! — and drags it into your mouth like a dog on a leash, and then makes it do tricks in there, the best of which is making Moxie taste good. It doesn't work without the lemon, though; the citrus crimps the Moxie's sweetness, and without it, the drink's a sickening mess.

CANADIAN! The big quiet guy on the American whiskey scene. We drink an amazing amount of Canadian whisky, but it's largely under the radar because mixologists haven't discovered it (and mainly it's your dad who's drinking it).

Here's a funny thing: it's also the favorite booze of my son and his 20-something friends. When they found out I had a cabinet full of Canadian samples, we became fast friends, and I learned a little something about what "those kids up at college" are drinking. Too much, actually, because they drink Canadian mixed with anything that comes in a two-liter bottle. I've tried to help by buying them good ginger ale and a bottle of Crown Royal.

Because despite the bizarre drinking habits of the folks I served at the Timberline bar in Iva, Pennsylvania, back in the 1980s, who drank Canadian with grapefruit soda — except for the one woman who stipulated grapefruit juice, because "it's healthy" — I think that's the way to mix a Canadian highball: with ginger ale. As the Canadian whisky guru Davin de Kergommeaux insists, the stuff's usually chock-full of rye; serve it up like rye! I do tend to give it a squeeze of lemon to deal with Canadian's usually sweeter character. But ice it, pour it big, and let's have a party.

JAPANESE! We've already talked about this one. The Japanese highball is blended whisky and soda, the "soda-wari." They mix it, they put it in cans, they even serve it on tap in some bars, because it's huge, and people drink it by the mug. They really get the whole highball thing, pushing it down to beer-strength levels. I love that idea: whisky cocktails by the mug.

CRAFT! Really? The wonderful handcrafted whiskeys that the distillers slaved over, sang to, and did only the best things for: you're going to put them in a highball? You bet you are, because one of the biggest things going for craft whiskey is the money-making white whiskey — unaged or lightly aged spirit — and that stuff, like Mencken's Tennessee tipple, is just begging for something to turn it into a drink. Get an unpretentiously good and reasonably priced one, like Finger Lakes Distilling's Glen Thunder corn whiskey, ice down a couple of ounces, and top it up with Pepsi, Dr Pepper, or cream soda. It's darn near a blank canvas, so paint the boozy drink of your dreams.

MINT JULEP

Throw Away All That

IT'S A BIG, BEAUTIFUL glass of bourbon — really, it's 3 or 4 ounces of whiskey — in a silver cup with shaved ice and mint. If that's not a Kentucky snow cone, I don't know what is.

There were once a lot of arguments over the mint julep: whether to muddle the mint, where the drink originated, what was the original liquor, and the best way to construct one. My favorite recipe was this, from Louisville journalist and editor Henry Watterson.

"Pluck the mint gently from its bed, just as the dew of the evening is about to form on it. Select the choicer sprigs only, but do not rinse them. Prepare the simple syrup and measure out a half-tumbler of whiskey. Pour the whiskey into a well-frosted silver cup, throw the other ingredients away, and drink the whiskey."

It has an admirable directness, but once you've had a well-made julep, you'll understand why people used to be mad about them. I do muddle the mint, gently, briefly, with a full teaspoon of table sugar, in the bottom of a chilled silver julep cup (glass works, but silver's so *fine*).

Then I cheat: I use a Hamilton Beach Snowman ice shaver. A steal at 20 bucks! It's a motorized device that shaves pucks of ice pretty quickly and keeps them cold. So I shave until I have a cup full of snowy ice crystals, and then I pour in the delicious bourbon. You'll want something that can stand up to the melting ice, so even though you're pouring 3 to 4 ounces — your call — you might want to go big and bold: Knob Creek, Wild Turkey 101, or Old Forester Signature. Stir till the glass frosts up (if you've chilled it properly, that won't take long). Then top it up with ice. Stick more sprigs of mint in the top, after you've given them a quick spank to release their aroma.

If you give the drink a straw, use a pair, and cut them so they're just an inch over the lip; that way the drinker has to get his or her nose right down in the mint, and that's an essential part of the drink. The sugar takes the edge off any bitterness from the mint, and the mint enhances the character of the bourbon. I often find hints of mint in bourbon, and the herbal quality of the mint also works well with the vanilla and corn of the whiskey. It's a fun, fun drink, but watch it: a big julep is about two Manhattans.

This drink makes me laugh, and not only because it's so good. Here you've got these whiskey snobs telling you that you've got to drink it neat, and no water, and certainly no ice, yet here's one of the most traditional whiskey cocktails there is, and it's just stuffed full of ice, designed to chill the bourbon till it's smoking with cold. It is to laugh.

One cautionary tale: be sure of the source of your mint. I got to like these drinks so much that I grew a large patch of mint in our backyard, big enough to roll around in. I made mint juleps, I made mint tea, I put mint in my bourbon highballs. Then one day I was making a julep, standing at the kitchen sink, muddling with my specially bent iced tea spoon, when I looked out the window. There was our springer spaniel, Barley, furtively lifting his leg on my mint patch.

I was off juleps for over a year.

FRISCO

Thanks, David Wondrich

DAVID WONDRICH IS a cocktail writer, in the same way that Grantland Rice was a sports writer. He's a damned genius, is what he is, and he ferrets out historical details that make reading his stuff about cocktails fascinating even if you're a teetotaler, assuming you're one with a sense of humor.

He writes a column for *Whisky Advocate*, covering a different whiskey cocktail every issue. I've learned a lot about cocktails and American history from editing him. One that's become a favorite was this little beauty I'd never heard of before: the Frisco. It's simple: put 2¼ ounces of bourbon and ¾ ounce of Benedictine in a shaker with plenty of ice, and shake the bejayzus out of it. Strain into a chilled glass, and twist a shave of lemon peel over it. Done.

As will you be after more than two. That's a Manhattan's worth of bourbon there, son, and Benedictine's got a lot more zap to it than vermouth, if you're counting. But the Frisco is so beguilingly easy to drink that it tends to disappear faster than a Manhattan. The golden glow of the Benedictine's herbal magic surrounds the bourbon and smooths off the rough edges, enhancing the oak and vanilla.

I keep the formulation handy in a file on my cell phone, and when I see a bar with a bottle of Benedictine — they're not every-where, unfortunately — I'll ask the bartender if she or he wants to learn an easy new recipe. If I keep this up, I may be able to spread the good news across the country. Give me a hand.

IRISH COFFEE

From Shannon to San Francisco

IF YOU'VE EVER BEEN to the Buena Vista Cafe on Fisherman's Wharf in San Francisco, you must have had the Irish coffee the BV is famous for. It's hard to miss the connection, with the framed newspaper and magazine articles on the walls. The bartender — likely Larry Nolan, who's been making Irish coffees here for over 40 years, hundreds a day, or maybe his brother Paul, who's been here only about 30 years — will be lining up the mugs on the bar and prepping them with the requi-site two cubes of sugar for the next round. And just to hammer it home, there are rows and rows and rows of bottles of Tullamore Dew standing shelved and ready. The Buena Vista has made its name on Irish coffee, and in all the times I've been there — morning, after-noon, late night — I've never had anything else. They've perfected it, and such devotion must be recognized.

They didn't invent it, of course. That is recorded history, and it happened in the dark days of World War II. A transatlantic four-engine seaplane leaves the dock at Foynes, Ireland, aiming for Newfoundland. It heads down the cold, gray River Shannon, lifting into the sky. But the flight is a nightmare of storms and contrary winds, and the pilots make the decision to turn back. Ten hours after they left, the exhausted passengers trudge back into the terminal.

Barman Joe Sheridan sizes them up and decides that they need something more than coffee. He drops a nutritional dose of sugar in the black elixir, along with a healthy and stimulating dollop of the water of life, and floats a whipped spoonful of cream — more nutrition — on top. The Irish coffee is born, and Sheridan has made his name.

How it got to the Buena Vista is recorded as well. Pulitzer Prize–winning *San Francisco Chronicle* columnist Stanton Delaplane had an Irish coffee at the Shannon airport (this was after the days of the seaplane flights), and after his return home he talked to the owner of the Buena Vista, Jack Koeppler, about it. They decided to re-create the drink.

As Delaplane told the story, after *hours* of experimentation they captured the drink. Here's how. Start with the mug. You can buy special Irish coffee mugs these days; they're stemmed glass mugs, with a handle. Clear glass will let you see the cream float, but ceramic works, too. Pour hot water in the mug to heat it. Dump the water, and put in two sugar cubes (or 1½ teaspoons of sugar). Add 1½ ounces of Irish whiskey (or 2 ounces, depending on how cold the day is) and about 5 ounces of coffee, up to an inch below the rim. Stir.

Then carefully float a layer of whipped heavy cream on the top. This is one time you really should get heavy cream and whip it by hand; don't use the spray-can stuff. Sheridan is supposed to have said that the secret was to use cream that was a couple of days old; take that with a grain of salt. And if you don't really want to whip it, you can pour it carefully over the back of a spoon held just above the coffee. The point is, don't just stir the cream in; float it.

Does Irish coffee have to be made with Irish whiskey? You could probably substitute a gentle Scotch, like Auchentoshan or Tomintoul, but why? You can, after all, simply drop a shot of any whiskey in your coffee with no ritual at all. The fellow who taught me bartending swore by it: "Catch the buzz, stay awake to enjoy it," he told me many times as he poured Old Grand-Dad into a hot, black cup.

Irish coffee is more than that. It's an original, an icon of Ireland. And there's nothing like it when you're sitting with friends, late on an evening, telling tales of the day you've had.

RUSTY NAIL

Sweet and Solid

COCKTAILS ARE, classically, a simple mixture of spirits, sugar, bitters, and a bit of water. Too complicated for the Rusty Nail! It's liquor (blended Scotch) and liquor (Drambuie Scotch liqueur) over ice. Done. You'll have to find your own favorite ratio of ingredients. Start heavy on the Scotch side of the equation, maybe 3 parts whisky to 1 part Drambuie, and work your way toward sweet Scottish nirvana from there.

The reason the Rusty Nail is so easy is that all the hard work's already been done for you. Yes, the whisky's been made — and don't skimp on it; use a better blend to get the full potential here — but it's the Drambuie that's the star here.

Drambuie ("The Dram That Satisfies") claims to have been the private recipe of Prince Charles Edward Stuart, a.k.a. "Bonnie Prince Charlie." After the disastrous loss by the rebellious Scots at Culloden in 1746, the prince fled, pursued by English troops. John MacKinnon, *the* MacKinnon of Clan MacKinnon, helped him escape over the water to the Isle of Skye. The story is that the prince, in gratitude, gave MacKinnon the recipe for his personal blend of whisky and flavorings that became Drambuie. One hopes MacKinnon got at least a few swallows as a sample as well; he'd spend a year in jail for helping the prince.

Story aside, Drambuie's quite good stuff. It must be; after all, it's been in production since 1909, and there aren't a lot of liqueurs that have lasted that long, especially in the whiskey world. Flavored whiskeys are all the rage now, but it's a recent trend. Before Beam's Red Stag broke out, whiskey liqueurs were usually short-lived and not that popular, with the exceptions of Drambuie and Irish Mist, which have both established a small, devoted base of drinkers.

Drambuie's constituents are the subject of some mystery. All the Drambuie Liqueur Company Ltd. will say is that it is a blend of herbs, spices, and heather honey with a blended whisky. The whisky is itself a Drambuie blend; the company buys new spirit from malt and grain whisky distillers and ages it in bourbon barrels in its own warehouses (it currently has well over 50,000 barrels of aging whisky). That's the kind of thing you can do when you're independent. The company is wholly owned by the MacKinnon family (not the same MacKinnons as the originals who aided Prince Charlie) and has been since 1914.

I reviewed Drambuie not long ago for *Whisky Advocate*: "Intriguing herbal/medicinal nose, with notes of pepper, grass, dried hay, dried flowers, orange peel, and licorice. Sweet but lively and light on the palate, as the orange explodes and the whisky boldly appears, wrapped in honey and herbs. The finish is herbal and sweet as the whisky strolls off into the distance. Overall, quite complex and rewarding."

It was the first time I'd had it in years, and I realized a new respect for it. Add the Scotch for a Rusty Nail and you get more whisky flavor; if you use a nicely smoky one, like Johnnie Walker Black, you'll find it adds not just smoke, but more depth, more character, more satisfaction.

Then I tried the new Drambuie 15, made with 15-year-old Speyside malts (the first time the whisky itself has been given top billing with Drambuie), and I was very impressed. The whisky steps into the foreground, and the drink is lighter, even more herbal, and delicious. Not as much whisky is needed; I've had this 1:1 in a Rusty Nail, and it's an excellent drink. A 15-Penny Rusty Nail? No, I'd better leave making up drink names to someone else.

BLOOD AND SAND

Kinda Sticky

THE BLOOD AND SAND is one of the classic Scotch cocktails. There aren't many. The Rob Roy is really a Manhattan variation (I'd argue that the Bobby Burns is, too, but there's that dash of Benedictine; pretty cool). Still, this is the one that comes up every time someone tries to argue that Scotch just doesn't mix in a cocktail that well. "But there's the Blood and Sand," they'll say, and you have to deal with that.

Do you? The Blood and Sand strikes me as the kind of cocktail that wouldn't have survived with any real competition. I think it's mostly around because we need to have a Scotch cocktail, and it's easy to make. Why do I say that? Take a look at the recipe. It's all equal parts: ¾ ounce each of blended Scotch, fresh-squeezed orange juice, Cherry Heering, and sweet/Italian vermouth. Shake it, strain it, and garnish with a cherry. Easy. All you have to do at that point is choke it down. I say "choke it down" because in these classic proportions, the Blood and Sand is a gagger, extremely sweet, and so throttled by the cherry and orange juice that you can't even taste the whisky. What's the point?

I was deeply disappointed by the Blood and Sand, until I had the Dried-Up Blood and Sand at Emmanuelle in Philadelphia. Bar manager Phoebe Esmon heard about my disappointment and lured me down with an irresistible offer.

"I'll make you a Blood and Sand," she said, "and you won't like it. Then I'll make you ours. It's better." Esmon and partner Christian Gaal boost the Scotch to 1½ ounces (they use Famous Grouse) and dial back the juice and Cherry Heering to ½ ounce — "That's a *scant* ½ ounce of cherry, too," she said. "It takes over a drink." And they garnish it with a big curl of orange zest, not a cherry.

The difference was obvious and delicious. The first one was sticky; the "Dried Up" version was a blend of flavors that kept the mind active. The Scotch and vermouth were now solid parts of the drink, the same kind of blend as a Manhattan but with the interesting interaction with the juice and the cherry added, and now they were not dominating.

The Blood and Sand cocktail was first made to promote a 1922 Rudolph Valentino bullfighting movie. It was silent, and black and white. Movies have changed; why not

cocktails? Try the new version. As Phoebe said, "You don't really want a drink when the blood's still fresh. Wait till it's dried up a bit. Then have a drink."

PENICILLIN

Good for What Ails You

THIS IS WHAT'S CALLED a "new classic" cocktail. But some would say that if you take a close look, it's roughly a whiskey sour made with blended Scotch, honey syrup (and some ginger) instead of sugar, and a float of Islay malt on top. Not a whiskey sour, but not far off, either.

Oh, heck, it's not, and that's why it's a new classic rather than just a variation. Because with something that works this well, that whining comparison I made above sounds like, "Well, a Harley-Davidson, that's really just a bicycle with a motor on it." Yeah, but . . . no. There's a quantum leap's worth of difference.

The good thing about "new classics" is that we usually don't have to go through the detective work to figure out where they came from. The Penicillin is documented: it was created in 2005 by Sam Ross, when he was working at the Milk & Honey bar in New York City. We even know the original recipe, because Sam shared it with everyone. And here it is:

Muddle three slices of fresh ginger in a shaker glass. Add 2 ounces of blended Scotch, ¾ ounce fresh lemon juice, and ¾ ounce honey syrup (equal parts honey and hot water: stir till an equal consistency, chill), and shake with ice. Strain into an ice-filled rocks glass and float ¼ ounce of Islay single malt on top (Laphroaig 10-year-old seems to be the usual choice, but don't feel constrained; Caol Ila should be considered). Some bars get calls for these often enough that that they make up a honey-ginger syrup to save time; it still tastes great.

When you get the first whiff of this, you know why there's no garnish: There's no point. Lifting this drink is like standing downwind from the Port Ellen Maltings on Islay: *peeeeat!* Orange peel? Lemon peel? They might as well be encased in glass; you aren't going to smell them. You can't smell anything past that little ¼-ounce float.

At least, not until you start to drink, and things start to mix, and then you get the lemon, and the ginger, and you realize why this cocktail has become so popular. It's no one-trick smoky pony; it's got a lot going on, and the blend of flavors is well considered and synergistic. It really is a cure-all for the boring cocktail.

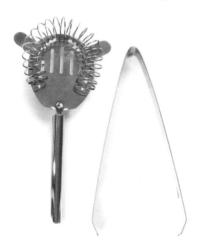

BOILERMAKER

There's Work to Be Done

THERE'S BEEN A LOT OF talk lately about "beer cocktails." I'm not against the idea *per se*; if someone can put one of my favorite drinks together with some other stuff that makes it taste even better, well, what's not to like? I've kept an open mind. I've tried plenty of beer cocktails and even invented a few that got published. One that I called Dry Season missed publication: Put ½ ounce of dry gin in a chilled red-wine glass and swirl it to coat, then add 8 ounces of chilled Saison Dupont. I thought it was worth including; my editor disagreed. Sigh.

But I don't generally hold with beer cocktails. As I said, it's not the idea, it's the execution. I have still, after a lot of tries, rarely had a beer cocktail that I'd rather have than a simple glass of the beer itself. There are two exceptions. One is the Red Eye, which pours tomato juice (or a good Bloody Mary mix) into a glass of light beer. It tastes a lot better than light beer.

The other is the drink you have before you: the boilermaker. It's a very simple beer cocktail: beer in a glass, whiskey in another. Sip the whiskey (or shoot it — it's your liver). Sip the beer. Repeat. Damn! That's a good beer cocktail!

I'm being somewhat tongue-in-cheek, of course, but as beer gets better and earns more respect with the general drinker, the workingman's boilermaker is getting more attention. Here in Philadelphia the revival started with the Citywide Special at a bar called Bob & Barbara's: a can of Pabst Blue Ribbon and a shot of Jim Beam for $3. And it did go citywide; other bars imitated it and then put their own spin on it. We can get a tallboy of Narragansett Lager and Old Crow; locally canned Sly Fox beer and Heaven Hill; or the High Beam, a Miller High Life and Jim Beam. It's not all bourbon, either: there's Pabst and Kilbeggan, and the O'Canada: Molson and Canadian Club. And of course there's always my reflexive favorite, the Guinness and Powers.

There's a reason we do this. Whiskey is good. Beer is good. Both is . . . better. The beer soothes the hot rush of the whiskey; the whiskey firms up the light flow of the beer. I like to take mine in about four sips of whiskey, alternating with multiple sips of the beer. Just remember: you're drinking for two.

It's no surprise why this is so good. Whiskey starts as beer. The grain-based beverages, father and son, Damon and Pythias, Batman and Robin. The Boilermaker and His Helper, to use an old name for the drink. That's what makes this cocktail work.

ONE MORE THING: THE FLAVORED WHISKEY RUSH

FLAVORED VODKAS ARE simply out of control. Thirty years ago the only flavored vodkas you'd see were horrible neon concoctions — cherry and lime, in the respective overly saturated colors — or the traditional bison grass or pepper-flavored infusions rarely seen outside eastern Europe. Today the shelves are full to bulging with flavors: cherry, pear, orange, apple, strawberry, tomato, whipped cream, cupcake, maple syrup, gummy bear, tea, coffee, salted caramel, and more. I just got a press release for a tobacco-flavored vodka (in traditional and menthol!).

Given the incredible success of the flavored vodkas, flavored malt beverages like Smirnoff Ice, and fruit-flavored beers, it was inevitable that someone would figure out a way to put flavors in whiskey and get away with it, despite the standards of identity. The legal dam against flavorings and adulterants has given way, and we're in a flood of flavored whiskey, the likes of which has never been seen before.

It started with honey — Wild Turkey American Honey was the first, followed by Evan Williams and Jack Daniel's — and progressed to cherry with Jim Beam's Red Stag and Evan Williams Cherry Reserve. Now we're seeing tea and cinnamon Red Stag, and Canadian Mist with peach, cinnamon, and maple flavors.

Dewar's took a hugely bold step, considering that the Scotch Whisky Association (SWA) has always had a very firm position on flavored whisky — that it's the Antichrist, essentially — and released a Dewar's Highlander Honey. It's officially labeled as a "spirit drink," but that's on the back. On the front, it's called "Dewar's Blended Scotch Whisky Infused with Natural Flavors." The SWA's objections that this dilutes the definition of Scotch whisky aside, the labeling on the front is the more accurate.

The success of these flavored whiskeys has opened the doors to this kind of flavor addition. As long as people keep buying them, and they are, in growing amounts, the distillers will keep making them, and adding even more flavors. I have samples of root beer and "Southern spiced" flavored whiskeys sitting in my sample queue right now, in aluminum bottles.

Well, is that so bad? It's hardly the Apocalypse. Just as with flavored vodkas, no one is holding a knife to your throat and forcing you to buy them. I have no problems at all finding unflavored vodka, after all. There's still more unflavored than flavored whiskey on the shelves and in the warehouses for us to buy, and there always will be.

When I approach flavored whiskeys, I try to keep Drambuie and Irish Mist in mind. This could be good, I remind myself. What I'm looking for is a genuine, natural flavor that blends well with the whiskey. On that basis I think the original cherry-infused Beam Red Stag works; the cherry flavor tastes real, like the housemade cherry-infused whiskey I remember tasting in the Pennsylvania Dutch bars back home. Similarly, the honey/whiskey mix in the Jack Daniel's Honey tastes authentically like honey and Jack Daniel's, not an artificial honey flavor shoved into the whiskey.

This may damage my reputation among whiskey geeks, who commonly express their dismay and disgust with flavored whiskey by referring to the Beam juice as "Red Gag." So be it. Truth be told, I poured some of my sample on the rocks, stirred in a few dashes of bitters and a splash of vermouth, and found it better than most of the Manhattans I've tried to make (told you I can't make cocktails). I'd rather *have* a Manhattan, to be sure, but the stuff's not all bad.

The more important consideration about flavored whiskey, as the SWA clearly fears, is whether it will somehow damage the image or reputation of whiskey in general. My first thought on that is that almost all of the people who are buying and drinking flavored whiskey were not whiskey drinkers before, and most of those are not going to become unflavored whiskey drinkers.

Some will, though, either straight or in cocktails, which begs the questions: if we're going to wring our hands over flavored whiskey, shouldn't we be wringing our hands over whiskey cocktails? What's the big difference between root beer–flavored whiskey on the rocks and a Jack and Coke? How many Jack and Coke drinkers "graduate" to sipping whiskey? More to the point, why should we really worry?

I don't think flavored whiskey is ever going to replace straight whiskey for most of us. As far as I'm concerned, if flavored whiskey sells big, that means distillers can spend more money improving my whiskey, trying new things that will make the whiskey even better. Having talked to people in the business, I can tell you most of them feel the same way.

But let me know if you see a peach-flavored Macallan 18. Because that just might be a sign of the End Times, and I want to get a drink before we go.

WHAT GOES WELL WITH WHISKEY?

Much of the literature on wine, and a growing amount of that about beer, has to do with food pairing, the synergy of the "right" wine or beer with the "right" food. We've gone well beyond the basic "red with meat, white with fish" to deciding what goes best with ceviche (a Belgian saison), egg rolls (pinot grigio), or peanut butter cups (an export stout or port; really, try it). We charge into it with gusto, trying pairs and tossing aside the mistakes, to celebrate the wins with friends who "must try this."

hiskey has largely been left out of the fun. Some of that is the occasion; we generally drink whiskey when we're relaxing before the meal, or after it, well into the night. Whiskey is often thought of as the end to a meal, rather than an accompaniment. One of the best meals I've ever had, at the late, lamented Arbutus Lodge in Cork, Ireland, started with beer and periwinkles, moved into wine and a mustard-dressed saddle of hare, and ended with coffee, petits fours, and a glass of Jameson to fill in the corners.

But a large part of the issue is whiskey's bold flavors and bracing burn of alcohol heat. Some people — most people — never get past the Wall we discussed in chapter 4, or they choose to drink their whiskey as a cocktail or highball, which is fine, but not the same thing. Whiskey is powerful in the flavor arena, but so are big red wines and imperial stouts, and they can be paired. Whiskey just requires a bit of thought, some different expectations, and an adjustment of consumption.

For instance, we think about acidity levels, tannins, and fruit when considering wine pairings; we think about bitterness, residual sugar, and fermentation aromas when considering beer pairings. With whiskey pairings, you have to consider the alcohol level, the age, the amount and type of wood influence, the weight, the peat level (if any), the sweetness, the base grain influence, and whether the whiskey needs a bit of water to bring out the full flavors.

These considerations aren't as clinical as all that sounds. When it comes to actually making a decision, it's more in the moment, a prepared seat-of-the-pants decision. You have a knowledge of the drink in question, a feel for it, and you consider how it feels in your mouth and how it presents to your nose, and you aim to pair it with a food.

It's something you'll get better at. I have; I came to Scotch whisky rather late in my career, after starting my whiskey journey in American bourbons and ryes. But recently I provided Scotch choices to a chef for a tasting we were doing together with a variety of whiskies. He came back with what were mostly good pairings, but one leaped out: a Dalmore 12-year-old accompanied by a dark chocolate crème brûlée with a candied orange garnish.

I didn't think, "Hmmm, normal strength, no peat, no issues there. Sherry casks will bring fruit and nutty character, bourbon casks mean vanilla and coconut; that all blends with the chocolate. The Dalmore spirit will bring citrus notes that the garnish will accent. It's weighty enough to stand up to the creamy richness; should be okay." No, I just looked at it and thought, "Brilliant!" It's visceral, after a point; and it was an exceptional pairing, I'm happy to add, the best of the night.

Pairing can take several directions. A whiskey can complement a food: think smoky Scotch whisky with smoked salmon, sweet bourbon meeting its mother grain in Indian pudding, or a smoothly mellow Canadian with a handful of freshly roasted nuts. These are usually the simplest, most direct pairings, and the only way they go wrong is when the whiskey or the food pushes the pairing into overload.

Another way to go is to use whiskey to cut down any overwhelming characteristics of a food. My favorite example of this is Irish whiskey and bacon. Not in a recipe, although that works well, too, but just a brunch munch of good bacon — meaty Irish rashers or crispy applewood-smoked pork belly — and a sip of Irish to complement the sweet pork and cut the fatty richness with its light spirit; some single pot still in the mix works even better with its grassy, fruity notes. Similarly, I love fresh bluefish, but it can be quite oily, and the darker meat is intensely flavored. Meet it with a solid Scotch blend, a Johnnie Walker Black or a Chivas Regal, and it settles down.

When you're pairing with food for a full meal, you'll want to go the distance. This is when I often take the highball route with a Scotch and soda or Kentucky tea (2 parts water to 1 part bourbon). As you have probably picked up by now, I'm a beer drinker as well as a whiskey drinker, and these dilutions give me the option to drink whiskey like it's beer. I still get the whiskey flavor — and the pairing, to complement or cut against the food — but it's low enough in proof that I can also quench a thirst or cleanse my palate between bites. One of the best pairings I recall was a sampling of different country hams — intense, dry, salty — with a tall glass of Kentucky tea made with 1792 Ridgemont Reserve. It would have been a very short night if I'd tried clearing and refreshing with straight bourbon, but the watered whiskey worked beautifully.

We're going to look at some pairing ideas for the various whiskey groups, and while I always encourage you to drink your whiskey the way you want to, I'm going to leave cocktails out of the pairings, except for the highballs I've already mentioned. A cocktail is already a pairing in itself, and you can go a

lot of places from there. Cocktails are great for meals, but that's a much more personal choice.

The most important thing to remember about food and whiskey pairing — and beer and wine pairings as well — is to be fearless, be bold, and not overthink your choices. After all, what's the worst that might happen? A bad pairing? It's a mistake you won't make again, and there's always another meal. Then again, you might have an experience like my friend Sam did when he took a waiter's casual recommendation of Clynelish 14-year-old with a plate of oysters on the half shell. He still gets that same look on his face when he talks about it, years later.

So be daring. Think, take an exploratory sip, and then dive in. If the water's shallower than you thought, well, that's how you learn. Be philosophical. Put the glass aside (with a cap, if you worry about oxidation). The food's fresh. Eat it, enjoy it. Then have the whiskey, and relax. Whiskey and relaxation is, I promise you, the second-best pairing you can make. The best, of course, is always whiskey and friends.

SCOTCH WHISKY

YOU CAN RARELY GO wrong with a whisky and a cuisine that have grown up together over centuries; a people rarely develop a drink that tastes terrible with what they eat every day. Witness the Bavarian brotherhood of lager beer, roasted chicken, and noodles; the French affair of wine, cheese, and bread; and the Belgian mania for funky spontaneously fermented beers with mussels.

Therefore, it's not surprising that Scotch whisky is, in general terms, a great match with lamb, fish and shellfish (smoked or not), sweets, citrus (the Scots were early and devoted producers and consumers of orange

A FEW DROPS

I was with a group of journalists at Ardbeg when I was first introduced to the pleasures of whisky in oysters. Notice: not whisky *and* oysters, but whisky *in* oysters. After our tour we were led outside, where a man was deftly shucking oysters, freshly harvested from the waters just offshore. We were magnanimously poured a dram of Ardbeg Lord of the Isles, a 25-year-old whisky that was sweet, smoky, complex, and magnificently rounded. It was wonderful with the fresh, briny richness of the oysters.

Then one of the distillery folks suggested we dribble a few drops of whisky into the oyster before tipping it up and into our mouths. What an eye-opening amazement! Right *in* the oyster, the whisky suffused the whole experience, spreading synergistically through the shell and putting peat in the sweet meat. I became addicted. The Bowmore people have been doing oyster pairings lately at such events as WhiskyFest and Tales of the Cocktail, and they encourage you to fork the oyster from the shell first, then add the whisky to the shell liquor only and shoot that; an oyster luge, they call it.

However you do it, you should try it. I'm about to go out for a dinner of oysters right now as I write this, and I'm packing a small flask of smoky Teacher's single malt from the Ardmore distillery: oysters, beware!

---

marmalade), and oatcakes, the national snack. It would be easy to produce such a list, a bottle of "Scotch whisky," and proclaim the pairing job done.

Not so fast. First, as you may know (and certainly will by the time you finish the book), Scotch whisky is no monoculture. There are light blends, sherried single malts, smoky peat monsters, austere antiques, and wine-finished exotics. Scotch whisky presents the palate with a wonderful array of choices and can present the cook or the diner with a broad set of choices. Pick your whisky, set aside a large glass of pure water for mundane drinking when you're not savoring a sip, and enjoy. Seafood, whether you've smoked it or not, loves an Islay or other peat-smoked whisky; the liquid will grab it and wrap it in a cloak of richly enticing smoke. Smoked salmon and oysters are an easy match, but simply prepared fresh seafood of almost any type marries well with peated whisky, including the smokier blends, like Black Bottle or Johnnie Walker Double Black.

If you're feeling carnivorous, I'd advise you to go to the more flavorsome, even gamey meats: beef, lamb, venison, and game birds like duck or pheasant. Prepared simply — roasted, grilled — these meats pull the caramel notes out of the malt. I think peat tends to take over this pairing to the detriment of the meat, so I lean on the unpeated side with these.

If you have a dessert choice such as the dark chocolate crème brûlée I mentioned above, things will fit together pretty well. Unless your whisky is hugely heavy in sherry or wine finish influence, or smoky as a barbecue pit, sweets should be an easy pairing. A peaty

whisky can actually work nicely with a dark chocolate that's not overly sweet. Oatcakes, digestive biscuits, sugar cookies, shortbread, and other grain-based treats pair naturally with a liquor made from grain, so experiment without fear to find your favorites.

There's also a traditional Scotch whisky-laced dessert called *cranachan*. It's toasted pinhead oatmeal, heavy cream, and raspberries soaked in honey and whisky, layered in a small dish and chilled. It's wonderful, and it's easy, and I advise you to try it soon.

If you prefer cheese at the end of a meal, you'll do well as long as you stay away from the most pungent of raw cheeses. Cheddar, Gouda, Swiss, and a favorite of mine, Hoch Ybrig, all pair up easily with Scotch whiskies; it's more a matter of determining your individual favorites. For instance, you'll notice I didn't add any blue cheeses. Some tasters insist they work well with Speyside whiskies' malt and fruit, especially for whiskies aged in sherry casks. For me they simply don't work; they end up making the whisky taste metallic and the cheese taste sweet. Obviously some

people disagree. Again, this is about *your tastes*, and the only way to determine them is to experiment.

JAPANESE WHISKY

JUST A NOTE ABOUT JAPANESE whisky here. While Japanese whisky is, indeed, different from Scotch whisky, there are unmistakable similarities. Part of the reason that malt whisky similar to Scotch has thrived in Japan is that the cuisine is complementary. It is largely grain- and fish-based, both of which are eager matches for malt whisky. Stick to those, and it's hard to go wrong, but think also of some of the accompaniments to Japanese food: ginger, soy, and miso all will cleave to the right whisky. Again, experiment, and you'll find your happy pairs.

BOURBON AND RYE

BOURBON IS PRETTY EASY (and for this chapter, anything said about bourbon goes for Tennessee whiskey, too). You can put a bourbon glaze on any of the sweeter or bland meats — pork, chicken, turkey — or on salmon, and it makes a sticky, delicious meal that boosts the flavor of the meat and the whiskey you're going to drink with it, which is perfect for food pairing. It works on tofu, too, and you can only imagine how happy I was to learn that: more flavor in tofu!

Keep it simple: ½ cup of brown sugar, ¼ cup of Dijon mustard, and 2 tablespoons of bourbon. Whisk that up, and dab it on generously. Feel free to play around with that. You can use butter instead of the mustard if you prefer; you can substitute maple syrup for the brown sugar. Add some Worcestershire sauce or ketchup, add a couple of shots of hot sauce if you want, but try it straight up first. This

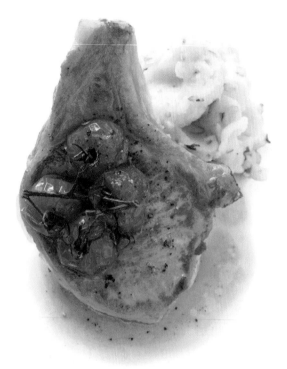

works fabulously well on ribs, but don't put it on too soon. Wait till they're almost done.

You can also keep it *really* simple and grill chicken or pork chops like Jim Beam master distiller Booker Noe used to do it. He'd get some nice, thick chops going on the grill, and just before they were done, he'd take a bottle of bourbon — he used his own Booker's brand, but it's a bit high proof for open-flame grilling for most of us! — and splash it liberally on the chops, and then he'd cover the grill for a minute. The chops get a great bourbon flavor and a little layer of char that's just delicious.

Enough cooking advice! As I mentioned earlier, pork is a slam dunk with bourbon; chicken, too. The sweetness of the meat will pair up with the whiskey and make it all luscious and juicy; happy mouth time. If you want to put some sauce on the meat, either at serving or during the final phase of cooking, sweet fruit sauces (apricot and plum especially) work great with bourbon.

Needless to say, cooking pork low and slow is perfect with bourbon; that's right, I'm talking about barbecue, cooked slow over a smoky wood fire. Pulled pork: lay some bourbon sauce in there. Ribs: cut the delicious grease with a sip of bourbon or a big pull of Kentucky tea. Burnt ends: bourbon cuts the char a bit (believe me, it knows about char). Whether you're using hickory, apple, cherry, or oak (I like a blend), that wood smoke is calling right out to the oak in the liquor. The same thing goes for smoked bacon.

Side dishes can be bourbon magnets, especially if they're a bit sweet. The mother grain, corn, is especially versatile, since it doubles as a grain and a vegetable. You can win with creamed corn, cornbread, and grits (and all the great things you can do with grits and cheese, shrimp, maple syrup). The Mexican-style *elote*, which is corn on the cob grilled (or boiled) and slathered with mayonnaise, cheese, and chili powder, is delicious with bourbon, if a bit messy.

I am not a fan of sweet potatoes, but sweetened up with brown sugar or maple syrup (another bourbon lover), they're great with the red liquor. Just about any vegetable (that isn't bitter; stay away from escarole and similar greens) will cozy up to bourbon if you add some butter and brown sugar, or some ham or bacon bits; baked beans, if you haven't figured that out already, are great, and again, you can slosh some whiskey right in there.

Desserts? Absolutely! Bourbon is one of the whiskeys you can pour right on ice cream, especially vanilla or the extra-rich French vanilla. A bourbon sauce makes bread pudding a decadent mess of hot whiskey love, and I've seen more than one dinner crowd reduced to satisfied groaning by the combination.

Now, I did say rye up above. I have not done a lot of experimentation with rye whiskey, because I tend to drink it up before the

WHISKEY DINNER

Not too long ago, my wife and I invited two other couples to our house for a whiskey dinner. The friends we invited had mentioned that they'd like to learn more about whiskey, and I was only too happy to help with that. I decided to do it in the format of a dinner because it's more convivial and more likely to generate easy conversation than a simple tasting. I like to come at things from the side sometimes, rather than take them head-on.

I wanted to introduce them to all four major whiskey types (Scotch, Irish, American, and Canadian), so I planned the menu accordingly. We started with a Highland Park 12-year-old; a bit of peat, but nothing overwhelming, and a beautifully varied range of citrus and malt flavors. I served it with water crackers, a farmhouse cheddar that had a hint of tartness to it, and a filet of salmon I'd hot-smoked over alder wood that morning; rave reviews as the cheese caught the fruit and the fish brought out that wisp of smoke a bit more. There were also some cornichons and olives, but to tell the truth, those didn't work out so well.

Next was the main course: Elijah Craig 12-year-old bourbon, with a bourbon-glazed pork tenderloin, fresh-cut corn, and bourbon sweet potatoes. The bourbon is one of my go-to bottlings: big, unabashedly sweet and barrel-wrapped with vanilla and bit of oaky spice. I served it in rocks glasses and gave the guests the option of adding cool spring water or ice on the warm summer evening.

The food reflects my philosophy on bourbon and food pairings: you can never have too much bourbon! Pork's sweetness works well anyway, and the bourbon glaze adds a caramel and burnt sugar flavor that boosts the whiskey's character.

Corn always works with bourbon; it's the mother grain, it can't miss — unless you put too much salt to it. I don't care for well-salted corn on the cob with bourbon, so when I do have that, I'll skip the salt and just do butter; Mexican-style *elote* is also good. The sweet potatoes were dead simple: boiled and mashed with pumpkin pie spices and brown sugar to taste, and ¼ cup of the Elijah Craig. Again, rave reviews, but this was a no-brainer.

Dessert was great. My wife Cathy had picked up some baklava at the market, dripping with honey. We served that gently warmed with glasses of luscious, single pot still Redbreast, and the sweet, fruity whiskey snuggled right up to the pastry. It emphasized the honey and nuts but shaved the sticky sweetness to a lighter level. Redbreast was the whiskey I got the most questions and comments on that night; the baklava didn't hurt.

Then it was time to relax, and I brought out a bowl of fresh-roasted, lightly salted cashews and some carefully poured drams of Canadian Club 30-year-old. It's rare, and I may have been cheating a bit by "introducing" Canadian whisky with such an exceptional bottling (in fact, I recall advising you against just that sort of thing). But it possesses all the qualities of the CC 20-year-old, and as more of the high-end Canadians start to slip into the U.S. market, it's a fair preview. And did I mention how well Canadian whiskies pair with high-quality roasted nuts? Richness and wood wreathing make the nuts float in the mouth, a synergistic blend that kept us munching, sipping, and talking well into the late evening.

It was a great night. Whiskey can make a dinner, and food can be a fantastic way to show off whiskey's flavor qualities. Have some fun, have some food, have some whiskey.

food gets served. But I did partake in a Knob Creek Rye–sponsored dinner in 2013, and I learned one thing: rye will go with most of the stuff bourbon does, but ease back on the sweets throttle. "Dry" and "rye" seem to rhyme for a reason. So pork belly? Great with rye. Maple-infused pork belly? Better go bourbon.

One thing that is amazing with rye, and it almost seems a cliché, is pastrami. Spice to spice, it's a complement thing; when you have a nice cut with some of the tasty fat, the rye will cut that. It's so good.

IRISH WHISKEY

BECAUSE THERE ARE ONLY a few Irish distillers, I'm going to shortcut you here. They're all good, but there's definite similarity to Scotch in some cases.

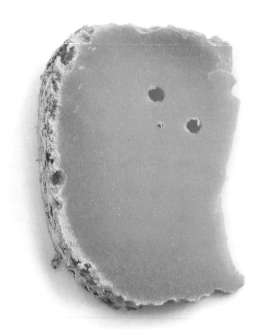

The Bushmills whiskeys are born close to Scotland, and they pair like Scotch. So go back to the Scotch whisky section and look at whatever works with unpeated malts. It all works quite well with Bushmills, and remember: Black Bush is sherried, and the 16-year-old has three woods in there, so match appropriately. I'd add that the standard bottling is quite good with cold ham, in a way I'd never think to try with Scotch.

If you've got the Cooley whiskeys in front of you, the pairings for the peated Connemara are similar to the peated Scotch whiskies; The Tyrconnell pairs like an elegant Speyside (and is genius with anything with honey in it); and Kilbeggan works a treat with trout.

It's the Tullamore and Midleton whiskeys that are different, because of the blending in of single pot still whiskeys. I find that the grassy, fruity character of those whiskeys makes them great with a large variety of cheeses, including the blues that I just can't handle with single malts. They're marvelous with older hard cheeses such as Mimolette and aged Gouda, and pair up well with the nutty flavor of Swiss cheeses, especially when there's some fruit nearby. A glass of Green Spot, some fresh brown bread, a crisp apple, and a chunk of Prima Donna make a very pleasant tasting indeed.

You'll find them equally at home with fish, especially with a milder flavored one. Place a dish of trout or halibut (or fresh cod, if you can find some) prepared with lemon and chervil, and potatoes in their jackets, beside a glass of Jameson 12-year-old. The whiskey's smooth but complex mix of malt sweetness, oak-aged roundness, and green freshness will support the fish's subtle flavor.

Irish whiskeys shine in the dessert course. Redbreast will dress up almost any type of sweet, from chocolate to lemon to simple sweet pastry. You can even serve the everyday bottlings, standard Jameson or Powers, with most desserts and know that you've got a good match going.

CANADIAN WHISKY

CANADIAN WHISKY IS a bit tougher to pair than others. Not because of how it tastes, or what Canadians eat, but because of how people generally drink Canadian whisky: with a mixer. That's how Canadian distillers have sold it, that's how Canadians and Americans drink it, and it works pretty well that way. But then you're "pairing" with something that's already been paired, and it gets odd.

For myself, as I mentioned above, I think Canadian whisky goes great with good roasted nuts. The flavors combine well, and it's even better with smoked nuts. I think it's the distinct wood character in the better Canadian whiskies, the real oak and hewn wood aromas; they pick up similar characteristics in the nuts, and I really like that.

Canadians also go very well with sweets, particularly baked goods: cakes, pies (pecan and hickory nut pies are great with a glass of Canadian), and cookies. My favorite pairing in this category are spiced cookies — gingersnaps, gingerbread, and the cinnamon-topped snickerdoodles — and nut cookies, like Russian tea cakes. The sugar is there, and it caramelizes, and the spice picks up the rye zing. You may feel odd eating cookies with whisky, but the feeling never lasts longer than the first half of the cookie.

Not to run the whisky down, but Canadian actually goes well with beer, a wide range of it. It's big enough to stand up to most beers, but not as prickly as an Islay Scotch or a brash young bourbon, so the blend is good. I remember a story from the 2008 presidential campaign where Hillary Clinton had a beer in one tavern and not long after a shot of Crown Royal; I thought she should have had them together!

COLLECTING
WHISKEY

The idea of whiskey collecting has been catching on and the prices of "collectible" whiskey at auction are rising. There are now regular auctions in New York, Edinburgh, and Hong Kong, and whiskey has become an investment property to some collectors. Auction houses learned about the money to be made by auctioning fine wine years ago (they make their money off fees and percentages), and have recently discovered that fine whiskey holds a similar interest for aficionados and collectors.

The numbers are astonishing. Consider this, from a March 2013 press release from the Whisky Trading Company, which was then raising money to purchase a pool of three thousand select rare bottles as an investment:

Whisky auction houses in the UK alone saw 14,000 bottles sold in 2012, a huge jump from just 2,000 in 2008. By 2020, this number is estimated to grow by 114 percent to 30,000 bottles. Globally 2012 saw around 75,000 bottles auctioned valued at £11 million, and this is expected to double in volume to 150,000 bottles in 2020 with values trebling to £33 million, suggesting that the trend towards premiumization will continue.

The projections seem overly optimistic about how many rare bottles there are (and that none of us will drink them). But if 14,000 bottles were auctioned in the UK in 2012, out of 75,000 auctioned in the world, that's a lot of rare whiskey being auctioned and shepherded into people's collections.

Of course, people collected whiskeys long before auctions. There are the miniature collectors, who like the little 50 ml "airline" bottles and try to collect as many different ones as possible. There are single-brand collectors who want all possible bottlings of a brand: different labels, years, ages, one-offs. There are the "dusty hunters" who cruise the aisles of liquor stores, looking for whiskeys that never sold and may still be in inventory (at the original price!); you'd be surprised at what people still find even today.

Why do people collect whiskey? There's a commonality with the people who collect coins, and cookie jars, and license plates. The right whisky has as much history and as interesting a story to tell and can be as visually appealing, given some of the labels and bottles.

Whiskey certainly has the variety that is like catnip to the collector: hundreds of different distillers (many more than just the ones that are still open), and labels, and blends, and finishes, and ages. There are anniversary bottlings, commemorative bottlings, special packages — decorative decanters, throw-back crockery jugs, elaborate metal-studded wood and leather presentation boxes, luxury crystal — even personal bottlings.

Like the best collectibles, whiskey has stability. Given a good closure, whisky can last over 100 years in an unopened bottle. A collector or investor can buy a bottle with reasonable confidence that it will be in similar condition in 10 to 20 years, a necessary assurance to create a market.

What makes whiskey even more interesting to collectors and investors is that there is a finite supply of the desirable bottlings. Only so much whiskey was distilled in any given year; a smaller amount made it into single malt bottlings (still the most desirable, though bourbons and blends are starting to get some interest); a smaller amount of those have been opened; and a smaller amount still is in unopened, undamaged bottles. And of course, every time someone gives in to the desire to actually try the stuff, there's one less bottle, which only puts the price higher.

That last point works both ways, though. While there are things that are made specifically as "collectibles," or things with minuscule intrinsic value that are fiercely collected (like stamps), whiskey is not particularly cheap, nor was it made to be collected. In fact, as several distillers have said in the face of the collecting craze, "We make it to drink!"

I've taken that to heart, and you won't find very many unopened bottles in my "collection." Whiskey writer Jim Murray refers to his collection of thousands of different whiskeys as his "library," and that's an image I embrace.

THE MOST COLLECTIBLE WHISKIES

These are the distilleries that make the whiskies collectors dream about, whether for rarity, for excellence, or for sheer character. I picked the brains of my friend Jonny McCormick, Whisky Advocate's auctions and collecting expert, to corral a few good bets for collectors. (But remember: they're bets. Please consider the risks, including the substantial one that you might just give in to temptation some night and open the bottle!)

1. The Macallan

Consistently at the top of the heap.

Bottles: The Lalique bottlings are out of range for most, but the annual Easter Elchies bottlings are a good bet.

2. Bowmore

The Black Bowmore is many a collector's white whale.

Bottles: The Black is pricy but will surely still appreciate; the older Feis Ile bottlings and the 1979 Bicentenary are steady gainers.

3. Ardbeg

Loyal fans and great whisky drive a desire for older bottlings.

Bottles: The 17-year-old is prized, pre-1984 distillations are coveted, and the Committee bottlings are almost sure things.

4. Brora

Silent, but the beauty still shines in the hearts of collectors.

Bottles: Anything, really; it's hard to go wrong with a good silent distillery, and Brora's appreciation is slowly growing.

5. Springbank

A bit eccentric; very popular with "drinking" collectors.

Bottles: The Local Barley seems to be a sleeper, and the older 21-year-olds have a special cachet.

6. Port Ellen

Rarity and heavy peat are a lure for collectors (especially when so many keep opening their bottles).

Bottles: Again, it's hard to go wrong with a silent distillery, especially when the prices of the official releases keep going up.

7. A. H. Hirsch/Michter's

The top bourbon on the list. A long-silent, beloved Pennsylvania distillery; bottles are harder and harder to find.

Bottles: The 20-year-old is rarer, but the "blue wax" 16-year-old is most sought after.

8. Any older Japanese malts

Older Japanese malts (and the aged blends) are doing very well right now as the world finally realizes just how good these whiskies are. Many of the bottlings are simply beautiful.

9. Glenfiddich

A popular malt with lots of fans, and a lot of stock for special bottlings.

Bottles: Snow Phoenix (a one-time bottling) is still appreciating, as are the older special bottlings, like the still affordable Havana Reserve.

10. Any older aged bourbons or ryes

Look for anything 15 years or more old, with Pappy Van Winkle and the Buffalo Trace Antique Collection at the fore. Prices exploded in 2013, but they're just getting started. This and Japanese are the new frontiers of collecting.

TOO VALUABLE TO SELL

I was lucky enough to be invited to the U.S. launch of the Mackinlay's Shackleton Rare Old Highland Malt, at the Explorer's Club in Manhattan. I distinguished myself by almost knocking over New Zealand's ambassador to the United States; it was quite a night. We were celebrating the release of a copycat whisky that had been created because the incredibly rare original was too valuable to consider selling.

A New Zealand archeological expedition to Antarctica in 2007 was conserving the hut of Sir Ernest Shackleton's 1907 polar expedition when they found, buried in the ice under the hut, three intact crates of whisky. Under the protocols that governments have agreed to on Antarctic research, the whisky could not be removed from the continent except for conservation or scientific purposes. One crate was taken to New Zealand, where it was carefully thawed over two weeks;

10 of the 11 bottles inside were full and intact. Three of them were taken to Whyte & Mackay's spirit laboratories in Scotland for examination by master blender Richard Paterson.

After chemical analysis and careful nosing of very small samples extracted by needle, the lineage of the whisky was determined, and Paterson began choosing similarly made modern whiskies to re-create the flavor of the original. The result was the whisky we had that night: lightly smoky, quite fruity, and refined. Fifty thousand bottles were produced, and part of the purchase price of each one went to the Antarctic Heritage Trust for conservation of early Antarctic exploration sites.

And the original case, with the three ever-so-slightly-lighter bottles reverently returned from Scotland, was taken back to Shackleton's hut, and put back in the ice.

You can take a bottle down, pour a dram — or just a taste — and enjoy it again, remind yourself of what its qualities are. But of course, once you've opened the bottle, its value on the auction circuit drops to zero.

No, to have a whiskey collection is to have bottles on the shelf that you are not opening. Some collectors will buy two bottles; one to keep, one to drink. Some will buy as many as they can afford, either to trade for other desirable bottles or to sell as the price goes up. There's been whiskey "flipping" going on over the past 5 years or so, when buyers will scoop up as much of an allotment of a rare whiskey as they can get their hands on, then turn right around and sell it at a profit to whiskey fans

A packaged bottle of Michter's Celebration bourbon retailed for $4,000 per bottle.

unfortunate enough not to be around when the bottles hit the shelves. That's not just greedy; it's often illegal — selling whiskey without a license is an offense in a number of states and countries — and it's certainly bad karma.

Distillers and bottlers drive this kind of collecting with releases of ultrarare, ultraexpensive whiskeys: the Dalmore Constellation Collection (starting at $3,200 a bottle) and one-off Richard Paterson Collection (a dozen-bottle set for $1.5 million); Glenmorangie Pride 1981 (suggested retail: $4,400); the Bowmore 1957 (sold for $160,000). Small amounts of whiskey from old casks are bottled as miniatures to maximize the money (and the number of people who can own such a prized piece of whiskey history, no doubt). The soaring prices of these rare whiskies have, it is believed, helped to pull up the price of whiskey in general, and there is no end in sight.

That's what leads to arrangements where whiskeys are bought at auction — and never leave the auction house. They are kept, safe and secure investments, until the new owner decides to sell. I'll be honest: I can't fathom such behavior. I have investments, and I can't lay my hands on them even if I want to right now, but this is whiskey. I can go to my cupboards and pick up that bottle, feel the weight of it, and open it if I so desire. Investments like these remind me of the art auctions in the 1980s, where Van Goghs and Rembrandts sold for ever-increasing amounts and never left the vaults except during the auctions. That makes me wonder about the expanding pressure of a bubble, but prices continue to climb, even through the recent recession.

It's not all bafflement and billionaires, and I don't mean to leave you with that impression. There are the good collectors, who pursue the bottles because they truly love them and want to be able to open up the doors and turn on the lights and see every possible bottling of Ardbeg, or a wall full of whiskeys from closed distilleries that there will never be more of.

THE DECOY BOTTLE

I'm not encouraging you to be selfish, but it happens all too often. A friend comes over, you offer him a whiskey, and he likes it. So you offer him something better, and he likes that, too . . . and then he wants another, and then he walks over and starts free-pouring your Pappy Van Winkle's Family Reserve 23-year-old, and he tells you, "This stuff's not bad!"

And now you'll listen to me when I tell you: you need some decoy bottles. It took me a while to figure it out, but I had a friend who loved whiskey. Any whiskey. As long as we were drinking whiskey, he really didn't care if it was Black Label or Black Bowmore. So I started making sure I always had a bottle of Black Label; not that I have a bottle of Black Bowmore, but I do have stuff I don't want to roar through half a bottle at a time.

Know your friends, and know your tolerance for pouring your collection. And consider getting some decoy bottles.

These are most often the people who will want to share and spread the love, because they are evangelists of a sort; they have had their lives changed (or at least enriched) by an experience with a whiskey, and they want to help other people have the same kind of pleasure.

These are the pleasant eccentrics. They may have tattoos of the logos or emblems of their favorite whiskey. They'll certainly have plenty of branded clothing and glassware. Their whiskey is like their team. In advanced cases the distillery will know them by name and often roll out the welcome mat for them (and may give them advance notice of release dates).

WHY COLLECT?

MAYBE YOU FEEL THAT URGE, maybe you had that amazing experience with a bottle or a dram, and you want to start to collect. Think about what you like, and about what might be reasonable. After all, if you really like something that everyone else likes, there's not as much of it to go around, and the price goes up and up. So think again, and maybe you'll think of something that's not quite as hard to find. Just be sure it's something you like to drink.

Are you going to collect to drink, taking the library approach? Aim your collection in the direction you want, but leave some leeway at the sides for additional whiskies you learn you like; a drinking collection should be a bit more broad.

Are you going to collect to invest? Take the long view, because even in the best of times for whiskey investment — which are the worst of times for the drinker! — you're going to have to take a portfolio approach and be in play for years to realize serious appreciation. And there's always the threat of a bubble that will take the prices up and up until it bursts and prices crash well below where they were. Best to diversify; whiskey is no place for retirement investing, although it does offer the option of drinking the ones that don't pay off. (Try that with stock certificates.) Stick to reputable auction houses or individuals you know; as collectible whiskey prices go up, a growing number of fakes are entering the marketplace. *Caveat emptor.*

Are you going to collect for the pleasure of collecting? I hope you're buying good drinking stock as well; the idea of all those bottles just sitting there collecting dust makes me crazy.

Don't collect everything on the Internet! The best liquor stores are great places to learn about whiskey. They offer tastings, and the people running the whiskey section are often as crazy about the stuff as you are. You'll meet other enthusiasts, exchange information, and start to build a network of friends who can lead you to more and better bottles, and likely share them, too. Remember to pay it forward; offering tastes to friends works both ways.

THE WHISKEY AUCTION

IF YOU'RE GOING TO GO to an auction, be sure you understand what you're getting into. There's a fee to register, and you'll want to invest the time to check out the whiskeys on offer before the actual sale. Preparation is important; you'll want to see the bottles beforehand if possible. Check the condition of the label, the condition of the closure, and the level of liquid in the bottle. If it's below the shoulder, the bend of the bottle to the neck, chances are it's oxidized and won't be worth drinking.

You're going to need to know what to look for, especially today. Just as it was when wine began attracting big money at auctions, whiskey is attracting forgers and fakes. Beware an overly full older bottle; it might be refilled. Look out for misspellings on labels; it's usually a sign of counterfeiting. Keep in mind that single malt bottlings were somewhat unusual before 1960.

You can often find bargains in the bundles. Auctions sell single bottles of the really collectible stuff, but they also sell "parcels" of bottles, sometimes all one distillery, sometimes regional, and sometimes just a bundle of bottles. If you take a close look at the bundle, and know what you're willing to pay, you can make out okay if you're curious and want to try some new things.

If you find something good, think about how much you can spend. Then find out how much more you'll have to spend on the auction's fees, taxes, shipping charges (which can be astronomical), and storage charges. If you're in a foreign country, find out what the customs charges are for bringing whiskey home (and how many bottles your airline will allow). Now figure out how much you can spend again, and stick to your budget. You'll be growing your collection with some stuff you won't find down at the corner liquor store.

STORING WHISKEY

WHISKEY IS STABLE, as I said earlier, but it needs as much help as it can get. The bottles keep best in the dark, in stable temperatures between 55° and 75°F (13° and 24°C). If it's too damp, the labels will get moldy; if it's too dry, the corks will crack. Speaking of the corks, whiskey is not wine! Don't keep the bottles on their sides; the higher concentration of alcohol will cause the cork to deteriorate.

If you've got a growing tasting collection, you'll want to keep the whiskey in good condition after opening it. Keep the closures in good shape (in fact, if the cork from an emptied bottle is in good shape, keep it, just in case a cork goes bad in a live bottle). Oxygen is whiskey's enemy after the bottle's opened; it will change the color, aroma, and flavor of a whiskey over time. You can protect the whiskey with the same cans of pressurized inert gas that wine drinkers use (which is what I do), or you can get some glass marbles, boil them gently for 15 minutes, and let them cool, then carefully add them to the bottles to bring the headspace up to where it was before. It works, but you have to be careful when you pour. You can also decant, slowly, into increasingly smaller bottles.

If you're going to take care of your collection, think about where you're going to put it. If it becomes extensive enough, you're eventually going to wind up with custom shelving or off-site storage (climate controlled, and they do exist; check with a wine collector). If you have an investment collection, rather than a drinking collection, you'll have to think about security and insurance if it reaches this point.

THE PRICE OF WHISKEY

THAT BRINGS US TO the money talk, which is: why does whiskey cost so much? There are some good reasons, and some not-so-good reasons, but what we really want to know is why this one bottle is so much more than another. It's a very important question to the collector, because she'll want to have *both* bottles.

Start with age. Think of whisky as a class in school. Here's the Scotch whisky that was distilled in 1980, the Class of '80, and there are 500 barrels. Eight years later 50 of them are dumped for inclusion in a blended whisky; a year later, 100 more. A year later there are still 350, but they are no longer full; whisky has been evaporating. There is the equivalent of 300 barrels left in 1990. Two years later 200 are dumped: half for single malt, half for blending. There are 100 left. Five years later, in 1997, the barrels have lost more whisky; what's left is the equivalent of 70 barrels, and 40 are dumped for single malt. In 2010 there are 30 barrels left, with about 20 barrels of whisky left in them.

Thirty years ago there were 500 barrels; now there are only 20. They are rarer, the only ones left. They are worth more with "30 years old" on the label, because people will pay more for that. They are worth more because over the 30 years between 1980 and 2010, demand has dramatically increased for Scotch whisky. If the distillery has closed or been demolished in the intervening time, more increase is added, because the barrels can never be replaced once emptied. That's one way whisky gets more expensive.

It can become even more expensive if demand for a brand increases, or tastes change. A bottling can command a higher price if it is finished in a wildly successful way in a different type of wood. It can increase in price simply by virtue of being an amazing whisky because of the barrels, the warehouse position, the quality of the malt that year.

Whisky can also become more expensive by fiat, by a decision by management to charge more. If people still buy it, it was the right decision, and if enough people buy it, a growing number, that will be reason enough to raise prices again.

The collector, though, will find a way to increase her collection. She may trade lesser bottlings for the big score, whiskeys bought cheap and now sold dear to finance a purchase. Finding a way is important when you've got a collection going.

The important thing is to keep perspective. How much of your life are you willing to give to your collection; how much joy does it bring you? What's your exit strategy? I know several people who say their collection is done; they have enough whiskey to last the rest of their lives and then some. Others intend to leave it to their children (often with detailed instructions).

I've told my family that when I die they should bury me with a bottle of table bourbon and throw a wake with every other bottle opened up and set out on the tables. Pick out what they want to keep, and whatever's left, send it home with the guests. They make the stuff to drink, after all.

Well, here we are. You've made it to the end. I hope you realize that it's just the beginning, a jump-start to years of selecting, investigating, enjoying, and tasting whiskey.

I've tried to give you a condensed version of what I've learned and discovered about whiskey in the past 35 years. It should put you well ahead on your learning curve with some useful thoughts on how to taste whiskey, a better perspective on what the different versions of whiskey around the world represent, some ideas on how to enjoy them, and the fun (and risks) of collecting them. I've also given you some of my favorite whiskey stories, some contrarian views, and a certain amount of entertaining trivia.

But before you close the door and start out on the trip that never ends, I'd like to offer you a wee *deoch an doris,* a "drink at the door," or, as we used to say in America, here's one for the road. It's a stirrup cup of more goodies to help you learn beyond this book.

WHISKEY ON THE WEB

INFORMATION ON ALMOST EVERYTHING can be found on the Internet, and whiskey is no exception. There are distiller and company sites, of course, and they're of varying value; some are quite good indeed, some are barely there. The Macallan has a nice selection of videos that provide real detail on its whisky-making process, for instance (themacallan.com), and Buffalo Trace has a good set of similar videos narrated by the man who actually makes the whiskey: master distiller Harlen Wheatley (http://buffalotrace.com). (Those two got mentioned not just because they're good but

because they both have a one-click yes/no entrance exam about being of legal drinking age, not the annoying requirement of entering your birth date.)

You can get your whiskey information more than one distillery at a time at nonaffiliated sites. Whiskey bloggers are doing it for the love, mostly, though some of them are on a semiprofessional basis. Here are a few of my favorites, and why.

CANADIAN WHISKY
www.canadianwhisky.org
A collection of information and reviews of Canadian whisky by Davin de Kergommeaux, author of *Canadian Whisky: The Portable Expert.* I can tell you from personal experience, the man's knowledge of Canadian whisky is encyclopedic, and he's happy to share.

THE CHUCK COWDERY BLOG
http://chuckcowdery.blogspot.com
Chuck Cowdery's about as blunt as the name of his blog. He lays out what he sees and knows about the American whiskey business without much fancy footwork. He's got years of experience writing about it in *Whisky Advocate* and *Whisky Magazine* and in his book *Bourbon, Straight,* and he also publishes an excellent subscription newsletter, *The Bourbon County Reader.*

MALT MADNESS, MALT MANIACS, AND WHISKYFUN.COM

www.maltmadness.com,
www.maltmaniacs.net,
and www.whiskyfun.com

Loosely related; not sure how else to put it, but there's too much information to ignore here! It's a group of people who are incredibly passionate about Scotch whisky, who disagree and argue about it, and who want nothing more than to teach you more about Scotch whisky (and have some fun while doing it). An incredible amount of good information (including whisky reviews and distillery profiles, which are linked to the excellent Interactive Whisky Map).

SKU'S RECENT EATS BLOG

http://recenteats.blogspot.com

A prolific collection of reviews, opinions, and flat-out rants about a wide variety of whiskeys from all over. It's always interesting and sometimes alarming. But what "SKU" is also doing, which is a great public service to whiskey lovers, is maintaining updated and complete lists of both whiskey blogs and all American whiskey distillers and brands, from Jack Daniel's to the smallest bottler. He's driven, and we all benefit.

WHISKY ADVOCATE BLOG

http://whiskyadvocateblog.com

The blog of *Whisky Advocate* magazine, where I'm the managing editor. You get a lot of reviews and commentary from the editor, John Hansell, who's been at this for well over 20 years and has connections into the highest and lowest levels of the business. There are also hundreds of reviews of all types of whiskeys.

WHISKYCAST

http://whiskycast.com

Mark Gillespie talking to whiskey people. And Mark Gillespie rating whiskeys of every type. He takes every chance to do both, and his recordings are very high quality. This is a chance to see and hear the people who make the whiskey. And what else were you really doing over your lunch hour anyway?

WHISKEY BY THE GLASS

I WAS ASKED TO DO ABOUT 40 reviews for the book *1001 Whiskies You Must Taste before You Die* by the editor, Dominic Roskrow. I had most of the whiskeys in my cabinet and was able to request samples from the distillers on a few others. But there were three I didn't have, and their makers didn't either. I didn't worry; I just hopped on the train and went down to Village Whiskey, the whiskey bar in Philadelphia, and ordered a glass of each. It wasn't cheap, but there they were.

Plenty of bars have a half-decent selection of whiskey these days. It's part of the growing appreciation for whiskey; more people ask, more bar managers and bartenders are aware, and the next thing you know, your local has a Classic Malts display, some Four Roses Single Barrel, and a bottle of Redbreast. Life is good. But there are an increasing number of whiskey specialty bars. There's Bourbon's Bistro in Louisville, Delilah's in Chicago, d.b.a. in Manhattan (and New Orleans), Rickhouse in San Francisco, Jack Rose in Washington, Char No. 4 in Brooklyn, the stunning Dundee Dell in Omaha, and many, many more. Just yesterday I was in Kybecca, a wine bar in Fredericksburg, Virginia, that had opened an adjacent whiskey room only a few months before, and they already had over 50 whiskeys of a variety of types (I had a Yamazaki 12-year-old in celebration of its merely being there).

It started in the centers of whiskey: Scotland, Ireland (behind the curve, but catching up), Kentucky, and Japan. But you'll also find whiskey bars in centers of finance and power: New York, London, Toronto, Washington, D.C.; in centers of culture and fine dining: Paris, San Francisco; and, well, other places, like Omaha, Prague, and Philadelphia.

Unfortunately, whiskey doesn't yet have a resource like BeerAdvocate.com, where you can find thousands of specialty beer bars, searchable by area, with ratings and mapped directions. *Whisky Magazine*'s website (www. whiskymag.com) does have a section for finding whiskey bars, but because things are booming so much right now, it's hard to keep up; similar issues limit the list at the WhiskyCast site (http://whiskycast.com; see above).

As a former librarian, I suggest using Google like this: *[type name of city here] "whisky bars"* and be sure to include the quotes around "whisky bars"; it forces Google to look for them in that order. Use "whiskey" or "whisky" as appropriate for the country you're searching for.

That will actually yield reasonably good results, which can lead you directly to Step Two of the Finding Good Whiskey Bars program. Try one of the whiskey bars from your Google search, one that's well reviewed and shows a good menu (a low number of misspellings, whiskeys in the right classification and region). Then comes the fun part: talk to people who are also drinking whiskey, or the bartenders, about where else in town they drink whiskey.

That may seem rude, or not likely to yield a great result, but you'll soon learn that when you're truly a whiskey aficionado, you have more loyalty to the whiskey than to the venue. Smart bar managers realize that sharing knowledge is a positive strategy; when

there are more good whiskey bars, there is more good whiskey business, because we tend to talk about whiskey, and spread the whiskey gospel, and that means more people thinking and drinking whiskey. So strike up a conversation.

MAKING FRIENDS

YOU COULD ALSO SKIP STEP ONE, the Google search, and go directly to Step Two in your other whiskey resource: your favorite liquor store. Find the local store with the biggest selection of whiskey, a really deep one, and I guarantee you that the whiskey expert at the store will be able to tell you where the best whiskey bars are. Of course, at the really great whiskey stores, you may be able to sample right there — don't abuse the privilege! — which is the whole idea, right? Tasting to see what you want to buy and take home and taste?

Not quite. Remember, this is about tasting whiskey, and learning about it, and as I've already said, tasting it with other people is the best way, the most enjoyable. There are benefits to whiskey bars (and samplings at stores) that you won't get at home, like perspective, like comparison, like the benefit of someone else's experience. Just as a fencer doesn't get better by fencing beginners, you won't learn by tasting with people who know no more than you do.

The best way to do that is to find (or start!) a whiskey-tasting club. Again, ask at the store (they'll often sponsor or run one), or hit the web, or just find four or five whiskey lovers and start one. It's a great way to learn about whiskey, and a great way to share what you have and taste what someone else might have. As the distillers say about collecting, they make the stuff to drink.

You can also join a more formal tasting club: the Scotch Malt Whisky Society (there are chapters for a variety of countries; check the home website at http://smws.com). They're a combination club and independent bottler. Membership gets you their very special single-cask bottlings and access to member benefits like distillery travel deals, tastings in "partner bars," access to the society's headquarters in Edinburgh, and the magazine.

There are no rules about whiskey clubs, just that they're about whiskey. They can be as simple as five friends getting together every so often to share whiskeys; they can be as elaborate as uniform shirts and organized holiday dinners for 50-plus members. Whatever suits your desires and purposes. But it can be a lot of fun. There's something invigorating about being around people who are just as interested in whiskey as you are; we're still a relatively tiny group, and it's good to know that there are more of us out there.

That's the feel you'll get at a whiskey festival. I was at one of the very first: WhiskyFest New York, 1998. Hundreds of people in a ballroom in New York, served whiskeys by the master distillers and brand managers, the people who know the most about them. It was an eye-opening experience, and it's only gotten better. More festivals have cropped up; they are held around the world now.

The price quite often seems high, until you consider what you're getting. You'll have the chance to sample from literally hundreds of different whiskeys, poured by people who are eager and able to tell you lots of information about them; the chance to mingle with folks who are just as excited about this as you are; and the opportunity to make friends and expand one another's knowledge. It's a fantastic time.

BIRTHPLACE

WHISKEY FESTIVALS CAN ONLY be equaled by going directly to where the stuff's made. Touring distilleries puts it all together. I drank

Scotch whisky for years before I stepped into my first Scottish distillery, and I remember the way things I'd never really understood suddenly locked into place in my head. The sights, the sounds, the people, and, perhaps most importantly for me, the smells are all wonderfully exciting additions of knowledge you can get *only* by visiting a distillery.

These are popular tourist sites: The Midleton distillery gets 150,000 visitors a year, and the Jameson "experience" at the old Dublin distillery gets another 250,000. Even the distilleries out on remote Islay get tens of thousands of visitors.

There are organizations to help get you on your way. The Malt Whisky Trail will take you to eight Speyside distilleries and the Speyside Cooperage (www.maltwhiskytrail .com). Rather go peaty? Islay is waiting at their official website, and they know how many people want to see their distilleries (http://islayinfo.com). The Ireland Whiskey Trail is relatively new but makes up for it by offering a guide to Ireland's whiskey pubs and whiskey museums as well as tours of the distilleries (www.irelandwhiskeytrail.com). The Kentucky Bourbon Trail's ready to welcome you to Bluegrass Country (http://kybourbontrail.com), and Bourbon Country offers more information about whiskey bars and restaurants (www.bourboncountry.com).

The organizations don't cover all the distillers, though. If one you'd like to visit isn't on their lists, find more information through the distillery's own website; almost all the distilleries offer tours these days. The craft distillers are especially great about it; they know it's their best way of making friends.

If you can swing it, visiting a distillery is the single most important thing you can do toward furthering your understanding of whiskey. You'll see it, hear it, smell it, feel it in a way you just can't do by reading about it.

FINAL TOAST

Thanks for joining me. I've enjoyed writing this; the memories it stirred were fantastic. Which brings to mind, as promised, one last story.

I was visiting the Glenlivet distillery recently and talked to Ian Logan, the global brand ambassador. An affable guy, a big man, and cheerful; he knows a terrific amount about the whisky, the distillery, and the industry. We were done walking about the place and were standing there in the new stillhouse, which has these fantastic floor-to-ceiling glass walls looking across the valley where this whisky's been made for 200 years, legally and nonlegally.

We were doing that guy thing, just enjoying the moment without saying a word. I don't know what Ian was thinking about, but I was relaxed in being where a major landmark in Scotch whisky history took place, and still was taking place.

Then I asked him, thinking ahead to writing this book, thinking about just this place in it: "Would it be possible for a person to taste a whisky without knowing any of this? Not knowing where it was from, or who made it? Not knowing what went into it, how it was made, what made it that whisky, not even knowing the name? Would you get much out of it?"

He answered pretty quickly. "Oh, aye. You could, the whisky's that good." He paused, then looked out across the valley again. "But why would you want to?"

That sums up for me — why there are whiskey books, whiskey magazines, whiskey blogs and podcasts, whiskey festivals, whiskey tours. You could just drink whiskey, go through your whole life without learning more, and you know, you'd probably have a good life. But it takes only a little more to really enjoy it, because it's true what folks say: The more you know, the better it tastes.

Kermit Lynch, the wine importer and writer, has been known to have some strong opinions. One of them is that blind tasting is to wine (let's substitute whiskey) as strip poker is to love. I read an interview with him years ago — unfortunately I cannot find the exact text, though I had it taped to the wall by my desk for quite a while, until I moved and misplaced it — where he said that you should pick a wine and learn everything you can about it: where it was made and what the countryside is like, and taste the grapes, and ask who made it and how, what they're like and what other wines they make, and how long wine's been made there, and what the other wines in the area are like . . . and then you will know that wine, and what it tastes like, better than you ever can by simply drinking a glass of juice.

You could just drink whiskey. But why would you want to? Continue to learn, and taste your whiskey to the fullest. Cheers!

ACKNOWLEDGMENTS

This is my first book on whiskey. I've got a number of beer books to my credit, so writing a book didn't throw me. But it wasn't until I undertook writing a whiskey book that I realized how little — and yet how much! — I knew about whiskey. It's been an experience, and the people I've met were there when I needed to ask more questions.

Naturally, I didn't get here on my own. There are three people who got me here more than any other. John Hansell was the guy who made me drink whiskey in order to keep my job — imagine that — and created the magazine that gave me the job in the first place. The late Michael Jackson opened the category; there were whiskey writers before, but he popularized it, and did it so very well, and was good enough to give me lots of advice. And John Holl was good enough to think of me when his editor at Storey asked him if he knew anyone who might be able to write a whiskey book for them.

Then there are the writers and drinkers and mixologists I learned from, and discussed with, and drank a bit with. Foremost are Dave Broom and Chuck Cowdery, both of whom led me to insights on whiskey. But I also owe thanks to Jonny McCormick (who gets a special thanks for his huge help with the collector's sidebar), Mike Veach, Jim Anderson (for the hospitality and fun we had at the Anderson in Fortrose), David Wondrich (who gave me more confidence in mixing my own cocktails; I'm getting better), Davin de Kergommeaux (the best friend Canadian whisky ever had), Gaz Regan (bless your bushy face, sir), Phoebe Esmon, Gavin Smith, Fred Minnick, Max "Manhattans" Toste, Jim Murray, and Gary Gilman, possibly the greatest amateur drinks writer around.

I was helped immeasurably by the folks in the industry, and it's a long list that I know is incomplete: Jimmy and Eddie Russell at Wild Turkey; Parker and Craig Beam, Max Shapira, Larry Kass, and Josh Hafer at Heaven Hill; Chris Morris and the late Lincoln Henderson (miss you, you angry wonderful guy) at Brown-Forman; and at Buffalo Trace, Harlen Wheatley, Mark Brown, Kris Comstock, the incredible public relations team, and the late Elmer T. Lee, Ronnie Eddins, and Truman Cox — I'm so sad to know you won't be reading this. Thanks as well to my man Fred Noe at Beam, Greg Davis and Bill Samuels Jr. at Maker's Mark, and Jeff Arnett at Jack Daniel, as well as Tom Bulleit and Dave Scheurich, who is, I believe, the funniest man in the bourbon business.

The Scotch whisky industry helped me in my ignorance; I've learned a lot about Scotch whisky in the past 15 years, largely thanks to folks like George Grant at Glenfarclas, Dr. Bill Lumsden at Glenmorangie, Ian Logan at Glenlivet (thanks for a great philosophical moment), Richard Paterson at Dalmore (who taught my son a couple things about Scotch whisky as well), Willie Tait at Jura (who says I'm a great girl's blouse), Jim McEwan of Bruichladdich, Eddie McAffer and Rachel Barrie at Bowmore, Diageo's Dr. Nick Morgan, Rosemary Gallagher from the Scotch Whisky Association, and Highland Park's superwoman, Steph Ridgway, who pinned me.

In Ireland, it's a small list, but just as important. I'm indebted to Dave Quinn, who took the time to meet me at his brother's bar in Philadelphia (For Pete's Sake, and you should visit) to teach me about the Jameson range, to Fergus Carey . . . for a *lot* of things, but here it's for giving me my first sip of Redbreast, to Barry Crockett for making fantastic whiskey, to John Teeling for a great interview, to Ger Buckley for explaining coopering so it made sense, and to Colum Egan for a great laugh at WhiskyFest.

Canadian whisky is a short list too. Dr. Don Livermore taught me an amazing amount in just a few hours at the Hiram Walker plant, Jan Westcott got me in where I needed to be (though rarely by the most direct route), and Dan Tullio . . . well, hey, Dan makes Canadian cool. I'll tuck in Japanese whisky here: many thanks to Mike Miyamoto of Suntory for a great "Yamazaki Time."

Craft whiskey is impossible to cover, there are so many people. The standouts are Fritz Maytag, Bruce Joseph, and David King at Anchor, true pioneers along with Steve McCarthy at Clear Creek; Darek Bell at Corsair and Chip Tate at Balcones (always with the new ideas, those two); Dave Pickerell, who brought solid experience over from the mainstream to cross-fertilize with craft's mad innovation; David Perkins at High West, who has an amazing ability to keep things on an even keel; and my local hero, Herman Mihalich, who makes Dad's Hat Rye from the grain I drive past on my way to work . . . which is pretty cool. A special shout out to Scott Spolverino, an underappreciated distilling chemist who's destined for good things.

Now, some special thanks. My uncle Don Harnish was the person in my family who showed me that it was okay to drink, and really okay to drink whiskey. Thanks, Don, it's an important lesson. Mike Burkholder, who gave me my first Jack and Pepsi — Mike, look me up, I owe you a drink! My boon companion, Sam Komlenic, who proofed this manuscript with a whiskey lover's eye, and bucked me up during some dark moments — Sam, you're the best. My agent, Marilyn Allen, found *me* by looking at my picture and thinking, "He looks like a good guy to do a whiskey book." I'm glad you reached out when you did, Marilyn; it's been great. My editors at Storey, Margaret Sutherland and Nancy Ringer, who were ever so supportive, and more than patient when I ran over deadline (mind you, ladies, I *nailed* the editing deadlines!). The staff at *Whisky Advocate*: Melanie, Kathy, Joan, and Amy are the best friends a guy could have at a job. They didn't help with the book, which was an independent project, but they were very supportive, every day. Thanks!

Finally, my family. I want to thank my mother, Ruth, and my late father, Lew, for their support of a son who wanted to make a living out of writing about booze (which some of the family still doesn't mention). My wife's whole family has always been very supportive; now if I could just get more of them to drink whiskey . . . these samples won't drink themselves! My kids, Thomas and Nora, who are now not just my supporters, they're my critics, and fair ones (and Thomas is drinking good whiskey, too!).

My wife, Cathy, knows this is coming, but I'll say it as I always do: I couldn't do it without you. Thanks for 25 years of unwavering support. I'm glad you never insisted that I get a real job; this one's become more than real enough.

And to all my readers, my Twitter followers, my Facebook friends, the people who say such great things, and keep me honest as well: *Cheers!*

GLOSSARY

ABV. Alcohol by volume, the amount of alcohol in a spirit (or beer) as a percentage of the total volume. This number is doubled to yield the "proof" of the spirit.

ALDEHYDES. A group of aromatic compounds found in oak, with a floral or fruity character.

ANGEL'S SHARE. The volume of whiskey that is lost during the aging process by evaporation through the barrel.

BACKSET. See **setback.**

BARLEY. A grain that is relatively easy to malt, with abundant enzymes for converting starches into sugars and a husk that acts as a natural filter; thus well-adapted for brewing and distilling.

BARREL. In whiskey making, a container built from curved oak staves, usually charred, that imparts flavor and color to the spirit through chemical changes from contact with the wood and slow evaporation. In American usage the standard size is 53 gallons (200 liters), though craft distillers commonly use smaller barrels. See also **cask.**

BEER. The fermented, undistilled liquid that is the first step in making whiskey. See also **wash.**

BEER STILL. A single column still used for first distillation in making modern bourbon and rye whiskey. Also called a "stripping column."

BLENDED SCOTCH WHISKY. A blend of one or more single malt Scotch whiskies with one or more single grain Scotch whiskies. This is the familiar category of whisky that includes well-known brands like Johnnie Walker, Dewar's, and Chivas Regal.

BLENDED WHISKEY. In American usage a blend of straight whiskey and grain neutral spirits; it must be at least 20 percent straight whiskey. And no, that's not a lot.

BOURBON. American whiskey made predominantly of corn (51 percent or more), malt, and either rye or wheat; distilled to a maximum of 80 percent ABV and aged in new charred oak barrels at an entry proof of no more than 62.5 percent ABV; bottled at a minimum 40 percent ABV.

CARAMEL. Cooked and browned sugar; allowed as a coloring agent in European and Canadian whisky but not allowed in bourbon or rye whiskey.

CASK. "Cask" is the word used more often in Scotland and Ireland as the generic term for barrel. See also **barrel.**

CHAR. The thin layer of burnt wood on the inside of a barrel that has been treated with flame. Required for bourbon and other American whiskeys.

COFFEY STILL. A still in the form of two columns that takes in a continuous flow of wash or beer, passing it over a series of plates as steam rises through the liquid, heating and "stripping" the alcohol out of the liquid, to be condensed and captured as spirit. Also known as a continuous still.

COLUMN STILL. See **beer still.**

COOPER. A person who makes, repairs, or resizes barrels.

CORN. A grain native to the Americas; not easy to malt, but an inexpensive, flavorful source of sugars for fermentation and distillation. The major component in bourbon.

CORN WHISKEY. Whiskey made from a large proportion of corn in the mash, and most often aged for only a short period in either uncharred or used oak barrels.

CUTS. The points in a pot still distillation where the stream of spirit is diverted. The first cut is after the foreshots or heads have run; the second is when the feints or tails begin to run. The cuts are made to get the maximum amount of clean spirit. The heads and tails are often redistilled to recover all the alcohol.

DISTILLATION. The extraction and concentration of alcohol from a fermented grain liquid (see **wash** or **beer**) by use of controlled heat. Ethyl alcohol — ethanol — evaporates at a lower temperature than water, and the alcohol-rich vapor is condensed and separated from the remaining water and other chemicals.

DOUBLER. A simple pot still used by bourbon distillers to polish the spirit from the beer still.

DRAFF. The leftover grains from the fermentation and distilling process, most often used for cattle feed; there is a move to use it for biogas generation recently. Also called "spent grains" or "dark grains."

DRYHOUSE. Where the spent grains from American-style mashing distillation go to be dried and processed for animal feed.

DUNNAGE. A traditional type of warehouse in Scotland, with earthen floors.

ESTER. An aromatic chemical compound derived from aldehydes; can yield fruity, spicy, or smoky aromas.

EXTRACTIVE DISTILLATION. A technique in which water is added to high-proof spirit to float unwanted compounds off the top, leaving a pure spirit. Used by some Canadian distillers.

FEINTS. Final runnings from a pot still distillation. See also **cuts.**

FIRST-FILL. When barrels previously used for aging bourbon or wines are used for aging whiskey, "first-fill" refers to the ones that are being used for the first time, just after being emptied of the bourbon or wine. These yield whiskey with much more character of the younger wood and previous liquid.

FLAVORING WHISKY. The lower-proof, higher-flavor component of Canadian whisky.

FORESHOTS. First runnings from a pot still distillation. See also **cuts.**

GRAIN NEUTRAL SPIRITS. Unaged spirit distilled to 95 percent ABV. It may be bottled at that strength or diluted down to 40 percent.

GRAIN WHISKY. Whisky distilled to a very high proof, up to 94.6 percent, using a column or Coffey still, and aged in oak barrels for blending.

HEADS. See **foreshots.**

HOGSHEAD. A cask of 250 liters capacity, often built from used bourbon barrel staves for aging Scotch whisky. Also called a "hoggie."

LINCOLN COUNTY PROCESS. See **Tennessee whiskey.**

LYNE ARM. The bend and tube coming off the top of a pot still. The angle of the arm — downward, straight, upward — helps determine the amount of reflux a still develops, and thus the weight of the spirit produced.

MALT. As a verb *malt* means the process of germinating grain to convert insoluble starches to soluble starches and develop the enzymes needed to convert those starches to sugars. As a noun it denotes barley that has gone through this process.

MALTINGS. A facility where grains are malted; they are wetted, allowed to sprout, and then kilned to kill the sprout.

MASH. As a verb *mash* means heating a mixture of grains and water to allow the enzymes to convert starches to sugars. As a noun it describes the mixture of water and grains, especially after the conversion occurs.

MASHBILL. The "recipe" of American whiskeys; the ratios of the different grains that go into making a particular whiskey or group of whiskeys.

MINGLING. Blending together barrels of whiskey and allowing them to sit briefly together (a couple of days to a few months), to allow the different barrels to "marry" and become a harmonious whole.

MOONSHINE. Illegally produced whiskey, whether aged or unaged, though usually unaged. Unaged legal whiskey is *not* moonshine.

NEUTRAL WHISKY. The Canadian term for grain whisky. See also **grain whisky.**

NEW MAKE. Unaged spirit, right off final distillation. Also known as "white dog" or "clearic."

PEAT. Partially carbonized vegetation that has slowly rotted and compressed in bogs and swamps over centuries and millennia; boggy plants that are on their way to becoming coal. When burned, peat creates an aromatic smoke that is used to kiln and flavor freshly germinated malt; when the malt is mashed, fermented, and distilled, it creates a spirit with the smoky aromas and flavors highly prized in Scotch whisky. Peat from different areas gives different aroma profiles because of the varieties of plant life from place to place.

PHENOLS. Aromatic chemical compounds with a smoky or chemical aroma.

PORT. A fortified wine from Portugal; port casks (pipes) are used to age whiskey.

POT STILL. A batch-type still; essentially a large copper pot with a tapering column on the top that leads to a lyne arm and a condenser.

PROOF. See **ABV.**

REFILL. When first-fill barrels are emptied and refilled, they are called "refill" barrels. They yield whiskey with less of the wood's character and more of the distillery character.

REFLUX. A redistillation that occurs within the initial distillation; spirit falls back into the still before escaping to the condensers. Increase the reflux by a taller still or an upward-angled lyne arm, and a lighter, cleaner spirit is the result. Decrease the reflux with a squat still, or downward-pointing lyne arm, and a heavier, "meaty" spirit is the result.

RICKHOUSE. Warehouse as used in America, with arrays of wooden rails — "ricks" — to hold rows of barrels in place. They vary in size, with the biggest holding upward of 50,000 barrels.

RYE. Hardy grass that yields a richly flavored, somewhat bitter grain used in American and Canadian whiskeys.

SCOTCH WHISKY. Whisky distilled in Scotland from malted barley (and other grains, in the case of blends and grain whisky) to no more than 94.8 percent ABV; aged in Scotland in oak casks for a minimum of 3 years and bottled at a minimum of 40 percent ABV. Caramel may be added (for consistency of color).

SETBACK. The soured grains and liquid left over after column distillation, used for the sour mash process. Also called "backset" or "stillage."

SHERRY. Fortified wine from Spain; sherry casks (butts) are used to age whiskey.

SINGLE MALT. Whisky made from 100 percent malted barley, in pot stills, from one distillery.

SMALL GRAINS. The grains other than corn in a bourbon mashbill; usually malt plus either rye or wheat.

SOUR MASH. The American practice of adding the soured, spent grains and liquid from previous distillation to the newly mashed beer at the start of fermentation. This creates a more beneficial environment for fermentation (with acidic balance and yeast nutrients). All major American whiskeys use the sour mash process.

SPIRIT STILL. The still (or stills) used for the second distillation in making Scotch whisky; the output from the wash still is distilled again in the smaller spirit still.

STILLAGE. See **setback.**

STRAIGHT WHISKEY. American whiskey that has been distilled from grain to a final proof of less than 95 percent ABV, at a single distillery, and aged in oak barrels for not less than 2 years; these are minimum requirements that are most often exceeded in practice.

TAILS. See **feints.**

TENNESSEE WHISKEY. Tennessee whiskey is bourbon, except that before it is put in the barrel to age, it is filtered ("mellowed") through 10 feet of sugar maple charcoal, a step known as the Lincoln County process.

THUMPER. An alternative to a doubler, in which the vapors from the beer still are put through hot water before condensing. The condensation and bubbling causes a thumping sound, hence the name.

VATTED MALT. Former term for a blend of single malt whiskies without any grain whisky added. Now known as "blended malt Scotch whisky."

WASH. The fermented, undistilled liquid that is the first step in making whisky; this is the commonly used term in Scotch whisky making, while the Irish and Americans mostly use the term "beer."

WASH STILL. The still (or stills) used for the first distillation in making Scotch whisky; the fermented wash is put in the larger wash still. The product of this distillation is known as "low wines" and goes into the spirit still.

WASHBACK. The fermenting vessel in Scotch whisky making.

WORTS. The runoff from mashed and converted malt in Scotch whisky; full of malt sugars and ready to ferment and become wash.

YEAST. The marvelous little fungus that eats sugar and excretes alcohol and aromatics; the engine of fermentation, the necessary and natural precursor to distillation.

INDEX

Page numbers in *italic* indicate photos or illustrations; page numbers in **bold** indicate charts or graphs.

INTERIOR PHOTOGRAPHY CREDITS

© AA World Travel Library/Alamy, 132; © All Canada Photos/Alamy, 167;
© Antonio Munoz Palomares/Alamy, 207, 214 (left); © Attitude/Shutterstock,
fabric texture backgrounds (throughout); © Balcones Distillery, Laura Merians,
103, 179; © Bert Hoferichter/Alamy, 165; © Blaine Harrington III/Alamy, 47;
© Bon Appétit/Alamy, 221; © BWAC Images/Alamy, 69; © Cephas Picture
Library/Alamy, 135, 138, 150; © Chris George/Alamy, 158; © Chris Willson/
Alamy, 174 (bottom); © Corsair Artisan Distillery, Anthony Matula, 190;
© Daniel Dempster Photography/Alamy, 94, 149, 152, 159; © David Gowans/
Alamy, 115; © David Lyons/Alamy, 117; © David Osborn/Alamy, 88; © David
Robertson/Alamy, 30; © Denis Kuvaev/Shutterstock, parchment texture back-
grounds (throughout); © dk/Alamy, 224; © Dorin_S/iStockphoto.com, 168;
© Finger Lakes Distilling, 186; © foodcollection.com/Alamy, 222; © Gavran
333/Shutterstock, 208 (left); © graficart.net/Alamy, 11; © Hemis/Alamy, 25;
© Ian M. Butterfield (Ireland)/Alamy, 96; © i food and drink/Alamy, 148;
© Jan Holm/Alamy, 32, 109; © Jeremy Sutton-Hibbert/Alamy, 77, 173, 174 (top),
176, 177; © Jiri Rezac/Alamy, 8, 112; © Jo Hanley/Alamy, 90; © JTB Photo/
Superstock, 101; © Keller + Keller Photography, 70, 196–199, 201, 204, 205, 208
(right), 209–213, 214 (right); © L Blake/Irish Imag/agefotostock.com, 126–127;
© Lenscap/Alamy, 155; © Lev Kropotov/Alamy, 219; © LOOK Die Bildgentur
de Fotografen GmbH/Alamy, 118, 129; © Madredus/Shutterstock, wood plank
backgrounds (throughout); © Mar Photographics/Alamy, 50; Mars Vilaubi,
131; © Martin Thomas Photography/Alamy, 122; © Marti Sans/Alamy, 203;
© Mary Evans Picture Library 2008, 14 (left); © Mary Evans Picture Library/
Alamy, 14 (right); © McClatchy-Tribune Information Services/Alamy, 229;
© Mira/Alamy, 16; © Mountain Laurel Spirits, Todd Trice, 185; © Nicholas
Everleigh/Alamy, 202; © Niday Picture Library/Alamy, 19; © Northwind
Picture Archives/Alamy, 17, 92; © Paul Bock/Alamy, 41; © Peter Horree/Alamy,
43, 140–141, 154, 157; © Rachel Turner/Alamy, 184; © Ranger Creek Brewing
& Distilling, 180; © Rawan Hussein/Alamy, 215; © Robert Harding World
Imagery/Alamy, 27; © Robert Holmes/Alamy, 108; © South West Images
Scotland/Alamy, 82; © St. George Spirits, 182–183, 189, 193; © Superstock/
agefotostock.com, 128; © Trevor Mogg/Alamy, 175; © Victor Watts/Alamy, 89;
Wikimedia Commons, 15

OTHER STOREY TITLES YOU WILL ENJOY

The American Craft Beer Cookbook by John Holl
The best beer-friendly recipes from breweries, brewpubs, and taverns
across the United States.
352 pages. Paper. ISBN 978-1-61212-090-4.

Cellaring Wine by Jeff Cox
A sourcebook to create a system for selecting wines to age, storing them
properly, and drinking them when they are just right.
272 pages. Paper. ISBN 978-1-58017-474-9.

Homemade Liqueurs and Infused Spirits by Andrew Schloss
Over 130 intriguing and original flavor combinations and 21 clone recipes
for big-name brand liqueurs.
272 pages. Paper. ISBN 978-1-61212-098-0.

Tasting Beer by Randy Mosher
The first comprehensive guide to tasting, appreciating, and understanding
the world's best drink — craft beers.
256 pages. Paper. ISBN 978-1-60342-089-1.

Vintage Beer by Patrick Dawson
Everything you need to know to build a beer cellar you will savor for years to come.
160 pages. Paper. ISBN 978-1-61212-156-7.

The Winemaker's Answer Book by Alison Crowe
A reassuring reference that offers proven solutions to every winemaking mishap,
written by *WineMaker* magazine's Wine Wizard.
384 pages. Flexibind. ISBN 978-1-58017-656-9.

These and other books from Storey Publishing are available
wherever quality books are sold or by calling 1-800-441-5700.
Visit us at *www.storey.com* or sign up for our newsletter
at *www.storey.com/signup*.